LOW TOX
LIFE
FOOD

murdoch books

Sydney | London

To literally everyone. May we be or
meet the people who grow our food in a
regenerative way as we learn more about
the critical importance of true partnership
with nature to our very existence. See you
at the table, on the farm, in the community
garden, by the compost bin, at the markets
or in your vegie patch as we send ripples
of change out into the world.

LOW TOX LIFE FOOD

ALEXX STUART

BESTSELLING AUTHOR OF *LOW TOX LIFE*

How did we get here?

What's best for our planet?

Change starts with us

Let's cook!

Introduction

Want to know a little secret? When I set out to write this book, I originally thought it was going to be about the highest carbon-emitting foods around the world, thus helping us discover a 'low-carbon diet'. I'd spearhead a mission to find the worst-offending foods, celebrate the foods with a halo around them, write some lovely recipes so we could feel proactive in doing something good for the planet, and hooray – goals kicked and progress made. A catchy title and a blueprint (we humans love a good list or protocol, don't we?): 'I'm busy, just tell me what to do!' All you need is to add a celeb, an accompanying workout plan and an interview with Oprah and: success! Or so I thought – but my investigations revealed the need for a different story.

I was gentle on myself and my earnest but flawed endeavour. As I began, I was soon reminded – just as my humanities degree had taught me 25 years earlier, every time I sat down to prove a point in several thousand words at the end of a semester – that this much is true: very little is black and white. There would be no reductionist ranking of all the foods, no 'evil' and 'sin-free' allowing us to arrive at a point where we could get 10 points and a gold star for having the perfect low-carbon diet. That safety we crave in seductive absolutes wasn't there, but something much more deeply rewarding and satisfying was.

   While it was quite easy to rate and rank foods from conventional agriculture, it didn't show the whole picture – kind of like a study concluding that 'red meat increases colon cancer risk' without distinguishing the healthy whole food eaters, who eat pasture-fed beef with a wide variety of colourful vegies and lead active lifestyles, from eaters of hot dogs and fast food burgers who drink two colas a night or processed beef sausages packed with preservatives and colours while they sit still for hours at a time, day after day. There was a ton of information about the evils of beef, which was considered the root of the planet's problems, emitting huge amounts of carbon and methane, but then there were stories of farmers using animal grazing techniques to reverse desertification, restore grassland health and recover soil health, restore healthy water systems and cool

the land's temperature. I'd find one piece of research that said almonds were terrible for the planet and we all had to feel guilty for eating them or drinking almond milk, but I'd then read about almonds produced using regenerative organic agriculture in areas with healthier natural rainfall and pollination, teeming with biodiversity.

In one report, avocados were not only creating horrible human rights abuses in Mexico and Guatemala, but also destroying the planet through deforestation, all so that they could be flown around the world in order for posh people to eat expensive smashed avocado on toast in a cafe in Europe. But if grown locally as a part of an agroforestry operation, avocados were a hardy tree that required little pest control and offered good cover protection to other plants, making them a great source of nutrient-dense food when eaten close to the source.

All this time we'd been fighting about *what* the food was and how bad it was for the planet, but it becomes clearer by the day that in order to have a productive and holistic conversation about the effect of produce on emissions, we need to take into account *how* it's farmed and *where*. We can't continue to let a trend in food or trend in agricultural methods – heck, a trend in beliefs even – lead to deforestation to 'feed the world' or create localised hunger. It seemed so horribly broken, a system that would rob people of their native foods, driving up local prices to export that food to satisfy a hot new trend on the other side of the world. There is so much more to consider in prioritising produce for our shopping baskets; and why something that might be good here might not be so great there, is just the tip of the iceberg.

So that neat little idea I originally had for ranking foods was getting messier by the minute and was about to get messier still, when I found two other major players we really need to consider here. Firstly, it's not just about what we should eat – the pear or the cashew or the chicken – but what we should do to stop wasting so much darn food. A vast quantity of food we produce or buy is subsequently wasted, either at the farm gate, rejected or without a customer; in the supply chain; or rotting away in our home fridges or landfill. This could all be nourishment for us, or for the hungriest global citizens, or for the soil through regenerative composting programs. Instead, it's a huge emissions burden. In fact, if food waste were a country it would be the world's third largest carbon emitter, behind the United States and China. I do believe that's what we call an elephant in the room.

And another elephant in the room when it comes to food and emissions burdens: processing. If we're going to have a truly productive, holistic

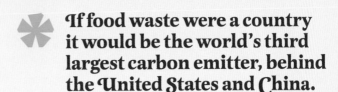

If food waste were a country it would be the world's third largest carbon emitter, behind the United States and China.

discussion about how our daily food habits impact emissions, fan the flames of the plastic crisis and harm global biodiversity, we have to look at the whole basket of food, not just the produce in the basket. A startling fact impossible to ignore is this: about 50 per cent of the products in an average shopping trolley in developed countries can be categorised as 'ultra-processed foods' – heavily processed food-like products that provide 'energy' but often very little in the way of nutrition, and/or often with a helping of various additives and preservatives to ensure pleasing textures, taste and shelf stability. How many emissions could we save if we simply stopped eating what provides no benefit in the first place and if we gave up complex processed delights for farm-to-table produce that's as local as possible?

And so, my dear reader, if you've made it this far through the introduction in the bookstore, where they're looking at you uncomfortably and wondering if you're actually going to buy this thing, here's where we're at so you can decide if you want to stick around for the rest of the journey. I am passionate about us all finding common ground despite all our different beliefs about food, our preferences and our sense of what suits our bodies best. And I believe we can all come together over three centring principles that will drive massive change. I'm so exhausted by the arguments that lead us away from making the accelerated change we need in order to help our species recover its health and our planet remake healthy ecosystems and regain its resilience. So if you want to link arms and do the work we can all do together, here are the three most important themes for making a difference to people and planet through our food choices:

1   It's not just what the produce is, it's how and where it's farmed.
2   It's not just what we buy, it's how much we throw away.
3   It's not just the produce, but the ultra-processed foods we don't even need.

In addressing these three themes, we're going to focus on four key areas so we can build a powerful collective of people creating change from our shopping baskets. These four themes will support us in our all-important quest to bolster human health by crowding out the voices of the ultra-processed foods that often call our names:

1   The many regenerative forms of farming that not only provide food for our family tables, but also repair and build fertile landscapes teeming with biodiversity.
2   How to connect with the forms of farming that are working to build ecosystem health and biodiversity, with lots of tips on sourcing and how to keep a produce-focused diet exciting and motivating all year round.
3   Food waste and how we can turn a challenge into a deliciously creative endeavour.
4   Meal inspiration from some beautiful farms around the world, along with some of my family's favourite recipes and new ones created just for this book, so you can address global issues at your family table. Flavour makers, adaptable staple recipes and feasts – I've got you covered.

This last point is so important, because one of our major barriers to eating well for ourselves and the planet is feeling overwhelmed in the kitchen and by food management. Some of us have a skills shortage or we've been utterly convinced by the food industry that we're somehow above cooking. Getting into the kitchen and developing your cooking literacy is a big, big part of the repair process that lies ahead, for you and the planet.

What I hope to help you discover, when it comes to caring for our planet from our plates, is that *how* our food is produced and what we do with it is of critical importance for future generations. One thing I know for sure, from interviewing scientists, doctors and nutritionists over the years, is that there is no one diet that suits all 7.8 billion people perfectly. Are there overlaps in what does work? Absolutely. Do we still see people trying to convince others that their protocol is 'wrong' and vice versa? Absolutely. So enough with the climate diet wars, the 'You're a planet killer cos you eat meat' or 'What would you know anyway, angry vegan?' Let's come together where we overlap, to appreciate the forms of farming that leave our planet in better and better shape each year, and to enjoy whatever diet helps us thrive on a personal level and keeps our healthcare provider happy. Let's all source ethically and as best we can, ditching ultra-processed weirdness, managing our foods to avoid waste, and composting our scraps to create new life.

I want to invite us to avoid reductionist arguments and to get excited about where we're headed together. Peace and progress come when we focus on our common ground, embracing and accepting our diversity. When I was starting to write this book, I surveyed the good people of the Low Tox Life community on their goals in life. They very much confirmed that while we might eat differently, vote differently and have different life priorities, we also have shared goals that go something like this:

* to live prosperous, healthy lives
* to do work or have a career that supports us and our families
* to love and be loved in loving families and with strong and supportive friendships
* to enjoy clean water and food sources, fresh air, beautiful natural landscapes to immerse ourselves in, and access to the health care that we feel works best for us
* to live on a thriving planet.

So we're going to put down that bag of Sweet Chilli BBQ Prawn Sour Cream Chips (?!) or even those organic, gluten-free lentil chips, and instead finally get appropriately fired up about the magnificent marketing calendar nature has provided for us. We're going to recognise the people growing that food for all of us, and our planet, to thrive on. We're going to cherish our role in bringing it all together into delicious meals for ourselves and the people we hold dear. And we're going to stop acting like it's no big deal to waste it.

Are you in?

Let me start by telling you a little story about what got me engaged with where my food came from ...

CHAPTER

1

How did we
get here?

A step back in time

I was standing in the supermarket one day, 17 years ago. Pre smartphone. Pre 'cool app for looking up additives'. I was tasked with starting to eat a food mix avoiding gluten as an experiment, to see if it helped stop my chronic tonsillitis. It was a long shot, but a bit of emerging research was suggesting a potential link between non-coeliac gluten sensitivity and recurring tonsil infections. At that point in my life I was up for trying anything, given the alternative was continuing to get worse and worse bouts of tonsillitis with antibiotics no longer working. So I thought, *If I do three months and I don't get tonsillitis, I'll try another three months*, and so on. How hard could it be, right? I was smart. I had this in the bag.

I'd headed into the supermarket for my then very conventional shop of all the aisles. At the time, my favourite breakfast on the go came from a large juice box/tetra pack. My favourite 'I don't have time to look up a recipe' dinner came in plastic pouches you submerged in hot water and then served. My favourite movie snack was either a bag of microwave popcorn or crunchy malt-centred balls. As I stood there, I decided that, given I had no idea what contained gluten, I would look at every ingredient in each product. My practitioner had given me a little list of names that gluten could be hiding under, such as hydrolysed vegetable protein, glucose, certain preservatives or 'natural flavour'.

And so I began. Little did I know the Pandora's box I was opening. *The breakfast shake should be an easy one, surely. Isn't it just milk, chocolate and some kind of protein?* What I found was this:

> Filtered water, skim milk powder, cane sugar (4%), wheat maltodextrin, soy protein, vegetable oils (sunflower, canola), Hi-maize™ starch, inulin, fructose from corn syrup, cocoa, oat flour, mineral (calcium), food acid 332 (potassium citrate), flavour, 460 (Cellulose microcrystalline), 466 (Sodium carboxymethylcellulose), 407 (Carrageenan) vitamins (C, A, niacin, B12, B2, B6, B1, folate), salt

At first, I wasn't too worried and even felt clever: I saw wheat maltodextrin, barley and oats, and knew it was a no-go. Moving on. I thought, *I know, I'll check the other brand*, and it was pretty much the same situation, so that was again a no. *I can just make porridge, I guess. Doh!* Oats (17 years ago, no oats came from a facility that processed only gluten-free foods). *I can have an egg on toast.* No gluten-free bread to be found in the supermarket. *Hmm. Corn flakes?* Nope. *Barley malt extract. What the?*

Then I picked up my favourite movie snack, which I'd already figured at this point would be a no, given 'Malt' was in the name. But worth a shot:

> 74% milk chocolate and 7.5% malt extract. sugar, milk solids, cocoa butter, glucose syrup (sources include wheat), cocoa mass, barley malt extract, vegetable fat, emulsifiers (soy lecithin, 492), wheat gluten, raising agents (501, 500), salt, pectin, natural flavour (vanilla extract)

I guess I could just have the dark-chocolate-coated honeycomb bar instead. Nope. Wheat and wheat-derived glucose. *I like those chocolate-filled coloured buttons, how about those?* Nope, starch from wheat. *Geez, is it hot in here?!* Off came the sweater. I rolled up my sleeves now, determined to find something I could eat for my breakfast or for a treat among the things I liked at the time.

So the chicken, rice and vegie dinner in a pouch that was my busy-week fallback. Surely that was going to be straightforward:

> Cooked enriched long grain rice (water, rice, iron, niacin, thiamine mononitrate, folic acid), cooked white meat chicken (white meat chicken, water, isolated soy protein, modified food starch, seasoning [dried chicken broth, chicken powder, natural flavour], sodium phosphate, maltodextrin, salt), water, carrots, peas, cooked scrambled whole eggs (whole eggs, skim milk, soybean oil, corn starch, salt, xanthan gum, citric acid), green onions, tamari soy sauce (water, soybeans, salt, sugar), 2% or less of garlic, chicken broth, sesame oil, corn starch, sriracha sauce (chilli peppers, sugar, vinegar, salt, garlic, chilli extract, beet powder), potassium chloride, caramel colour, lime juice concentrate, salt

Say WHAT?! I thought it was chicken, vegies and rice; I thought it was just a yummy 'chocolate' treat; I thought it was just a protein-rich chocolate

milk drink to help me power through the morning. But looking up the ingredients in these things – all common go-tos for brekkie, dinner or a trip to the movies – made me feel extremely confused and sad about starting my gluten-avoiding experiment. I thought about how complicated it was going to be choosing 'food', and I was completely overwhelmed. As I continued, I kept finding gluten in everything, from my rice crackers to the biscuits to the frozen fish I liked, to the chicken stock … Gluten everywhere. I thought, *Oh my gosh, I am literally not going to be able to eat anything!*

Ever had one of those huge realisations that bring to mind a movie scene where the actor screams and the camera pans out to shots that then pan out further and further until they're still screaming and it's panned to outer space? That's what it felt like. I cried that night. I cried at a friend's who'd toiled over a nice lunch I couldn't eat. When it was time for the staff meal at work, which at the time was a beautiful restaurant and bar, and I had to have something specially made for me by the chefs, I felt rude and ungrateful. I started calling myself names and apologising incessantly for being a pain, just to try not to be such a pain to everyone. Ugh! This was going to be hard. I didn't feel safe, I didn't feel like I knew what to do, and I felt like a social burden – a food leper. If you've ever been in that position, I see you, I feel you, it sucks. If you're there now? Trust me, this is actually, in a way that might not seem possible right now, your ticket to food freedom.

A seasoned cook and produce lover reading this now might think, *Silly girl, roast a chook and some vegies and you would have been fine.* Easy to say when you know how to do that, but back then I genuinely didn't know how. Growing up, I had licked the chocolate cake bowl or, at most, helped put in all the ingredients for the cake. By the late 1980s, home economics had been taken out of my school curriculum because this subject was considered 'beneath women' and anti-feminist. In thinking about it, it's anti-human not to be taught a few good basic cooking techniques for sustaining yourself. All boys and girls should leave home knowing how to do that, yet as fewer and fewer of us did, the ultra-processed, packaged-food industry laughed all the way to the bank, having us believe we couldn't do food without them!

If I ever cooked from scratch, it was by slavishly following each step of a recipe in a book, gathering exactly what I needed to execute that recipe, looking at the page every five seconds to make sure I was 'doing it right', and getting flustered with timings. When you have no agency and not many cooking skills, trying to eliminate something like gluten can be very tough psychologically – especially 17 years ago, when gluten-free pantry staples were non-existent and advocates weren't there to lend a supportive hand and show the way. Later, when I started teaching people how to cook (how's that for a career plot twist?), I swore I'd never let anyone feel so helpless or silly for not having cooking know-how. But first, I had to figure things out for myself.

After a couple of big cries, a side helping of self-consciousness, and a whinge to my close friends and boyfriend for a few weeks, I put on my big girl pants and decided I wasn't going to do this as a victim. This didn't feel nice. I was bored by the broken record playing the poor-old-me tune over and over. I was going to find the silver lining. I was going to figure this out. And by golly I was going to learn how to make yummy things and treat it as an exciting creative adventure (fake it till you make it). I ran a very swanky bar at the time and created cocktails so good that they won me competitions to fly me overseas. If I could make up to six different complex drinks at the same time while talking to two different waiting groups, then surely I could figure out how to cook dinner not only without stress, but with success.

I started with pan-frying meats (burnt on the outside, raw on the inside, of course!), overcooked vegies, and fried rice that you'd more accurately call 'fried glue' – which my boyfriend, now husband, was very sweet to say was 'fine'. I'm actually shocked we made it past #gluericegate!

But slowly, my love for cooking began to develop. The challenge of 'nailing food' was exciting to me. My first big food-education epiphany was that the easiest way to avoid gluten was to learn to cook produce well. You don't have to pick up a capsicum, or butter or a steak and read the ingredients, after all. I became obsessed with what the chefs were doing in the kitchen where I worked. At every opportunity I tried to learn, and when they used wheat flour to thicken something or bind something, I started to research what I might be able to use instead to produce the same effect.

I went from being someone who thought Charcoal Chicken or my mum were the only people who mysteriously knew how to produce a great dinner, to being the person who could darn well do that herself. It was fun. I was in my element. It was such a creative time. I used recipe books to learn the basic principles and classic cooking techniques, and from there I was determined to really learn how to bring things together myself. I wanted to reach that wise moment where I could say, 'If I put this in, then that, mix it with that, add those things and slow-cook for three to four hours, or sauté for 10 minutes, something delicious will eventuate with 100 per cent certainty', and have the confidence that it would. And? I got there. If this sounds completely impossible to you right now, then stick with me, baby, and you'll get there too.

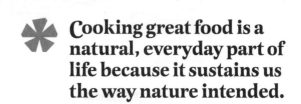

Cooking great food is a natural, everyday part of life because it sustains us the way nature intended.

To me, getting to that point where you can be a confident 'rustler-upper' who can make good meals when other people might look around and think there's nothing to eat, is where the ultra-processed food industry loses its hold over us. It's powerful. It's also where food waste in our homes starts to decline dramatically. See how the themes start to intertwine when we reconnect to produce and cooking?

Now I was really starting to understand flavour, the chemistry of different ingredients interacting with each other, and I'd sold off my proverbial shares in the local chicken shop! I was going to make it on my own, and the important mental shift I made during this time was that cooking great food wasn't something you did when it was a special occasion or when you 'had time', it was a natural, everyday part of life because it sustains us the way nature intended. So why wasn't it the norm? I really started to want this to be the reality for everyone. I still do. We are most definitely not there yet – either mentally, in the skills department or with more complex issues such as access, education and food sovereignty – where farmers and consumers all have a say in how our food is grown and sold, away from the control of the ultra-processed food industry.

Cooking great food is a natural, everyday part of life because it sustains us the way nature intended. Not only did the gluten-free experiment make me learn how to cook, but the whole foods shift meant I also stopped getting tonsillitis. It worked like magic. I don't think any whole food is 'evil', and I'd never tell others how or exactly what to eat, but boy, did this work for me!

The gift in disguise was a big move away from ultra-processed foods in general. It wasn't just the gluten-containing ingredients I learnt about in that process of investigation, but all the additives, preservatives, fillers, thickeners and agents that were used, because I had to in order to figure out whether they contained gluten. I was shocked that as a 28-year-old with 17 years of formal education under my belt, I'd never once been taught how to sustain myself with the basics, or that what I put in my body could impact my health, or the planet's health either – as I was soon to discover. Little did I know that this was just the beginning of my food education.

The global picture

Part of the reason we don't learn to think about whole food versus
processed food is that until the recent past, real food never had to be
distinguished from non-food or processed food. Food has been food
for most of human history. Once we'd figured out the poisonous plants
and fungi, the extent of our processing throughout time has been in the
form of cooking, soaking, sprouting or fermenting to make things more
digestible or to preserve them for times of scarcity. Today, however, food is
a minefield. Over the past 150 years, much progress has been supposedly
made in farming, food manufacturing and processing, with the result not
only that we're now faced with navigating a much more complicated food
landscape, but also that our health has never been worse. Chronic illnesses
continue to rise, leading to important questions, including:

* How did it become possible that a colourant with known links to
  hyperactivity, attention deficit disorder and mood dysregulation could
  be freely used in a food or drink marketed to parents and children as
  'fun and exciting'?
* How did it become okay to treat meat with carbon monoxide to keep
  it looking pink and 'fresh' in the supermarket?
* How could we end up extracting oil from cotton seeds, once deemed
  toxic waste, and then be allowed, with no long-term testing, to market
  that oil as a 'great new product for flaky pastry'? And how did we get so
  fooled into believing it?
* How was it that a farmer couldn't sell their raw milk or meat from
  their farm to their neighbour, but Coca-Cola could completely legally
  sell and market their sodas to people all over the world, despite the
  abundance of research on the negative impact of excess dietary sugar?

Some epidemiologists believe that about 35 per cent of the global
disease burden can be attributed to diet. Where are the government
initiatives to promote fresh produce? Where is the investment and
education in vegetable gardens and keeping chickens, especially in lower
socioeconomic communities, which are often lacking in fresh food thanks
to what are known as 'food deserts'? It makes no sense for taxpayers to
continue funding public healthcare costs with all major diseases on the
rise, and yet diet is not focused on at all in most public health discourse.

While the lighting might be perfect here, the combined ingredients tally for these products is just under 100, and many of those have shown negative health effects in nutritional studies.

There is no preventative communications strategy for instilling produce-over-products in our children. If you want a food education for your child, you'd better be a good fundraiser, with a kitchen garden program costing the average school around forty thousand dollars a year. We humans seem to be under the spell that solutions to many of today's disease epidemics are solely to be found in new scientific discoveries of pharmaceutical drugs to 'combat disease'. Sure, there will always be a place for this important research and these interventions, but where is the light shone on diet, knowing its weighty impact?

Over the past two years, I've seen one ad, on community TV in the country, made by an Indigenous Australian community group, talking about how important it is to support our immune system with lots of fresh healthy food. One lonely ad. Not a government message. Not a health association directive. Something has to give. Luckily, as chefs Ann Cooper and Jamie Oliver and other real-food champions have shown us, we don't need to wait for someone else to give us the green light on change from within our homes and communities. The real power here is not in thinking big so much as starting small. Starting with me and going from there. *I can't make a big difference out there* should never dampen our spirits when we can make a powerful difference right here and with our very next meal. So let's make this one of our campaign slogans moving forward: From products to produce!

Me being me, knowing how to cook now and having happy tonsils didn't mean I was 'done'. My curiosity had been piqued. I wanted to try to figure out the food system and I wanted to help others do the same. The more I looked into things, the more I started to see how much about our modern-day foods – how they were made and what was allowed in them – just didn't make sense for the human body to thrive. I was sad that I hadn't been smart enough before to question what I was putting into my body. I was angry that there didn't seem to be many checks and balances when it came to what was used in packaged foods. I was frustrated that food labels could promote a product as healthy by using unregulated star ratings or saying it was 'free from' something. (People giggle in my talks when I say an organic gluten-free cheesy puff is still a cheesy puff, and an organic chocolate cream cookie is still a chocolate cream cookie, mmkay? A 'free from' on the label, doesn't answer the real question to ask, which is: *What's in this?*)

I started to dig a bit deeper and climb a bit higher up the chain. I was angry to learn that people who decided on and wrote health and food guidelines and recommendations for governments were legally allowed to, and often did, take money from multinational processed-food companies.

Let's make this one of our campaign slogans moving forward: From products to produce!

I was also horrified to discover that those companies were allowed to contribute unlimited funds to political campaigns in many countries around the world. These companies have budgets big enough to place ads across traditional and online media, too. I was shocked to learn that the former head of a processed-food or agricultural chemical company could join a department of agriculture or health, and vice versa, creating ties and networks that truth and justice find hard to penetrate to this day.

It seemed that behind all the glossy ad campaigns about irresistible snacks to help take the pressure off our busy modern lives, what the packaged-food industry really cared about was capitalising on trends and extended shelf lives; being the architects of increased responses in our brain's reward centres so we'd come back again and again; and, of course, increasing profits and market share. And to achieve those ends it would use whatever legal way it could. Add the pressure of stock market performance and constantly trimming costs from the bottom line, and we end up with grapes in an apricot-flavoured cereal and an apricot vapour sprayed into the pouch just before it's sealed – because grapes are cheaper, don't you know? And yes, thanks to an ex–food technologist friend I've interviewed on the subject, this is a very true story.

When the share price and profits become more important than the impact on people, animals and planet, we have to ask ourselves: *Did we maybe stuff up when building this system?* Profit is great for a business, but when it comes at the cost of other success metrics, such as health, worker ethics and planet resilience, we have problems.

The picture is improving today, thanks to consumer pressure and to some hardworking ethical brands that are putting people and planet alongside profits rather than prioritising profits at all costs. These companies are starting to produce packaged foods that can actually serve as legitimate stopgaps for the modern family in those busy weeks. But the reality is still, for the most part, that the food industry is not designed to be health-giving. If we're lighting up reward centres in our brain without flooding our bodies with nutrition, we end up full but unnourished. And our health eventually declines.

A man I'll talk about more in a little bit, a certain Lord Northbourne, had this to say of the direction food was taking way back in 1940:

> *One strange consequence of the prevailing loss of real quality in food is that a great many people, even relatively poor people, eat habitually far too much ... Malnutrition is rarely nowadays a quantitative phenomenon. The organism can never be satisfied with the fearsome, tainted, bleached, washed-out, and long-dead material with which it is supplied, and being unsatisfied calls out for more. In vain does man distend his stomach with an excess of such things – what he must have is not there.*

Translation? The human body will never be satisfied with long-life, dead food (our ultra-processed foe!), but we will therefore ironically reach for more of it to try to be satisfied, always in vain. It's sabotaging our health and it's also very good for business because production costs are cheap and shelf life is long: such is the mixed-up, muddled-up world we live in.

When I started, deciphering the ingredients on food packaging was so complicated, it was the perfect motivation to plunge myself into the arms of good, honest produce. Would I have made that leap in the end anyway? Who knows, given we humans tend to wait for apocalyptic moments to create the changes that will serve us better? But I did and I'm grateful. I've been able to help others do the same, and for that I'm also grateful. Maybe, with this book, I'll be able to help you too, or if you're already across this, perhaps it will be comforting to know that the message is spreading. Perhaps you can think about your next circle of influence and support your friends, family, patients, employees ... The sky's the limit when it comes to the ripples of change. Was I done learning? Nope, not even close.

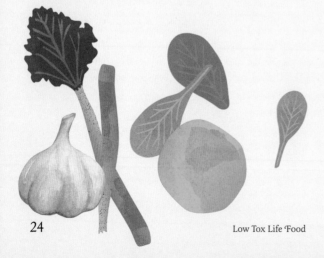

Low Tox Life Food

The dirty world of produce politics

Once I had my boy 11 years ago, I wanted to do my best for him and our family, which led me to look into how our whole foods were produced and what the best foods for babies were. I fortuitously picked up *Wholefood for Children* by my now dear friend Jude Blereau, which led me on to many more books by incredible investigative authors, such as Marion Nestle, Michael Pollan, Joel Salatin, Gary Taubes and Michael Moss. I then understood, even more deeply, how great an influence the food industry now has over people, the media and government officials. If you're completely new to looking into additives and processing agents in your food, have a look at these authors' brilliant books, which I have listed, along with many others, in the Further Information section at the end of this book. You'll also find more in the food chapter of my first book, *Low Tox Life*.

My deeper level of inquiry into how whole foods were farmed and produced opened me up to how agriculture had transformed since the industrial revolution to involve more and more poisonous chemical inputs, a newer technology called genetic modification, worse and worse conditions for the great majority of farmed animals, live export of cattle to faraway countries in horrid conditions, and workers practically enslaved on minimum wages that barely paid their bills. And then I learnt about the role lobbyists from various food associations played in influencing policy-makers when food pyramids were being developed, especially early on.

So while I left the ultra-processed food landscape confident and empowered, in looking more closely at produce I was stepping into another minefield. Turns out there were wars going on between the associations representing various types of produce. And those wars in boardrooms would lead to us ordinary folk becoming more confused than ever before about food, more robbed of our natural instincts and age-old wisdom about what's good for us and what helps us feel nourished and well. This was enough to make my head spin, because I had thought that produce was the simpler, safer option. And while of course it *was*, compared to the boil-in-a-bag dinners with ingredients lists a mile long, I was about to discover a whole new can of worms – or lack of worms as the case may be.

In her book *Death by Food Pyramid*, Denise Minger sheds light on how the original food pyramid design came about. It tells the story of how Luise Light, head nutritionist for the United States Department of Agriculture's (USDA's) new food pyramid project in the early 1980s, had fruits and

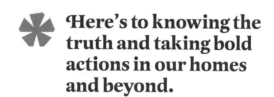

Here's to knowing the truth and taking bold actions in our homes and beyond.

vegetables at 5–9 daily serves and grains at 2–3. When the pyramid was published, those numbers were flipped, with grains at 6–11 serves per day and fruits and vegetables at 3, essentially because the wheat lobby was louder and more affluent than the fruit and veg farmers. Isn't it quite stunning that whole generations, through being so grain-focused, missed out on critical micronutrients from eating a large variety of plants?

If you ask most people, as I have when coaching clients over the years, to map out their typical daily food in childhood, it would be a bowl of cereal or eggs on toast, a sandwich for lunch with a simple spread, some kind of cracker snack or chip in the afternoon, a piece of fruit and a rice- or pasta-based dinner with some sort of protein and veg sauce. Not much room for vibrant colourful foods and all their powerful micronutrients, is there? Not much room for high-quality, nutrient-dense proteins or omega-3s fats or fat-soluble vitamins A, E, D and K. Very little space for B12, to support nervous system health and energy. It's criminal that we were led down this path, through government recommendation no less, and that no one was ever held accountable for the toll on health taken by reduced nutrient variety and increased refined carbohydrates and therefore packaged food.

When, at the beginning of talks, I ask a room of about 100 parents whether they remember more than one child with a food allergy, eczema or ADHD when they were at school, one or two people put up a hand. When I ask them then if they can think of more than one child with any of those conditions in their children's school classes today, everyone's hand goes up. I ask them to keep their hands up if it's their child? Roughly three-quarters of the room's hands stay up.

When you see room after room of parents confirming the same contrast in health challenges from a generation ago to now, you really have to think about the major changes in the way we live, what we put on our skin, what we're breathing in and what we're eating. The reduction in food quality and change in agricultural methods are contributing to the decline in children's health not only directly but also through its effects on their parents. Nothing is black and white, but it is emerging that the impact of food on gut health affects our overall health, which in turn affects our sperm or egg quality, and then affects the health of our children. As well as the food type and quality, we must also look at what chemical inputs are used when produce is grown and when it is processed, marketed and distributed. Fresh food spoils quickly, so achieving the longest possible shelf lives means, by default, food devoid of vibrancy and life. It's not difficult to see how human health has suffered, leading to greater numbers of children with chronic health issues.

Do we know the perfect diet? People are still arguing over what that looks like – low-carb, keto, vegan, paleo, Mediterranean, wholegrain-focused – but I don't see the point, given there's no evidence of any one diet working perfectly for 7.8 billion people across the globe at all stages of life and through all challenges, whether physiological or perhaps logistic or financial, that might pop up over the course of a lifetime. Dictate what everyone *should* eat, and you bring up ethical food sovereignty concerns. Michael Pollan's famous blueprint of 'Eat food. Not too much. Mostly plants' seems to be the soundest, and still leaves everyone the flexibility to find what works for them within that framework.

What's bad for us is bad for the planet

The final revelation on my journey towards whole food was that there was another big casualty of ultra-processed foods and intensive, chemical-fuelled farming: our planet. We're all down here fighting about paleo versus vegan but missing the developing consensus that at current degradation levels we have about 60 years of healthy topsoil left. It's not going to matter what produce mix you think is the best for human health if we can no longer grow or raise any produce at all.

Without healthy topsoil, the earth loses its ability to take in the sun, filter water, produce plants, feed animals, feed us and store carbon. The poorer our soil becomes, the less nutrient-rich our food becomes, so this is a big deal. Yikes! I don't want to start having to eat Space Food Sticks in my old age, sitting in front of an air-conditioning unit. You don't either, right?

As we will see in the next chapter, soil health and ecosystem management through responsible, regenerative agriculture play an important role in deep, fast planet repair. How on earth have we missed that memo for so long? Why are we instead caught up in the petty online squabbles of the diet wars, when the fight for better land management seems so much more important?

What excites me most is that the fight for regenerative agriculture is one we can mount together, whatever our food beliefs. I don't want to convert people to a particular diet, I want to see us all realise our potential of becoming regeneratarians – as author and filmmaker Damon Gameau calls it in his film *2040*. It strikes me that this first 15 years of social media has seen us all move into very separate echo chambers building ironclad 'truths' and fighting with the 'others'. The next chapter will surely fulfil the platforms' initial promise: to connect us better. When we feel connected, we fight less and we do more. But here's the thing: we have to want to connect. We have to be curious about where we overlap. We have to be willing to accept that not everything will be agreed upon but that for our planet and our health – both mental and physical – working from our commonality matters and it won't be breezy.

In my own journey I got to the point where I thought: *Am I brave enough to continue asking the questions? This is hard. Why do I have to play a part in opening people's eyes to all this stuff? Can't I just keep teaching people how to bake pretty gluten-free treats and yummy family dinners, call it lucky that I know how to source of good food for my family, and leave it at that?* Well, nope. I'm going to endeavour to do both.

The good news is that we can actually work to improve our own health at the same time as the health of the planet by focusing more on where our produce comes from. And that's one of the major things we're going to do in this book.

You might be thinking, *Isn't fixing the planet through our food choices as simple as just not eating meat?* Nope. If only we could remove one food type from our diet and get to say, 'Yay! I'm making a difference. I'm a good eater.' To regenerate topsoil, water systems and our planet, and to increase biodiversity on the land, animals and plants work best together – which we'll explore in the next chapter.

Just as no one food is advantageous or evil for all people, and we generally find that different people thrive on a variety of whole-food-based diets around the world, no one type of food will be the lone saviour or lone baddie. We've seen articles condemning everything from avocados to almonds to cows. In those cases there are very clear examples where farming them has hurt farmers, animals, bees and our planet, but what is always missing is the big picture: *how* are these things farmed? What methods and chemical inputs are used? How far does the food travel? How is it processed and used? What is the social impact on a country of increased demand? Is land, particularly forest, being cleared to produce this food? Sometimes yes. Sometimes no. Nothing is black and white. It is complex and many factors are involved. Once we define what helps more than hinders the health of our planet, we can find the overlaps and embrace food diversity. We can start our passionate journey towards sourcing as best we can, and letting go of the *I want it now* mentality of expecting to have any food, from anywhere in the world, on any day of the year. If we're to make progress, our attitude needs to look different; our expectations of immediacy, convenience and access need to relax. I believe with my whole heart that we can do this.

I completely understand people who can't and won't eat meat because of their beliefs. Should we put an end to factory farming and live export? Yes, I believe we should. But simply ditching the meat completely fails to

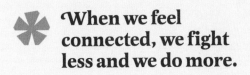

When we feel connected, we fight less and we do more.

address the role animals play in building a healthy landscape, the nutritional benefits of these foods, how all the plant foods that remain in the diet are farmed, how we are to produce enough nutrition from plant foods alone to feed the world, and what protein foods we use to replace those meats. The food industry is champing at the bit to provide meat replacements for people who have the best intentions of caring for the planet, but at what expense to human and planetary health? The latest talk of the town – cultured synthetic meat – begs at least two questions. What about the vast amounts of energy it takes to run warehouses of temperature-controlled culturing operations? How much land clearing would have to occur to make room for these warehouses? How would we manage the herd animals in order to maintain the world's grasslands? Who would manage that and how would they earn money if they weren't selling the meat from the animals?

Many people – and even whole cultures – do well as vegetarians, so this is in no way a dig at dietary choices. But it is a call to think of the bigger picture. I know no one would wish that a woman's business be taken from her in a country where a woman can keep a cow but is not allowed to own land or tend crops. I often think of the privilege so many of us have of being hyper-particular about our food choices. Oh, how lucky we are!

When it comes to ready-made, plant-based packaged foods, while some use simple ingredients from good local sources, many are just another ultra-processed-food disaster. I saw plant-based 'meat' burgers at the supermarket recently, when I went to look at what was on offer for people cutting their meat intake or going vegan. It was like one of the ingredients lists of my early food education years:

> Mycoprotein (54%), wheat flour (calcium, iron, niacin & thiamine), sunflower oil, water, potato protein, pea fibre, wheat starch, wheat gluten, firming agents (calcium chloride, calcium acetate), natural flavours, kibbled chilli, parsley, salt, yeast, garlic powder, onion powder, tomato powder, spices (cayenne pepper, white pepper), stabilisers (carrageenan, sodium alginate), rice flour, spice extracts (black pepper, cayenne, ginger), colour (paprika extract), raising agent (ammonium carbonate)

What happened to a simple roast sweet potato and lentil burger if we wanted or needed a meat-free option?

Or here's a chicken-free butter chicken I found online:

Low Tox Life Food

Meat free butter chicken style curry (57%), cooked mixed grain rice (43%).
Meat free butter chicken style curry contains: water, chicken style pieces
(25%) [water, soy protein isolate, wheat gluten, soy protein concentrate,
pea starch, pea fibre, seasoning (salt, rice, spices, sugar, dextrose, maize
starch, herbs, thickener (1442), yeast extract, vegetable powders, smoke oil,
natural colour (caramel 1))], coconut cream (20%) [coconut cream, thickener
(415), stabilisers (412, 407)], red masala sauce (14%) [onion paste, water,
tomato paste, sunflower oil, garlic paste, ginger puree, spices, salt, acidity
regulator (330), garam masala spice, natural colour (paprika oleoresins)],
tomato paste (10%) [tomato, acidity regulator (330)], sugar, lemon juice from
concentrate, corn starch, tandoori marinade (0.5%) [natural colour (paprika
oleoresins)], garam masala spice, salt

We are being sold this as 'planet-saving, cruelty-free food'? Really?

It seems that a slogan like 'Leading the way with plant-based foods' is
interchangeable with 'Leading the way with ultra-processed foods'. I saw
what was basically margarine the other day re-marketed as 'plant-based
butter'. Genius after the scientific research walloping that industrial seed
oils have received over the past decade. We must be wary of that as we
make our choices. Plant-based still doesn't answer the important question
we should be asking: so what's in it then? Where do the ingredients come
from? How are they farmed? Plant-based is to the 2020s what 'all natural'
was to the 2000s and 2010s. In other words, it means very little by way of
health and environmental care, and doesn't even hint at the full picture
regarding the product's potential impact, from the ways the raw materials
might be farmed to how far they then travel to be processed, additional
ingredients, packaging and final product transportation.

Wouldn't it be better, if you wanted to reduce your meat consumption or
refrain from eating meat, to eat like the traditional vegetarian communities
around the world, focusing on well-prepared wholefood legumes, nuts
and grains as a protein source? I yearn for simpler meals. What happened
to a delicious chickpea curry with vegies and rice? And who doesn't love
a cauliflower schnitzel? I guess the cauliflower and chickpea farmers'
produce isn't as sexy. Ever see that ad for the 'hot new chickpea' on the side
of a bus? Nobody did. It doesn't exist (much as I think chickpeas are one of
the best foods in existence and I'm completely obsessed with hummus).

The ultra-processed food and food-tech industries are trying to hijack the
'eat for planet health' conversation. But just as a gluten-free cheesy puff is

still an ultra-processed cheesy puff, a lab-created fake prawn is still an ultra-processed fake prawn. Neither is particularly good for us, nor for the planet.

Those of us who are vegetarian or vegan still need to consider:

* the way the ingredients for these processed foods are farmed
* the fact that post-farm processing contributes to 18 per cent of global food emissions and returns no carbon to the soil
* that many of these ultra-processed plant-based foods contain hard-to-digest additives and proteins, and that even the vitamins they might contain are often synthetic forms with poorer bioavailability than nutrients from whole, unprocessed foods.

Another way the ultra-processed food industry dictates the planet-loving narrative is with the words 'cruelty-free'. Here, they falsely appeal to people's desire not to cause harm to animals, but it's not the whole truth. Things die for us to eat. Things die for other creatures to eat. What about all the rabbits and deer that are killed on farms for peas to be made into pea protein that is sold as 'cruelty-free' and plant-based? The millions of mice killed in wheat fields by tractors and sprays? Is that not cruel too?

While the vegan chicken curry doesn't contain animal flesh, often these ultra-processed foods come from agricultural practices that are no better at helping us address our topsoil crisis, which means they are contributing to climate change just as much as any intensively produced food – not to mention the human rights issues one often finds in developing countries. Whichever way we eat, to truly heal the planet, those of us lucky enough to be in a position to choose must get to the bottom of where our food comes from and lay it all bare. We can still prefer to be a vegan or an omnivore in all this, of course – especially as we start to explore the many different forms of regenerative agriculture in the next chapter. It's really important that we respect what sits right with people in their food choices, but however we eat, it is important to consider what we're sourcing and how it comes to be.

To move forward productively and united in our common values and goals, we need to ditch the ultra-processed madness and make produce sexy again. I want to see an outrageously luscious lentil pie ad on TV, or be targeted on Facebook with a punnet of strawberries instead of a Chicken Teriyaki Chip! Toss out the processed-food marketing calendar and fall in love with nature's marketing calendar. Let's get super excited about the upcoming 'strawberry season launch'. It's beautiful to know that towns

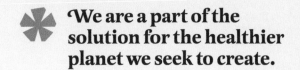

We are a part of the solution for the healthier planet we seek to create.

in heavily agricultural areas around the world have festivals to celebrate produce. Why can't this happen in cities? Let's show pumpkins the door after five months of enjoying every possible pumpkin dish, saying, 'Thanks, see you next year. It was great, but I think we need some space!' Let's flirt with the incoming spring peas and asparagus for our next delicious dalliance of the year.

Imagine if we stepped into the power of this: that by buying some organic, biodynamic carrots, coriander, lentils and rice, and some biodynamic or regeneratively farmed meat, then making a beautiful slow-cooked meal with some spices and vegie stock, we're directly supporting regenerative farmers, allowing them to continue to nourish the earth and build topsoil. And, as a bonus, we're flooding our bodies with foods that support us and our families to thrive. How powerful are we, right? We are a part of the solution for the healthier planet we seek to create.

The ultra-processed food industry would have well-meaning people believe that lab-created fake meats, made from soy or textured wheat proteins and other processed ingredients grown using methods that deplete topsoil, are 'climate friendly' food. Yet very often these ingredients come from monoculture farms using pesticides and herbicides that contaminate waterways, and employing methods that send carbon into the atmosphere. Sometimes they don't, sure – there are always category champions doing things better – but we need to be aware and choose wisely.

Just as they convinced us we needed diet sodas to lose weight and make 'healthier' choices, they are trying to tell us that ultra-processed imitation foods will save the planet. My words here are absolutely not about shaming vegans. Not one bit. My vegan friends, vegan doctor friends and the vegans in our Low Tox Life community are some of the most passionate and creative whole foodies I know. I'm aiming here for a frank examination of what's *truly* good, not just what we're told is good. Omnivores, too, need to take a long hard look at where most of the meat they eat comes from. One thing the research unequivocally shows is that we could all do with a drastically more diverse and nutrient-rich fresh diet.

Please don't feel bad if you've been duped by big food marketing. Most of us have been duped by the industry at some point. You're not a bad person or a silly person in this scenario. We're all just doing our best to navigate what it means to be a good human in today's world. And what I've learnt over the years, through studying and learning from incredible experts from farmers to nutritionists, doctors and public health officials, is that the answer isn't what the shiny packets and promises of the food industry would have us believe. No one is to blame other than the system that got us here and all of the complex factors that make up that system. If we keep trying to pin the blame on someone, put people down or shame people for eating a certain way, we'll die trying to find the guilty party. Now that we're here we need to look inwards, work out how best to act from our personal power, and all move forward together.

Is anyone else exhausted by the food fighting? I get it, our war-like blueprint is buried deep. We've been trained to find the right people and disparage the wrong people, unearthing every shred of evidence to support our conviction. But here's the thing: food is complex. It's not just about 'eating and getting full', it's about health, it's about culture, it's about geography, it's about equal rights, it's about agriculture, it's about politics and it's about the health of our planet. There are a lot of layers there, which is why we can't have a win–lose mentality on the subject of food. I yearn for all of us to come together, focused on how our food is grown and where it comes from rather than fighting about what it is and trying to be better than each other. By uniting and focusing on what works to create robust soils for growing healthy foods, we become agents for carbon sequestration and thriving farming communities all over the world – right from our dinner plates!

Some of the biggest industrial food producers in the world are starting to see that while the agricultural practices of the last century might have contributed to the degradation of approximately half of the world's topsoil, agriculture is our best chance of reversing that degradation. Farmers everywhere are being called on to change, with great education programs to help them get there, both locally and internationally.

Imagine if, from now on, meat-eaters in the privileged position of being discerning about their food choices only ate it if they knew how it was farmed. Imagine if meat-eaters brought a whole variety of plant-based whole foods into their diet for a greater range of micronutrients and prebiotics? How soon would this stop feeding the beast that is factory farming and increase the range of plants grown on farms, thus increasing biodiversity and healing more landscapes?

Our job as caring human beings

So here's what the task ahead is starting to look like, with baby steps and building from there:

1 To leave all that processed weirdness out of our trolleys. Did you know that globally, only about 33 per cent of the food we consume is whole food or minimally processed? The remainder – yep, a whopping 67 per cent – of the food we consume is processed or ultra-processed. Imagine not only the greater good we can do with a trolley rethink, but also the dollars that will free up!

2 To source as much of our food as possible from regenerative farms that are actively working to reverse desertification, build healthy topsoil, raise happy animals, and farm healthy and diverse crops for healthy and diverse ecosystems. The key here is starting wherever you are with whatever you can – aim for progress, not perfection.

3 To bring a whole lot more variety into our diet. Relying on meat, dairy, sugar, corn, soy and wheat as our main events continues to drive high-chemical-input monoculture crop farming and cruel and destructive factory farming. By bringing in variety from local growers, we will send a powerful message that farmers can and will thrive on mixed farms (the importance of the mixed farm is coming in the next chapter), and that there is demand for a broad spectrum of healthy whole foods.

4 To not waste the food we buy. On average, we are wasting one in every five shopping bags worth of food from our shopping, which places an enormous burden on the planet's resources – not to mention our hip pockets. A sizeable percentage of all food emissions globally is due to food waste – either in the supply chain or by us. We gotta get smarter here!

5 To compost everything we don't eat, so that it doesn't end up trapped in landfill.

Low Tox Life Food

You'll see time and again in this book that moving forward isn't about big grand gestures, shifts and policy changes 'out there', but about what happens right here in our kitchens and at our tables with friends and family. With that loving, home-prepared meal, made possible by connecting with the people who grow its ingredients or by growing them ourselves, we can create ripples of change. Through a deeper connection to our food, where it comes from, how we manage it at home to avoid waste, and what we choose to leave out of the trolley altogether, we can dramatically impact both human and planetary health. I have a huge amount of optimism that we can do this, and I'm excited to journey with you through this book.

We're going to find common ground no matter how you prefer to eat or what your beliefs. You might not want to make every recipe. That's okay. This isn't a prescription. It's an invitation to explore what's working to create a healthier planet and to ensure more nutrient-dense foods into the future, so our children and their children can thrive. It's about falling deeply in love with whole, nutritious foods and the land from which they come. It's about full food-system transparency and the deep happiness that comes from knowing more about the people who are responsible for growing your food.

The variety of foods you can incorporate into the recipes means there'll probably only be a couple you can't or won't eat. I want us all to remember – as we look to play a more meaningful role in supporting the healing of ourselves and our planet – that we have a lot more in common than we have differences.

All sorts of people profit from pitting us against each other. It sells more products, it boosts algorithms and it grows 'reach'. Let's not die fighting to be right in comment threads, but instead make progress by starting with what we know to be good and true, and from there making space for our bio-individual needs, diversity and shades of grey. Let's reconnect with each other, and celebrate our overlaps and our desire to do right by people, animals and the planet. It's time for connection and regeneration.

How the following chapters work

You might be thinking, *What's the plan from here, Alexx? How are we going to do this?*

Firstly, we're going to explore farming systems and practices that heal and regenerate landscapes. In knowing the different types of farming and their names and terms, we'll be better equipped to seek out produce grown using these methods, both in our communities and online. It'll get a bit technical, so if you're not that way inclined, I've got you covered with a crib-notes section starting on page 58.

Secondly, we're going to explore how best to connect to foods grown using these practices, no matter where you live in the world, as well as make a list of foods to focus on and try to incorporate more. We'll also step through some of the major cooking 'blocks' that hinder our full appreciation of and connection to produce, seasonal eating and cooking from scratch.

Thirdly, I'm going to arm us all with ways to make the most of all the foods we have in our pantry and fridge, so that we can use it more wisely and treat it with the gratitude it deserves. Some will be little things to add to meals, in the form of sauces, dressings and marinades; others will be basic templates, or what I call 'adaptable recipes', with a 'choose your own adventure' element; and the remainder will be recipes to follow – something for every mood. There's nothing like a few great go-to recipes to help put all the theory into practice with the people you love, at your table and theirs.

You've heard me say 'regenerative' and 'mixed farms' a few times so far. Let's now go on a little tour of the major methods of farming that have allowed farmers to prosper, biodiversity to flourish, animals to roam on pasture and enjoy life, desertification of land to be reversed, local water systems to thrive, flooding and run-off issues to be prevented, soils to become rich and fertile again, and more. It's a story of hope. It's a story of regenerative farming practices being used by more and more farmers, from those with small acreages right through to large-scale operations, who are achieving wonderful results not only for their land but for their business, as their farms become more resilient and productive. And it's a story that lays the foundation for healthier people and a happier planet, as we all work to increase our support for these methods from our homes around the world.

CHAPTER

2

What's best for our planet?

A way forward for us all

Can I cram 30-plus books' worth of information into 10,000 words here, I wonder? Well, no. It's going to be impossible to go into huge amounts of depth here, thanks to the inherent intricacies of the topics in question: the evolution of agriculture; the transition of economic systems towards growth as the number one measure of success; the Renaissance and then the industrial revolution's impact on food and agriculture; the intersection between military poisons and farming; the stealing of indigenous lands, and the loss of deep indigenous understanding in the process; the damage to and potential for restoring healthy water cycles; the serious magic and complexity of soil; the case for promoting biodiversity in farming, both in terms of nutrition and the climate crisis; and the magic of true fertilisation and regeneration of land ... You get the picture. There's a lot going on when we start trying to understand how we got here and where we need to go.

I've therefore included a Further Information list at the end of the book for you to continue learning if, like me, you enjoy delving deeper, or if you need to in order to change your habits and understand the best way forward. I always find if I truly grasp the why, I'm far more motivated to move on to the how, what, where and when of change. Bring on the deeper thinking, the grey-area magic, and the realisation that the argument about plant-based versus omnivorous diets is keeping us distracted from the exciting progress to be made. I often say that big oil, plastic and food have us right where they want us, pitting us against each other in order to keep the focus squarely off them.

Everything that is in nature – and remember, that's us too – is in a giant cycle and circle of life. We cannot have life without death and decay. There's no agriculture I've been able to find where something doesn't die, be it a worm, slug, rabbit, deer, mouse or frog in crop agriculture or animals for producing meat. I completely understand someone's desire to be as kind as possible to our planet. It's my desire too, so while some of us won't ever want to eat animals, some will, some have no option but to do so, and progress means moving forward where we agree.

Ethical, regenerative sourcing, reducing ultra-processed foods in our home, turning would-be food waste into new meals or life-giving compost – that's our big overlap. That's our huge opportunity for locking arms and making massive progress in cleaning up the food system, improving the treatment of animals in agriculture, repairing the soil and healing our planet. My favourite comprehensive agricultural history lesson, which includes profound evidence that we can effect radical and quick change together, came in the first chapters of Charles Massy's *Call of the Reed Warbler* – it should be taught in schools, and not just the agriculturally focused ones!

There is much we can learn, and I urge you to seek out many more teachers. But when I ask myself what would be really useful for us all to know, to inform how we work to source our food and to level up our awareness from this point on, this is what floats to the top:

* A good understanding of the types of farming that are giving more resources back to the planet than they use.
* A collective recognition that monoculture farming (one crop on one piece of land) and the use of agricultural chemicals have led to a rapid degeneration of land and biodiversity over the past few centuries – and that seeking out regeneratively farmed foods turns the tide.
* A focus on what regenerative practices we can cultivate ourselves, from a backyard vegie patch in the country to a little balcony in the city.
* A realisation that when we started to package long-life foods for global distribution, we began to lose cooking skills, which perpetuated a cycle of greater and greater dependency on ultra-processed foods.
* An awareness that when we started to normalise eating perfect-looking produce and whatever we feel like, we catapulted food waste levels into the stratosphere.

We can all make a difference from today by learning some basics in these areas, improving our understanding, raising our awareness and changing our habits over time. This is a journey towards a recognition of and support for what's good and true, and a healthy discernment of what's shiny and new. So let's now take a trip back to some key moments in recent history that help us understand how we came to be so disconnected from nature, seeing her as subservient to our needs, and no longer as our partner. Please do note that this history doesn't cover the indigenous wisdom lost in colonisation. I've shared some valuable resources on this on page 292.

A few key turns in recent history

During the First World War, all sorts of poisonous gases were created and used as a gruesome means to wage war and win battles. So horrific were the deaths and injuries these gases caused, in 1925 almost all countries signed the Geneva Gas Protocol, which prohibited the 'use in war of asphyxiating, poisonous, or other gases, and of bacteriological methods of warfare'. The protocol did not ban the development, production or stockpiling of such weaponry, however, and here's where this matters: it didn't ban these toxic substances from agricultural use – only from combat.

The creation of explosives and lethal gases grew exponentially during the Second World War. These included the first organophosphate compounds, known as 'nerve gas', developed in 1937 in Germany as it geared up to declare war. After the war, the manufacturers of these compounds repurposed them for use as pesticides, as a way to create a stable market for their ongoing sale and use. Shortly after the war, the first chlorine-based herbicides were created to kill broadleaf plants, with the promise of increased food production. This was rather handily timed with a demand for America to 'feed the world' due to the food shortages in Europe, and so farmers planted monoculture fields of grains that could be easily processed into long-life biscuits and crackers to be shipped overseas. Farmers were subsidised for this endeavour, and some of these subsidies still exist today.

After the Second World War there was also a huge excess of petroleum in America. Scientists found that it could be used to create synthetic fertilisers, which the chemical industry started to market as an easy tool for farmers, luring them in on the promise of bigger yields and easier farming. Unfortunately, though, the plants weren't healthier, and the weaker a plant, the better target it becomes for pests – kind of like the way we humans can be more easily knocked down by the flu if we're very run down. Luckily, we now had 'cool new products' to address weak plants.

So the war on pests and weeds grew, bringing a wide array of pesticides and herbicides onto the scene. These also polluted the air and the water because, shockingly, only 2–3 per cent of the products hit their target – a pest or a weed – while the rest affected the surrounding environment.

Many politicians and farmers were seduced by the promised benefit of these chemical inputs. The tides are turning today, but even back when these compounds were introduced, a few gents were alarmed by where the use of such things might lead.

Regenerative-thinking pioneers

A few key figures sought to define a different path into farming's future at this time of accelerated chemical input use. Here are some of their stories in brief (but see also lowtoxlife.com, my podcast and Further Information on page 292).

BIODYNAMIC PIONEER
RUDOLF STEINER (1861–1925)

An Austrian-born philosopher, artist and education pioneer, Steiner was the founder of plant-based remedy and personal care company Weleda and of biodynamic farming. He taught that the best approach to agriculture was to 'farm as one organism'. In 1924 he ran a seminal eight-part agriculture course teaching his principles, thus becoming the godfather of biodynamic farming. Adolf Hitler spoke publicly against him as early as 1921, declaring him an enemy of Germany. Steiner died shortly after, but his disciple Ehrenfried Pfeiffer flourished in Switzerland, and in 1938 wrote a book explaining Steiner's teachings, *Biodynamic Farming and Gardening*. He said 'the cultivated field is a living organism, a living entity in the totality of its processes'.

AGRICULTURAL PIONEER
GEORGE WASHINGTON CARVER (1865–1943)

Born into slavery and orphaned at an early age, scientist, botanist and agricultural pioneer Carver forged an inspiring path, becoming the first black college student at Iowa State University, then a professor of agriculture at

Tuskegee University, where he developed a pioneering agricultural research centre. After the boll weevil beetle migrated into the cotton-growing areas of America from Mexico, devastating many farms, Carver helped farmers implement his crop rotation techniques to grow a greater variety of crops, repair soil and build the resilience of the land and of farming businesses. He didn't stop at educating farmers: he also published public recipe ideas for the new peanut, pecan and sweet potato crops, to increase their uptake and marketability. Global leaders and pioneers of the day turned to him for agricultural advice, including Theodore Roosevelt, Franklin D. Roosevelt, the Crown Prince of Sweden, Mahatma Gandhi, Henry Ford and Thomas Edison. *Time* magazine declared him a 'Black Leonardo da Vinci' in 1941.

REGENERATIVE PIONEER

WALTER JAMES, LORD NORTHBOURNE (1896–1982)

Walter James, who was also the 4th Baron Northbourne, was an Oxford University graduate, long-time farmer, silver Olympic medallist, painter and poet. He visited Ehrenfried Pfeiffer in 1938, inviting him to present the first conference in England on biodynamics. Northbourne then wrote *Look to the Land* (1940), cautioning against 'chemicalisation', government intervention and centralisation of the food system. He maintained that farming was an intimate labour of love for the local land, and was one of the first to write about distinguishing between conventional and organic farming. He said that 'Farming cannot be treated as a mixture of chemistry and cost accountancy' or conform with 'the exigencies of modern business'. Most tellingly, he wrote, 'Nature will not be driven. If you try, she hits back slowly, but very hard.'

And boy, is nature hitting back hard right now! It's time to learn the lessons and turn the tide.

J.I. RODALE
(AND SIR ALBERT HOWARD)

J.I. Rodale (1898-1971) championed the organic agriculture movement in America. A New York entrepreneur who had always suffered ill health, Rodale one day decided to buy farmland in Emmaus, Pennsylvania, and move one of his businesses there. His enthusiasm for organics and working in partnership with nature rather than against her or dominating her culminated in the creation of the renowned Rodale Institute. Here, researchers carry out some of the most advanced trials of regenerative agriculture versus conventional farming, along with other research that benefits farmers around the world.

Rodale was influenced by the work of British botanist Sir Albert Howard (1873-1947), the first Westerner to document the Vedic Indian techniques of sustainable agriculture. Howard wrote passionately about the necessity for healthy soil, and the use of natural methods like composting and cover cropping for food production and farm resilience. Inspired by Howard, Rodale 'decided that we must get a farm at once and raise as much of our family's food by the organic method as possible'. He noticed that as the health of the soil improved, so did his own health. He was so inspired by these results that he went on to create the organic movement in America, publishing the first issue of *Organic Gardening and Farming* in 1942.

Unheeded cautionary tales

Imagine if the clever work of these cautionary tale-tellers had gathered momentum since then. Instead, conventional chemicalisation of the food system prevailed. Lord Northbourne's warning about treating nature as something to manipulate and dominate can still be heard today.

Let's return to our place in nature instead of placing ourselves outside the system as managers, trying to analyse costs and benefits, profit and loss. These pioneers and many like them have shown us the path, and modern educators are furthering their cause around the world.

Making our biggest impact

The ecological impact of producing a food on, say, emissions or water usage, will change a great deal depending on key factors such as the farming method used, biodiversity, water cycles and location. The health impact of foods on each individual depends on their existing health, age, stage of life and genetics. It's important to remember this as we home in on the three areas where we can truly make a massive difference:

1 **eliminating food waste and composting scraps**
2 **using whole foods to cook from scratch**
3 **upgrading our food sourcing whenever we can.**

These three areas of focus give us all a job we can do from today, no matter our location, budget or time constraints. Can we all master all three? Most of us, probably not. But the beauty of having all three to focus on in doing better for our health and for the planet is that we can all start somewhere and do something. Your way of making a difference becomes somewhat of a 'choose your own adventure' situation.

Perfectly imperfect is how we're proceeding here. All progress is regenerative because it's all stepping us closer as a collective to eliminating waste (*big* emissions saver); eating simpler, less processed food (*big* health saver and emissions saver); and eating from local farms that are working to repair and regenerate the landscape with nature as their partner rather than slave (*big* win for planet health, farmer health and our health).

I'm still figuring out where some of my produce items are going to come from so that I can have a truly regenerative shopping basket, and sometimes budget constraints work against my ideal. I still buy that packet of crackers for the mezze plate when friends are coming over and I don't have the gumption or pantry stocks to whip up some crackers of my own. I still sometimes have a whoopsie on the food waste front and wish I'd listened to myself two days earlier when that thing could have been saved and relegated to the freezer or drowned beyond recognition in a soup or stew. Thank god for compost, turning it into a resource instead of a waste, as we'll discuss in more detail at the end of this chapter.

Does this mean I berate or shame myself for what I'm not achieving? Nope. If you were coaching a team of six-year-old basketballers, would you chastise them for the couple of things they did imperfectly while they were getting the

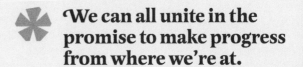

'We can all unite in the promise to make progress from where we're at.

hang of things or when they were obviously trying their best? Of course you wouldn't. You don't want them giving up the sport before they've begun. Encouragement is key as we move forward.

At this point I feel It's important to mention that choosing regeneratively farmed produce is a privileged position. Not everyone can pick and choose where their produce comes from, although as you'll see, there are lots of ideas here for how to connect more deeply to your food sources and to create savings and opportunities by forging links with your surrounding community. In the urban food deserts you find in many developed areas around the world or in many regional areas where there are big mono-cropping farms shipping all the food they produce 'out', sometimes the supermarket is the only option – for now. Maybe you're in a mining town where you can't grow anything in the dirt around you. Maybe you're not a confident vegie gardener yet, even if you have the best soil ever.

Different people. Different stages. Different skill levels. Different capabilities. Millions of imperfect humans moving forward. We can all unite in the promise to make progress from where we're at. So if you ever find yourself asking 'Where to next?', remember:

* Packaged foods with simple ingredients lists always trump those with encyclopedic ingredients lists.
* Packaged foods labelled 'Made from local ingredients' or with at least a very high percentage of local ingredients always trump those with overseas-sourced ingredients.
* Local produce always trumps processed packaged foods, even if it's conventionally grown.
* Seasonal produce grown locally always trumps overseas or faraway-grown produce.
* Reducing your food waste to nothing tops having any.
* Regeneratively farmed produce that we don't waste tops it all.

That, my friends, is the journey ahead. Let's all pledge to do more with the lives we're living, to do our best to reconnect to skills like cooking, growing and composting, and to focus more on the provenance of our food.

Demonise processed foods, not farmers

It's important to note that at this point in history, most farms are not kept according to regenerative philosophies. This means that farmers might read this book who are using conventional farming methods, lots of chemical inputs, and perhaps genetically modified seeds and their accompanying herbicides. To those farmers, however they're farming right now, I say thank you for your hard work. I mean it. Producing food is a big job that most wouldn't have the stamina to manage for a day, let alone a lifetime. Nothing here is intended as a personal criticism of anyone. We're all only ever doing what we can based on what seems to be the best way forward. All I ask, as you read this, is that you keep an open mind. While this chapter won't provide nearly enough depth for an agricultural professional, I hope it will serve as a springboard for research, for connecting to local farmers who are already achieving positive results with regenerative methods – be they small- or large-scale and in any part of the world. My first suggested stops for the agricultural professional? Allan Savory's *Holistic Management*, Nicole Masters' book on soil, and Charles Massy's *Call of the Reed Warbler*. All are by experienced farmers and scientists.

If we can see farms as an important site for reversing our planet's loss of topsoil and biodiversity, in a way that still provides farmers with a healthy and stable income, while perhaps also increasing the resilience of their farms, then surely we're off to a good start!

So many articles I've read over the past few years have demonised asparagus and beef farmers, accusing agriculture of inflicting various degrees of damage on the planet and concluding that we should eat in such a way as to minimise this damage. Over the same period, I've seen 'plant-based' ultra-processed foods increasingly touted as the silver bullet for minimising our dietary impact on the planet. I just picture row upon row of temperature-controlled warehouses culturing trademarked synthetic meats, refrigerated trucks running around the world delivering processed frozen plant-based meals, and trendy meat-free burgers with funky names being shipped frozen and sold in a country 15,000 kilometres (9000 miles) away. It's an entrepreneurial bandaid, not a deep, healing solution, unfortunately.

Has anyone done an emissions calculation on Beyond Burger patties? Actually, yes. In their book *Sacred Cow*, Diana Rodgers and Robb Wolf cite a Michigan State University study of a farm called White Oak Pastures in

Shown to reduce labour costs and increase yields and profits in the short term, monoculture farming seemed a boon for agriculture in the 20th century. Now, with just decades of topsoil remaining, farmers the world over are moving back towards a total-ecosystem-health approach. They're farming many different plants and species together, and increasing topsoil levels, nutrient density in food, farm resilience, farmer income and even yields once well established.

Georgia, USA, where they raise 100 per cent grass-fed beef. The net total emissions on the farm were *minus* 3.5 kilograms (7.7 pounds) of CO_2 per kilogram (2 lb 4 oz) of fresh meat. Hang on, so you mean to tell me that I'd need to eat a White Oak Pastures grass-fed beef burger to offset the Beyond Burger? Yes, you would. I'm not trying to have a 'gotcha' moment 'against' people who choose a vegan diet. When we create an 'other' and an 'enemy', we commit to stagnation and fighting, not progress and repair. I just truly believe we should all be able to come together in our quest to do better for the planet while eating whatever we prefer or need, guided by our health practitioners, religious beliefs or tastes – that's everyone's right. But it *is* a gotcha moment against those narratives that try to create a bad guy in our food choices and food recommendations. Over the years, for example, eggs have been as bad as smoking one day and essential to a healthy diet for their omega-3s, choline and vitamin D the next. Is it possible that the fast and ultra-processed food markets are cleverly trying to hijack the 'save the planet' conversation in order to tear us even further away from the not-as-sexy, non-trademarkable, much less profitable world of produce?

If we start looking at the impact of produce on the planet using an overall cost–benefit analysis, that brings us to the types of farms that are using the planet's resources and natural systems to produce food, but *at the same time* regenerating those systems and improving them. Consider these points:

* Most reports about carbon emissions from food don't consider the contribution of synthetic fossil-fuel-based fertilisers and other chemical inputs such as pesticides and herbicides, or their role in the degradation of soil in the long term.
* Many reports on carbon emissions aren't focused on the broader ecological impacts of the forms of farming that are poisoning waterways and the air and reducing biodiversity.
* Most 'water cost' reports on food don't factor in rain that would be falling anyway. This explains why one report will say each kilogram

(2 lb 4 oz) of beef requires 1500 litres (400 gallons) of water to produce, while another will say that with better overall water retention on the farm (rather than allowing it to run off), it takes 98 per cent less water. They also don't factor in the benefit of the ruminants trampling the soil, thus allowing the water that does fall to sink into the landscape, meaning more plants (grasses/legume/clover and whatever else is grown on the pasture) grow more quickly and capture more carbon.

* Not enough reports about the cost of farming show the increased carbon sequestration and biodiversity to be gained by using farming methods proven to regenerate landscapes.
* Reports about animal emissions in farming don't consider the impact of leaving grassland fallow over time: compacted soil that allows water to run off, taking topsoil with it into rivers, for example.

Nothing is black and white. Surely now, when we should be trying to return the whole planet to a thriving state, is not the time for reductionist thinking.

This doesn't mean we should dismiss reports or researchers who are trying to figure things out and ascertain where our focuses should lie. But it does mean that we should look to who is funding the research, what areas it is focusing on, and how this fits into the big picture. It's like a savings account: sure, you might make some withdrawals to buy what you need or want, but what about all the savings you put in as a result of your good habits? Some farming methods are excellent at making metaphorical deposits back to the land.

Biodiversity loss – a big concern

A 2019 UK report showed that agriculture has been the main offender in the dramatic loss of wildlife, reducing it by a whopping 41 per cent. The report emphasised that this decline was driven by the change from mixed farming to intensive monoculture farming practices, where the farm grew in size and specialised in either animals or grain or seed.

When you plant fewer crop species on wide-stretching fields, you lose a lot of cover crops, hedgerows, ponds and dams, which leaves the farm more susceptible to pests because there are no birds and other animals to eat them. The reliance on pesticides on monoculture farms in the UK has *doubled* over the past 25 years, and the figures are similar elsewhere. One of the pesticide families now restricted in Europe, neonicotinoids, is believed by Dutch and German scientists to be responsible for a massive loss of insect population, including bees, all over the world. In Germany the loss has been 76 per cent in the past 27 years.

We don't just have a climate crisis, we have a biodiversity crisis, thanks to all the land clearing over the past few decades and the shifts in agriculture since the world wars of the 20th century. But perhaps, instead of abandoning agriculture and farmers by investing in the huge tech race towards lab-created foods, we need to give farmers every tool they need to restore health to the local ecosystems and land they manage. And if the governments of the world aren't going to do that yet, how do *we*?

By giving them a big market of people longing for whole, nutritious food from biodiverse regenerative farms. When farms are healthy, landscapes are healthy. When you have healthy landscape after landscape, you have a healthy planet because of the increased carbon-capturing capabilities of healthy soils, more efficient water cycles and better land cooling. The soils teeming with nutrients also produce more nutritious foods, which means humans are satisfied and deeply nourished at a cellular level. By connecting our plates to farms that are increasing biodiversity and ecosystem health, we can capture more carbon in soils, put an end to the sixth mass extinction and improve our own health.

What the heck are we waiting for?

But the yields

In the past, regenerative methods have been criticised for their poorer yields. But could regenerative agriculture be done on a global scale without harming yields and thus be able to 'feed the world'? Yes, it seems it could, especially given that biodiversity-rich farms seem to be more resilient to drought and adverse weather, thus making harvests less variable.

This is just one example of why we should be making a case for large-scale education on regenerative farming methods. Farming free from chemical inputs has come a long way in the past few decades. As I prepared to write this book, I became aware of story after story of farmers around the world who had reversed desertification; increased topsoil; returned rich, fertile soil to their landscapes; and restored water cycles – all while producing delicious, nutrient-rich food and an environment more resistant to pests and excess weeds. Farmers of both animals and plants could be a part of the climate solution we so desperately need right now.

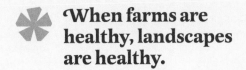

When farms are healthy, landscapes are healthy.

But the animals are destroying the planet

'Project Drawdown', a not-for-profit research and advisory body founded by Paul Hawken and Amanda Ravenhill in 2014, is one invaluable resource I've come to refer to regularly. Hawken and Ravenhill's bestselling 2017 book of the same name is a must-read. Project Drawdown describes 'drawdown' as the future point in time when greenhouse gases levels in the atmosphere stop climbing and start to decline steadily. This is the moment when we begin the process of stopping further climate change and averting potentially catastrophic warming. It is a critical turning point for life on earth. Interestingly enough, among all of Project Drawdown's climate-forward solutions, several involve animal agriculture. Were these bought and paid for by animal-industry lobbyists? No. The research is simply showing us that farm animals have a very strong and positive role to play in maintaining healthy regenerative landscapes, thanks largely to their poop and trampling the ground.

So there are significant overlaps in a focus on farming methods that design for and encourage biodiversity, and those that draw carbon back down into the soils where it belongs. The forms of farming that improve biodiversity also improve carbon drawdown. Winning!

Let's go on a big-picture-thinking tour of farming methods that produce high yields of nutritious food for good health, resilient farms and food security. Methods that create farms with rich, healthy soil supporting a myriad of different plants and grasses, brimming with a biodiversity that improves the longer and longer they are farmed this way. Methods that also focus on the health and wellbeing of the farm worker and owner.

We'll start with a quick snapshot of the major forms of farming that tick both the biodiversity and carbon-drawdown boxes, followed by a more thorough examination for nerds like me who want more detail. So prepare for a magical tour of regenerative farming methods.

What is regenerative agriculture?

'Sustainable' means taking as much as we give. Problem is, we've taken much more than we've given for a long time now. The planet will continue with or without us, but if we're to stick around, regeneration is critical – giving more than we take, restoring and healing. While in the coming chapters we will upskill in how to source regeneratively grown produce, minimise food waste, turn scraps into new life and cook from scratch, it's important to familiarise ourselves with the different terms used in regenerative farming methods. That way, we can source produce more confidently and also understand what we're contributing to by making swaps whenever we can. Understanding the 'why' helps put a fire in our belly.

Regenerative agriculture, in its many forms, works to cultivate healthier soils and build topsoil, improve water retention and water systems, increase carbon sequestration, and ensure more resilient operations for the farmers as well as fair working conditions for all who work on the land. Decentralisation and food sovereignty are also both important in the many different approaches.

Simply put, the following systems do a whole lot of good to improve communities, our own personal health and the health of the planet. And we can do this while pursuing whichever way of eating we've found works best for us.

Regenerative agriculture 101

If you want just a brief look before you start digging into the recipes, the following 'crib notes' on the main regenerative agriculture methods are just the ticket. For more in-depth coverage of these systems, see pages 64–86. I must say, though, that these methods are just the tip of the regenerative agriculture iceberg.

We still have much to learn about indigenous food security principles and agricultural methods around the world. As we celebrate anyone who is doing great work in rekindling a deeper connection to land, we should take any and every opportunity we get to amplify indigenous wisdom and stories.

Low Tox Life Food

Getting to know regenerative agriculture methods

Here's your in-brief rundown of the regenerative methods you're likely to encounter in reports, articles and out and about talking to farmers.

Regenerative organic agriculture

ORIGINS Founded by Bob Rodale, Pennsylvania, United States, 1970s

WHAT IT MEANS Farming in a way that respects workers, animals and the land, while working to consistently improve the landscape, regenerating it and continually making it better rather than simply 'sustaining' it in its current state. (For more see page 65.)

Biodynamics

ORIGINS Founded by Rudolf Steiner, Austria, 1920s

WHAT IT MEANS The farmer sees the farm as one whole organism. The health of that overall organism depends on the health of the forest, plants, fields, animals, soils and compost. The role of the biodynamic farmer is to support the health of all of those parts, while respecting and enhancing the synergy between all elements of the farm, listening to the land and evolving as necessary over time. (For more see page 68.)

Agroforestry

ORIGINS Founded by J. Russell Smith, USA, 1929

WHAT IT MEANS Agroforestry is the study and re-creation of what we find in a healthy forest: layers, from canopy to undergrowth and leaf litter. An agroforest includes multiple layers of trees, crops, shrubs and sometimes animals, to create food and sequester carbon. Each layer provides some sort of food or benefit to the system as a whole, comprising predominantly perennial plants and species native to the area. (For more see page 72.)

Permaculture

ORIGINS Founded by Bill Mollison and David Holmgren, Australia, 1970s

WHAT IT MEANS Mollison and Holmgren described it as 'an integrated, sustainable and evolving system of perennial or self-perpetuating plant and animal species useful to mankind'. It has since evolved to encompass not just systems for growing and procuring food, but also 'consciously designed landscapes which mimic the patterns and relationships found in nature, while yielding an abundance of food, fibre and energy for provision of local needs'. (For more see page 73.)

Holistic management

ORIGINS Founded by Allan Savory, Zimbabwe, 1960s

WHAT IT MEANS Proper management of the wild and domestic grazing animals that evolved in and still inhabit the grasslands of the world, as the key to reversing desertification, restoring healthy grassland soils so as to engage them as a carbon sink. In one study, Holistic Planned Grazing yielded a 400 per cent increase in permanent soil carbon relative to conventionally managed neighbouring land. (For more see page 75.)

Silvo-farming

ORIGINS A European system that dates back centuries

WHAT IT MEANS Also known as silvopasture farming, silvo-farming is a form of agroforestry that includes grazing animals for the mutual benefit of trees, forage plants and animals. The farmer benefits from multiple income sources over the year, and the ground benefits from significant carbon capture. (For more see page 79.)

Natural sequence farming

ORIGINS Founded by Peter Andrews, Australia, 1970s

WHAT IT MEANS This repair system is the ultimate example of regeneration. It addresses land degradation and biodiversity loss by re-establishing natural water systems – which Andrews calls the 'chain of ponds – swampy meadow complexes'. These Australian landscape features were destroyed by European settlers in the way they used the land. Andrews's method is about harnessing the biological potential of a landscape by reading it intimately and observing all life and relationships upon it. (For more see page 82.)

Conservation agriculture or no/minimal till

ORIGINS Brazil and Argentina, 1970s

WHAT IT MEANS This is all about minimal tillage (ploughing and other cultivation methods) and disturbance of soil to protect it from erosion. Permanent soil cover, with crop residues and mulches for better nutrient cycling and carbon capture, is used in conjunction with crop rotation and intercropping (see opposite) for improved water usage, pest resistance and root system development. (For more see page 83.)

Regenerative seaweed aquaculture and marine aquaculture

ORIGINS Japan, 1600s

WHAT IT MEANS Seaweed can grow up to 60 times faster than land-based plants and can sequester 20 times the carbon. So farming seaweed has much potential to facilitate a rapid increase in carbon sequestration while also providing essential nutrients and trace minerals for humans and other animals. (For more see page 84.)

Urban organic agriculture

ORIGINS Various and growing in popularity

WHAT IT MEANS This is less a method and more an umbrella term for all forms of regenerative farming practices being performed in an urban setting. It's an exciting part of greening our cities and finding creative ways to localise food supply. (For more see page 85.)

Some more regenerative agriculture terms

You might also come across these terms, some of which are variations on those we've already seen.

* **Intercropping and polyculture:** The growing of many different plant species in tandem, to increase resilience to drought and extreme weather events, as well as to provide a wide variety of foods and nutrients to local communities. (For more see page 65.)
* **Water harvesting:** The practice of ensuring that every drop of water is captured and its release is slowed through the landscape to increase hydration of that landscape and prevent run-off (where the water lands fast and leaves fast).
* **Plant bordering:** A strategy that allows wild plants and weeds to grow as a border around a farm to encourage bees and beneficial insects, and minimise the threat of pests on the farm.
* **Push–pull pest management:** Regenerative farms of all kinds often employ this pest-management method to dramatically reduce, if not prevent altogether, the need for chemical inputs. Some plants act as pest detractors and others as pest lures, so for a crop often bothered by a particular pest, you would plant something the pest is attracted to that keeps it away from your cash crop.
* **Alley cropping:** The act of farming trees between harvest crops for greater biodiversity, pest protection and carbon capture.

An in-depth look at regenerative agriculture

Let's take a more detailed look at some of the most promising regenerative agriculture methods being worked with today. It's important to note that many of these more recent methods are refinements and inspirations from ancient indigenous wisdom – a little bit like a modern-day pop star being inspired by chord progressions and harmonies popularised by The Beatles. We're at the tip of the iceberg in acknowledging and championing ancient systems and land-management techniques. These sophisticated and truly sustainable methods were practised by indigenous peoples before colonisation, and shining a light on them will ultimately help us heal not just the earth and our broken relationship with our natural world, but some of the deep injustices of the past. This is not my story to tell, but I can recommend an important film on the subject, *Gather* (2020), as a starting point if you want to know more.

As we explore these regenerative methods in more detail, it's important to note that each one will work differently in different parts of the world, depending on the climatic region or microclimate. There is no 'one best way' for everyone, just as there's no one best diet for 7.8 billion people. We need to learn the lesson that we are caretakers of the land, not owners. And we must listen and partner and nurture. Nicole Masters, in her book *For the Love of Soil*, shows just how intimately we need to get to know the land in order to really help it, and us, thrive.

I don't know about you, but I feel a great peace in my soul and trust in my heart that everything's going to be just fine if we start to assume our place as part of a natural system, not as a person trying to manipulate the system to get what we want. That's the farming of the future. I'm just so excited to keep meeting amazing humans who are embarking on these journeys back to being one with the land and helping orchestrate the return of beautiful biodiversity, cooler landscapes, healthier water cycles and deeply nourishing whole foods.

Everything's going to be just fine if we start to assume our place as part of a natural system, not as a person trying to manipulate the system to get what we want.

Intercropping and polyculture

For hundreds of years, Indigenous American tribes have planted more than one crop synergistically, knowing that certain plants make each other more resilient and more efficient in their use of light, nutrients and water. When done right, this method aids in increasing biodiversity and sequestering carbon. Corn, beans and squash, known as the 'Three Sisters' and grown by the Iroquois of the north-east, are a perfect example. The corn makes trellises for the beans to run up, the squash leaves make a natural mulch to cover the soil and discourage weeds, and the beans fix nitrogen in the soil. Isn't that just amazing?

Regenerative organic agriculture

Robert 'Bob' Rodale, J.I. Rodale's son, coined the term 'regenerative organic' to describe a holistic approach to farming and to distinguish it from simply sustaining the land without synthetic inputs. He wasn't satisfied with the word 'sustainable', which was first used in reference to agriculture by Abraham Lincoln in the 1850s. All the way back then, before Lincoln was even president, he warned that bigger farms using big machines would not be able to sustain themselves in the long term. Bob agreed. In an interview in 1989, he said, 'I don't think the average person aspires to live in a sustained environment, they want to live in something that's expanding and getting better. So I think the idea of regeneration is more appealing.'

Bob's daughter Maria Rodale is a friend of mine and one of the wisest people I know. She is a wonderful champion for her dad and grandfather's legacies, continuing to advocate for and build awareness of the power of regenerative practices. Here's how she describes Bob's view:

My father came up with the idea of regeneration by observing nature. Nature has an innate tendency to heal itself. After a fire, for instance, nature has a process of healing and regenerating. He believed that people had the same tendency, for example when our skin heals after a wound. He saw our job as being to tap in to that natural process to heal ourselves and the land by farming and living regeneratively.

The Rodale Institute in Pennsylvania has been conducting critical research for decades, including the longest-standing trial of conventional versus regenerative organic in the world. Since 1981, this trial has assessed differences in yield, resilience to weather and pests, nutrient content and water usage. I've had the great good fortune of standing in that field, thanks to a dear friend who worked at Rodale for a time, and seeing the difference with my own eyes truly was a special moment. They have found, over the course of these trials, that the regenerative organic method wins in every way, all while avoiding poisonous run-off of synthetic chemicals into the waterways.

Soil health is the number one focus of regenerative organic farming, as the health of the soil contributes to the health of the plant and the nutritiousness of the food, which in turn impacts human and animal health, the resiliency of the farm and the health of our planet as a whole.

Any regenerative farmer or pioneer will insist on not relying on too fixed a definition or method, as they need to remain flexible to evolution over time, just as the landscapes they seek to regenerate evolve. There is one guaranteed constant: no genetically modified seed or synthetic pesticides or herbicides are used on the farm.

What is most beautiful to me about this philosophy is that it illustrates perfectly that there is no one ideal way to do things. What works on one farm in one climate will work differently somewhere else, and then differently even possibly the next year. Just as the best diet is one that addresses the reasons, seasons and lifetime, the best farming tweaks things within its basic principles depending on specific reasons and seasons.

From these regenerative agriculture principles have emerged a variety of methods that all unite in their ability to improve agroecosystems, in turn increasing the health of the planet as more and more farms adopt the practices.

Low Tox Life Food

REGENERATIVE ORGANIC AGRICULTURE CERTIFICATION

The Regenerative Organic Agriculture certification was created in 2018 by a non-profit alliance between the Rodale Institute, clothing company Patagonia and soap company Dr Bronner's. This goes above and beyond 'organic'. To be regenerative, a farm must practise the regenerative organic way, constantly improving the health of the farm, soil health, animal welfare and social fairness for all who work there. Regenerative organic agriculture, as defined in the new certification, rests on four basic principles:

1   **progressively improving all agroecosystems (soil, water, biodiversity)**
2   **creating content-specific design and making holistic decisions that express the essence of each farm (because as we've seen, there's no 'one size fits all' in farming)**
3   **ensuring and developing just and reciprocal relationships among all stakeholders**
4   **continually growing and evolving individuals, farms and communities to express their innate potential.**

Biodynamic farming

Biodynamics evolved from the work of philosopher and scientist Rudolf Steiner. It all began with his eight-part agriculture course in 1924. Steiner carved out a set of principles for farmers, using the best of contemporary scientific understanding while at the same time working with the spirit of nature. The philosophy has continued to develop over the century since, and can be applied anywhere food is grown, with local adjustments based on the size of the farm, the landscape and the climate.

Biodynamic farming is a method of organic farming that has a spiritual element. The farmer is in service to life – the life of everything on the farm. Although it is now a century old, it is truly a form of agriculture for our times, when we seek to repair and regenerate soil and land around the world.

The main tenets of the biodynamic philosophy

1   **A biodynamic farm is a living organism.** The health of the overall organism depends on the health of the forest, plants, fields, animals, soils and compost. The role of the biodynamic farmer is to support the health of all of those parts, respect and enhance the synergy between all elements of the farm, listen to the land, and evolve as necessary over time. Are you starting to see a pattern here with the forms of regenerative agriculture that help us create a healthy planet?

2   **Biodynamics cultivates biodiversity.** Annual and perennial vegetables, herbs, flowers, berries, fruits, nuts, grains, pasture and other forage plants, native plants, and pollinator hedgerows can all contribute to plant diversity, amplifying the health and resilience of the farm organism. Diversity in domestic animals is also beneficial, as each species brings a different relationship to the land and a unique quality of manure. The diversity of plant and animal life can be developed over time, starting with a few primary crops and one or two species of animals (even as small as earthworms or honeybees), and adding more species as the farm organism matures.

3   **Biodynamics brings plants and animals together.** While in a lot of industrial farming you raise either plant crops or animals, in biodynamic farming you combine the two, for overall farm health and greater biodiversity. Biodynamics recognises the imbalance that occurs over time when you farm 'either/or'. Soil, plants and animals work together to support balance and resilience in the whole landscape.

4 **Biodynamics generates on-farm fertility.** When you grow plants in living soil, they take up an abundance of nutrients from that soil, in a way that cannot be achieved with intensive chemical fertilisers or through hydroponic methods. Composting brings soil, manure and plant matter into a healthy cocktail that gives strength to the overall farming system. Composting is enhanced by herbal preparations unique to biodynamics, including yarrow, chamomile, stinging nettle, oak bark, dandelion and valerian. These all contribute to healing the land and to the cultivation of diverse microbes and fungi in the soil. Cover crops bring plant diversity and life to the soil through oxygen and nitrogen. Crop rotation brings an abundance of organism variety to the soil. Everything works together to strengthen the organism, the farm, as a whole.

5 **Biodynamics approaches pests and disease holistically.** Pests and disease don't have much opportunity to thrive in a healthy, robust farm organism. When there is a pest or disease, the biodynamic farmer uses it as an opportunity to identify an imbalance. While they can use biological interventions to manage the immediate situation, they then ensure that they identify the imbalance that caused the weakness in the first place. Making the necessary changes to management and practices will restore overall health to the farm organism. Modern medicine could learn a lot from biodynamic agriculture, I think.

6 **Biodynamically raised animals are treated with respect.** They are always cared for and fed food that is appropriate for their digestive system. Cows keep their horns and chickens' beaks aren't trimmed, for every part of the animal serves that animal's total health. Baby animals are fed the milk of the herd, not outside replacements or formula, and all animals roam and forage with plenty of space to thrive.

7 **Biodynamic preparations give life force to the soil.** And from here to the whole farm. You might have heard of some woo-woo-sounding preparations in biodynamics, like burning horns packed with manure, and wondered what the heck that's meant to do. But this practice, which dates back to Steiner's 1924 lecture series, is backed by a certain mixture of science and spirituality. Horsetail tea, for example, is used to prevent fungal disease in the soil. Horn manure is manure placed inside a cow horn and buried in the ground over the winter months to strengthen the life of the soil and the relationship between the soil and plants. Cow horns can also be filled with quartz crystals and buried over the summer months, then ground down into silica and added to the soil

with the intention of improving plant immunity, photosynthesis and ripening. These preparations and the composting treatments are used to bring plants into a dynamic relationship with soil, water, air, warmth and cosmos. The idea is that this will help them develop into healthy, balanced organisms with access to all the nutrients they need. This in turn should make them more resilient to pests, diseases and extreme climatic conditions.

8 **Biodynamics contributes to social and economic health.** It aims for the triple bottom line of social, ecological and economically sustainable growth. You might have heard of CSAs, community supported agriculture initiatives making highly nutritious food available to the community and strengthening the economic position of farmers through regular community purchasing. These were pioneered by biodynamic farmers.

DEMETER BIODYNAMIC CERTIFICATION

—

'Demeter' is the international logo used to signify biodynamic certification. The certification process ensures that the whole property is certified, not just the crop or the animals, and also that the farm reserves designated space to cultivate biodiversity.

Agroforestry

Also known as multisystem agroforestry, this is the study and creation of what we find in the magic of a healthy forest: layers. The approach was first articulated by J. Russell Smith, an economic geographer, in 1929. An agroforest contains multiple layers of trees, crops and shrubs to create food and sequester carbon. The idea is to study the natural relationships between all things in a living forest and re-create this in order to produce food for people while serving the planet. Some of the most robust agroforestry projects comprise seven layers: roots, ground cover, herbaceous plant, shrub, low tree, tall tree and vines. The plants in these layers are predominantly perennials and local native species. Every layer provides some sort of food or benefits the system as a whole. I mean, it just makes sense, doesn't it?

Agroforestry prevents erosion and flooding, restores degraded lands and soils, supports and protects biodiversity, and sequesters carbon. Farmers around the world are already seeing the benefits of this approach. Home gardeners can get really excited about this system, because the most resilient home vegie gardens and patches can be mini agroforests at work.

In the industrialised West, agroforestry is still a burgeoning industry, but for thousands of years, farmers around the world have observed that different things need to grow together. In Latin America, for example, coffee farmers traditionally knew that the plants needed to be grown in shade. In the 1960s, however, farmers were introduced to a special type of coffee plant that could thrive in full sun. It soon became apparent, however, that the new plants required frequent use of expensive fertilisers and were susceptible to pests. Today, most of these sun-grown coffee plantations have been abandoned. Agroforestry was the answer they were looking for, not more chemical inputs.

Some other agroforestry approaches include berry bushes planted between tree rows, the trees providing partial shade and protection for robust berry harvests. Or herbs such as coriander (cilantro), mint, basil, parsley and rosemary grown in the acidic soils of the forest floor. Or melons and squash of all types thriving between tree rows, or peas and beans climbing up the trunks of young trees. It's a food forest wonderland.

Another great example is the large agroforestry farm Stephen Briggs is establishing in Cambridgeshire in the UK. He's already finding that growing wheat in an apple orchard is reducing soil erosion and increasing carbon capture. The wheat yields in a normal growing season are comparable with those of a standard monoculture wheat farm, except for when something out of the ordinary happens. In 2019 high winds led to a 20 per cent loss of yield from monoculture wheat fields, while the agroforestry structure suffered only a 10 per cent yield loss. The trees provided a windbreak and lessened the damage. Stephen also plants legumes and flowers between the orchard rows and wheat, to attract beneficial insects and pollinators. He hasn't needed to use insecticides for more than ten years.

You can see that communities surrounding such farms are set to enjoy greater food security, while the farmer has greater income security, given they don't have all their eggs in one basket. And the planet wins, because the trees dig deeper roots and the soil has greater cover and suffers less erosion, which means healthy, carbon-sequestering soil.

According to research from the Project Drawdown team, an acre of multistrata agroforest can achieve comparable carbon sequestration rates to afforestation and forest restoration, with the added benefit of producing food. With a growing global population, it's easy to see the plus side of focusing on this double win.

Permaculture

Permaculture is founded on three principles:

1 **Earth care – rebuilding nature's capital**
2 **People care – nurturing ourselves, our family and the community**
3 **Fair share – setting limits to consumption and redistributing surplus.**

It's easy to see from Indigenous Australian history how close this is to what happened on the Australian continent for thousands of years before permaculture was devised. I'm very glad that someone did devise it though, right here in Australia, and that it has now spread across the world. The permaculture system for growing food draws on Indigenous wisdom and traditional cultural practices, pairing them with modern understanding and science. It is to me the form of regenerative agriculture that most embodies indigenous approaches to the role of humans in the overall 'system' of a local place or indeed the whole planet. In a similar way to agroforestry and silvo-farming, permaculture protects soil, maintains biodiversity and sequesters carbon.

The term 'permaculture' was coined in Tasmania in the 1970s by Bill Mollison and David Holmgren. As we have seen, they described it as 'an integrated, sustainable and evolving system of perennial or self-perpetuating plant and animal species useful to mankind'.

Permaculture has since evolved to mean not just systems by which we grow and procure food, but also 'consciously designed landscapes which mimic the patterns and relationships found in nature, while yielding an abundance of food, fibre and energy for provision of local needs'. Permaculture encompasses not just growing food, but people, their buildings and the ways they organise themselves. Over the years, the original vision of permanent or sustainable agriculture has evolved into permanent or sustainable *culture*.

This is similar to Allan Savory's concept of holistic decision-making based on the health of the whole planet or the whole local community. This yardstick can be used to design everything from farms to new towns. In his *Essence of Permaculture*, David Holmgren explains permaculture systems and their usefulness now and into the future.

One important principle is to capture local forms of energy, both renewable and non-renewable, taking advantage of surplus food, fuel and other resources when they are available and ensuring that systems are in place to sustain the community during times of scarcity. Permaculture aims to catch such immediate sources of energy as sun, wind and water, while using wasted resources from conventional agriculture and other human activities. In addition, it taps the major resource that is the knowledge and skills of older people.

Permaculture also invests in energy sources that can sustain the community into the future, such as fertile, humus-rich soil; trees and other perennial plants that yield useful resources including food; seed banks and arboreta; water-storage dams and tanks; passive solar buildings; and knowledge stored in the form of libraries and information systems. Together, these approaches will continue to sustain communities even after fossil fuels are exhausted.

The beautiful thing about permaculture is that we can take these design principles and apply them to a balcony garden, a community garden or a large farm, ensuring that the design brings abundance for us and strength to the ecosystem while encouraging biodiversity. The idea is to design the system so well that it reduces your need for input. It sure does sound like a metaphor for what we as humans need to do a whole lot better: design our lives so that we're not at full speed 24/7. When you design well, there's less to do. When you plant perennial vegies and the planting gets a little thick, you move the seedlings from the undergrowth into a new vegie bed, thus saving yourself from seedling cultivation. When you get a couple of chickens into the garden, they fertilise your food plants and eat weeds. Create no-dig gardens and use mulch for soil cover, and you prevent weeds even more. And less weeds mean less work.

This quote from permaculturist Robyn Francis sums up permaculture beautifully:

> *From a philosophy of cooperation with nature and each other, of caring for the earth and people, it presents an approach to designing environments which have the diversity, stability and resilience of natural ecosystems, to regenerate damaged land and preserve environments which are still intact.*

Holistic management

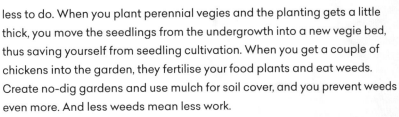

In the 1960s, Allan Savory, a Zimbabwean ecologist, made a breakthrough in understanding what was causing the degradation and desertification of the world's grassland ecosystems, which cover 30–40 per cent of the globe. Big grasslands occur in areas of the world where there is seasonal humidity and insufficient rainfall for trees and crops – much of Australia and Africa, and a large chunk of the Americas. Once upon a time, large tightly packed herds moved quickly through the grasslands, pursued by pack-hunting predators. Today, these herds are largely gone, and their absence has contributed to the degradation of the grasslands.

Savory was determined to figure out why and fix it. Over the next few years, he worked with farmers on four continents to refine the system of grasslands regeneration that he had successfully developed in Zimbabwe. By the early 1980s, he had called this system holistic management.

His book, *Holistic Management*, was one of the most pivotal, big-picture-thinking reads of my life. I highly encourage it, whether you're a farmer or not – I'm definitely not a farmer and I found it absolutely riveting. He talks about needing to define what the 'healthy whole' looks like, so that everyone can play their part in creating that healthy whole from their corner. The best businesses and governments do this, and when people have a healthy united purpose, they are much more peaceful, free, safe and secure in their lives, knowing that what they're doing makes a contribution to the healthy whole. The 'whole' can be a family unit, a business, a farm, a country, the cast of a movie, a baseball team ... the planet. Once we define what the healthy whole looks like and how it functions optimally, it's much easier for everyone to work in different ways to create a positive impact upon that whole.

While we see these healthy wholes in nature's ecosystems, many farming systems in modern agriculture ignore the natural, healthy 'whole', instead focusing on landscape manipulation to do what we want and need. This has led to a huge fall in biodiversity, desertification of grasslands and loss of healthy soil, which essentially means diminished food and water security. This is no small thing we're talking about here.

I was inspired to read the book after watching Savory's 2013 TED Talk, which taught me about desertification of the world's grasslands and its impact on climate change. Desertification, he said, was the process of land turning into desert due to such factors as over-grazing or no grazing. I was intrigued. We've come to accept that cattle farming is destroying the planet, but Savory – and now thousands of farmers practising holistic management – can see that we need cattle just as the grasslands of yesteryear needed those large wild herds, tightly packed to avoid predators. We need those herds for healthy ecosystems, including soil health and water systems, and it's about getting the management right. We've been doing it wrong, and this has led to destruction and desertification.

Savory talks about loving biodiversity as a child, and hating cattle grazing due to the effects it was having on biodiversity and the landscapes he loved so much. He went on to study ecology at university with the aim of figuring out how to eradicate cattle grazing and save biodiversity. After years of study, experimentation and trying to figure out the problem, he was shocked at what he found. It wasn't grazing that was the problem. It was the way grazing was managed.

You leave a bunch of cattle to roam, removing any of their predators to save them from death, and they sprawl out over a landscape, eating the grass, staying put in the one space. Eventually the grass is too short, the soil too exposed, and the soil dries out, no longer able to retain water, and a big release of carbon occurs into the atmosphere. If you leave a grassland completely untended, that is to say with no large herds coming through, that grass has to biodegrade to make way for new grass in the next rainy season, but the problem is it doesn't do that fast enough on its own, which causes oxidation that smothers the new grasses, leading eventually to the growth of woody vegetation and then desert sandy soil and lost water pooling just a few years later. *Argh!* Too much grazing in one spot, not enough grazing at all … Savory found the Goldilocks solution of 'just right', which can restore healthy grassland ecosystems all over the world. Because grasslands account for 40 per cent of the earth's land mass, and because of their ability to store carbon in their soils, they represent a huge opportunity for us to sequester carbon. From the Savory Institute:

> *For each 1% increase in soil organic matter achieved on the world's 5 billion hectares of grasslands, 64 ppm of carbon dioxide would be removed from atmospheric circulation …*
> *Proper management of the wild and domestic grazers that evolved in and still inhabit the grasslands of the world is key to restoring healthy grassland soils and engaging this carbon sink. In one study we have seen a 400% increase in permanent soil carbon on land under Holistic Planned Grazing, relative to the neighboring land managed conventionally.*

Savory remarked in one of his talks, 'People have a saying that it's the drought that causes the bare ground, but that's nonsense, it's the bare ground that causes the drought.' Surely it would make more sense to go to the root cause of drought and work from there to rebuild healthy ecosystems, rather than accept that we've lost 30 per cent of the world's arable land in the past 40 years and say, 'I guess we need to make ultra-processed food in a lab now.'

I do urge you to read Savory's book – it makes a wonderful audiobook and it taught me how to think of us all as a part of a whole, and then quickly see that our whole is broken. We're fractured, fragmented and disconnected – from each other, from our natural world. We don't even realise we are nature ourselves. Is it any wonder that we are all fighting each other when we don't have a clear vision for what a 'healthy whole' looks like and how we can each play a role in that?

No holistic management plan is the same from one area to the next or one country to the next, nor is it identical year on year, because the philosophy and practice require a deep relationship with and assessment of the land that is ever evolving. Again, this holistic management philosophy echoes ancient indigenous ideas about place, listening to the land and being one with it rather than trying to manipulate it.

WHAT ABOUT METHANE?

The Savory Institute has this to say about methane: 'An intact ecosystem effectively balances ruminant methane production and breakdown. While there are indeed excessive sources of methane from conventional livestock management, such as manure lagoons and land use changes (for example, conversion of forests and grasslands to croplands for animal feed), other than market-related transportation costs, Holistic Management requires none of those practices. Healthy, well-aerated soils – a characteristic quality of grasslands under Holistic Planned Grazing – harbour methanotrophs, bacteria that break down methane. Soil-based decomposition of methane may be equal to or greater than ruminant methane production, depending on animal density, soil type and soil health – exactly why a deep understanding of correctly managing the land one is on is crucial. The regenerative thinking and emerging research is that the benefits of eco-restoration through Holistic Management far outweigh methane emissions resulting from livestock.'

We can see, then, why methane plays such a big role in the environmental impact of factory farming. The soil is reduced to dust. There is no vegetation or biodiversity. The methane can't be broken down by methanotrophs and so it goes up, up, up. And even though methane is a part of a natural cycle while fossil fuels are not in any way, shape or form, we do need to address the issue that methane levels are greatly reduced if we farm in a holistic way. As a side note, there is exciting research suggesting that when cows are fed seaweed, methane emissions can be reduced by up to 80 per cent.

Silvo-farming

Silvo-farming, also known as silvopasture (or silvopasture farming) is a form of agroforestry that integrates trees and pasture into a single system. It has been around since ancient times and has been popular in Native American agriculture, as well as in Europe and Latin America. In parts of Europe over the past few hundred years, for example, pigs have been farmed in apple orchards. The pigs clear between the apple trees to make them easy to get to, while fertilising the ground and eating the odd fallen apple as an extra treat. In turn, the pigs have cooler living conditions with the shade from the trees, meaning they don't die of heat stress. The Native Americans had managed a wild ecology of mixed woodlands, grasslands and forests. They hunted wild game and cultivated gardens for staple crops.

Steve Gabriel, in his book *Silvopasture*, writes of how when the Europeans arrived in the Americas, they feared the great big forests, making massive clearings to enable ploughing. For centuries now, modern farmers have separated field and forest, but research is showing us it's time to bring the band back together. The system takes some years to establish, but the benefits are a regenerated landscape, a more secure and diverse income for the farmer, who can grow and sell animals, nuts, fruit and mushrooms at different times of the year, and greater resilience in times of drought or excess rainfall. There is shelter for the animals from the trees and additional products to sell from those trees. Atmospheric carbon is also better sequestered than if it were a forest or grassland alone. The whole is greater than the sum of its parts.

Steve Gabriel provides examples of silvopasture farming from across North America, illustrating its potential for creating healthier and more resilient farms and ecosystems. On an apple cider and asparagus farm in New York, turkeys are used to get rid of pests and for fertilising. On a nut and sheep farm in Minnesota, grazing the sheep in the understorey of hybrid chestnut and hickory plantings makes the nut harvest easier. Farmers use small ropes or moveable fences to keep animals grazing down to the desired grass level before moving them to a fresh area, so there's also a link to Allan Savory's holistic management.

Natural sequence farming

Natural sequence farming is the brainchild of an Australian farmer by the name of Peter Andrews, who many say is a man way ahead of his time. This farming method takes a 'whole landscape' approach, focusing on plants and water first – specifically, the movement of water and nutrients from the landscape's topmost point to its floodplain in such a way that the water can hydrate the whole landscape in the process. Andrews believes that with natural sequence farming systems, Australia could be carbon negative in a year. That is not a typo.

Natural sequence farming is not a blueprint or protocol for farmers to follow step by step, but, as seems to be the pattern with all regenerative practices, a deepened understanding of the land, water systems and carbon cycling, and using that understanding in a systems-thinking approach. It's always so terribly sad to think about the indigenous wisdom, in so many colonised countries, wiped out because white people like me muscled our way in and started doing things 'our way' on lands we'd never before known. Is it any wonder that things went so wrong?

Andrews has shown repeatedly that we can turn dry landscapes into thriving farms by observing the processes that have operated in the Australian landscape for tens of thousands of years, and working with them to restore health to the soil, the water systems and the food we produce. The result is a more resilient landscape and more productive farm.

I disagree that Andrews is ahead of his time – his time is now. From early childhood, Andrews was fascinated by the Australian landscape where he grew up in outback Broken Hill. When he bought an 80 hectare (2000 acre) farm in the upper Hunter Valley region, he tasked himself with creating the most sustainable farming practices he could, testing and developing his theories. He studied the cycles of fire, flood and drought on the land, and reintroduced natural landscape patterns and processes he imagines would have existed in Australia before European settlement.

Andrews believes that European-style heavy grazing along water courses reduced vegetation, which significantly increased water flow in streams and resulted in gouged streambeds and lowered water tables in floodplains. This means the landscape experiences dry spells that turn to drought conditions faster than they should, reducing biodiversity and, where fresh water once sat on top of saline water, salt is being released into the streambed. Andrews's natural sequence farming methods aim to reverse this chain of events. In his system, the stream flow rate is slowed by a series of interventions in the landscape, and water is retained to hydrate the landscape with a slow release.

Recent record drought in Australia further highlighted Andews's work in containing salinity, generating water savings, and reducing if not removing the need for conventional irrigation.

Work is underway to implement natural sequence farming more broadly across Australia in order to reverse desertification, improve farm resilience, increase soil health, avoid soil compaction, restore water health, sequester carbon, and maintain high biodiversity and diversity of habitat with the natural vegetation and water flows. Natural sequence farming has so far worked well in both grazing and organic crop agriculture, and it will be exciting to see where this will lead in Australia in the years to come.

 ## Conservation agriculture or no/minimal till

Conservation agriculture has its roots in Brazil and Argentina in the 1970s. It is guided by three principles:

1 **Minimal tillage and disturbance of soil:** This protects the soil from erosion by wind and water, increases soil humus content, improves water infiltration and conserves soil moisture, and cuts labour costs in the long term.

2 **Permanent soil cover with crop residues and live mulches:** This protects the soil from erosion by wind and water, improves the cycling of nutrients, prevents weed germination and growth, and increases organic matter accumulation and carbon sequestration.

3 **Crop rotation and intercropping:** For example, cereals like corn and wheat followed by legumes like beans and lentils. This allows for improved water use, because crops with different rooting systems use water (and nutrients) at different depths. It increases resistance to pests, because different crops are susceptible to different pests and disease, so the pests are kept guessing by alternating crops. And it improves fertility and yield. In addition, the legumes help fix nitrogen in the soil for the benefit of successive cereal crops.

I love the similarities between this technique and basic human nutrition. Conservation or no/minimal till farming works to strengthen the soil, increase its nutrient content and reduce erosion. A healthy diet needs nutritional variety – don't eat the same few things over and over again on repeat, eat through the full spectrum of whole foods to get all the vitamins, minerals, macro- and micronutrients you need ... It's no coincidence that healthiest forms of farming are similar, teaching us not to do the one thing over and over again but to cultivate diversity on the land. We're all natural beings, part of a big 'whole' planet.

Marine and regenerative seaweed aquaculture

Shouldn't we stop meddling with the ocean altogether? Well, no. Because we've played such a major role in creating the mess in the ocean, from plastic pollution to overfishing and coral bleaching from climate change, we must pay *more* attention to the ocean than ever before and help nurse it back to health.

Thanks to overfishing and climate change, the number of dead zones with dangerously low oxygen levels is increasing rapidly. In 1960 about 50 of these zones had been identified. Now there are more than 700. The ocean is a massive carbon sink. Like land-based plants, seaweed takes up carbon from its surroundings to use in photosynthesis, and buries carbon in sediment after it dies. As the ocean acidifies and warms as a result of too much carbon in the atmosphere, its ability to store carbon is impaired. The ocean has acidified by 26 per cent since pre-industrial times. The warming ocean loses oxygen, and marine life is threatened as a result. Shellfish are the first casualty.

The good news, though, is that we can work to restore balance and regenerate oceans through farming seaweed. Seaweed grows somewhere between 30 and 60 times faster than the average land-based plant and can, per hectare, sequester around 20 times more carbon. That's why seaweed needs to stay in the carbon drawdown conversation.

Scientist and author Professor Tim Flannery has said: 'One study suggests that if you cover 9 percent of the world's oceans in seaweed farms, you could draw down the equivalent of all our current emissions – more than 40 gigatonnes a year – and grow enough protein to feed a population of 10 billion people. That's a huge opportunity.' It sure is, and one begging for more research and action. Temperature rises on the coastlines have affected kelp forests over the past few decades, but their regeneration is definitely worth championing. Once established, marine permaculture farms have produced exciting and rapid changes in sea alkalinity as well as in the return of marine life. Just as a healthy land mass contributes to a stable climate, so too does a healthy ocean. Seaweed, along with seagrasses and mangrove swamps, which emerging reports also indicate as important, will play key roles in sequestering carbon.

Urban organic agriculture

All over the world, exciting food projects are blooming in the world's largest cities. Multigenerational city-dwellers, who have historically been cut off from wholefood sources, can now connect to fresh food growing on rooftops, balconies, in community gardens and on vacant lots. Urban organic farms and gardens can utilise local scraps to produce compost and regenerate long-abandoned soils to a thriving state capable of producing healthy plants. Many cities are 'heat islands' because buildings, roads and other infrastructure absorb and radiate more of the sun's heat than natural landscapes. This means many are experiencing temperatures around 4 degrees Celsius (7 degrees Fahrenheit) higher than outer areas.

One of the biggest issues in many cities, especially in poorer communities, is food deserts – where people literally have no access to fresh food. Have a good look around your own city or town. Are there areas where it is easier to access fast food than fresh food? Are there places where fresh food isn't available at all? In parts of my own city, for example, you can walk to four fast-food mega-brand outlets, but the supermarket is on the other side of a highway, which excludes anyone without a car. In these areas, the system is rigged against people making healthy gains through access to produce.

Urban farming projects are one way we can not only improve biodiversity in our cities and reduce the 'heat island' effect but also restore health to struggling communities and purpose to people. Gardens need you every day, and restoring that sense of community and purpose can be pivotal to mental health.

In Paris, in the 15th arrondissement where my relatives live, Nature Urbaine has launched as the largest urban farm in Paris, 14,000 square metres (more than 3 acres) of entirely organic gardens, farmed regeneratively. It is also the largest rooftop farm in the world. With more than 30 species growing, it will be able to produce 1000 kilograms (2200 pounds) of food per day, to be distributed to local residents and restaurants. Locals can also buy into an allotment for a small annual fee, and attend workshops to learn vegie gardening and composting. The City of Paris is rolling out urban food forests in the centre of Paris to produce free food for its citizens to enjoy. *Mais oui!*

Ron Finley, a celebrated urban gardening pioneer, gave a TED Talk that was pivotal for many in understanding the potential for the planet and community of regenerating abandoned public land, ripping out abandoned parking lots and replacing them with vegetable gardens. Ron grew up in south central LA's 'food prison', where you had to drive 45 minutes just to get a fresh tomato. He set out to change things, beginning with a verge garden outside his house and ultimately converting abandoned land in south central LA into fruit and vegie gardens. Ron has a vision for transforming food prisons into food forests. These in turn will help cool the city and create healthy soils that hold water instead of it running off and flooding the streets.

Far to the north-east, in Detroit, a 12-lot-row of abandoned houses was converted into an urban organic farm in 2012. By 2016, it had pumped out 180,000 kilograms (400,000 pounds) of produce that had fed 2000 households within 5 square kilometres (2 square miles). It has provided valuable volunteer experience for 8000 local residents, who have collectively put in 80,000 hours. What a beautiful step forward for people and planet, bringing communities together, cultivating healthier soil in the cities to trap water when it rains, and localising fresh food availability!

In Sydney, Australia, one of my favourite urban farm examples is Pocket City Farm – converted from the greens of a former lawn bowls club and now home to a bounty of fresh organic produce and delivering an interactive farming experience for local schools, businesses and people interested in growing food themselves. A greenhouse cultivates seedlings for the market garden and for members of the public to buy for home. A composting unit has been established to turn over waste from local restaurants and cafes. The street verge of the farm has been converted into a food forest, providing free produce for residents and passers-by to enjoy. They have a double-decker bee hotel with native stingless bees that work hard to pollinate the produce on the farm. You have to pinch yourself to remember you're in Sydney's otherwise very busy inner west.

The beautiful thing about these regenerative urban farms is that they're not isolated cases. There are hundreds of examples in cities all around the world, breathing biodiversity into the urban landscape. Do you know which community vegie gardens are closest to you? I urge you to go out, explore, connect and spread the good word.

Regenerative agriculture FAQs

· · · · · · ·

Phew! After all that information, your mind is probably teeming with questions. Here are some answers to the most common ones.

Q **Can regenerative agriculture really make a difference?**
I hope that after reading about all these significant forms of regenerative agriculture, you're feeling as inspired as I am. What fills me with optimism is that these systems exist and are set to save the planet. We don't need to create anything new or invest huge funds beyond the farming subsidy budgets common in the world already. We can start today and we must.

· · · · · · ·

Q **But how are we going to feed the world?**
You may have heard that we can't 'feed the world' with organics or regenerative agriculture. The yields are too low, they say. Yes, some research shows that monoculture organic farms have higher yields, but thanks to the refinement of techniques and a deeper understanding of how to return multiple species and plants to the one farm, the evidence is turning in favour of regenerative methods – especially if we're playing the long game, which with the estimated 60 years of quality topsoil left, we darn well ought to be.

It's worth noting that the term 'feed the world' came from America after the Second World War, when Europe had severe food shortages and America rose to the task of providing shelf-stable long-life food in the form of grains and flours to send across the Atlantic. When the need to export grain to Europe ceased a few years later, American farmers who had been subsidised to rise to the urgent call for food now had a huge surplus. The new market of cereals and snacks exploded, and shortly after we started feeding cattle, chickens and pigs grains – very creative!

· · · · · · ·

Q **Can we feed the world on regenerative ag?**
Yes. While yields can dip during the transition process, studies show that once the farms are in full swing, their yields are comparable to conventional

agriculture during predictable seasons. Excitingly, though, research published by the Rodale Institute shows that yields on regenerative farms are up to 40 per cent higher than on conventional farms during periods of drought, thanks to their more robust, healthier systems. Methods like permaculture design, silvo-farming and agroforestry, create multiple revenue streams and harvests throughout the year, compared to just one or two on a monoculture farm. This means the farmer is less at risk of losing a whole year's harvest and therefore builds a more robust business. What is hopefully abundantly clear now, after decades of intensive monoculture farming, is that in going down that path of pesticides, herbicides and genetic modification of seeds, we patently ignored how nature's systems worked. We've also patently ignored our part in nature's systems – we're in nature, not a figure apart from it trying to boss it into the things we want it to do for us.

The road we've gone down has made nature's systems weak and susceptible to disease, creating farms that require ever more artificial propping up with synthetic pesticides and herbicides. This has unfortunately led in many areas of the world to even greater vulnerability to weather, pest and diseases; it has eroded our topsoils to the point where they are void of microorganisms, and are no longer able to sequester carbon. To use the analogy of human health, the equivalent would be for us to be on multiple antibiotic treatments each year, stripping our microbiome of the beneficial organisms that support our immune system and brain (and this is a particularly fitting analogy, given glyphosate, the active ingredient of Roundup, was originally patented as an antibiotic). Add to that a diet full of junk food we don't even need in order to survive, and over time we become more susceptible to disease, no longer able to function optimally and be useful members of society. Our farming landscapes are in danger of no longer being able to function as bountiful producers. Our waterways are poisoned, with many communities in developed countries unable to access fresh, clean water.

It's time for change. You don't have to be a farmer to make that change, but they all need our support. As eaters, we can all do a tremendous amount, in the years to come, to secure the health of our planet and future generations. That might sound dramatic, but every lecture, every book, every report has taught me that now is a critical time. And rather than thinking about all the complicated things we could do – building machines to suck up carbon or growing synthetic meat in labs – perhaps the answer was there all along: we can make a world of difference as a collective from our plates, saying goodbye to all that waste, and hello to the farmers we're about to get to know a whole lot better.

Speaking of bins, when it is ever not the perfect time to talk compost?

A practical guide to composting and worm farms

To end this chapter on a big high about how you can be a regenerative champion from your apartment block, house or property, I want to share a contribution from a special guest star. I could have written a nice little to-do/not-to-do list on composting and worm farms, but the thing is, I'm not the best person for the job here. Australian readers will be familiar with Costa Georgiadis as, among other things, the presenter of the ABC's long-running *Gardening Australia*. For my readers overseas, I want to introduce you to this local Aussie champion. When I think about the person who's been most influential in the past 15 years in getting people connected with nature in Australia, it's Costa. His boundless energy and enthusiasm make you want to jump into a garden and get going.

Once, when we were both running a sustainability workshop at a local university, I was covering all the personal care and cleaning, and the disaster of things like microbeads and endocrine disrupters flooding our environment. Another friend and activist, Tim Silverwood, was opening students' eyes to the state of our oceans, and Costa was talking about composting and soil health. At one point, he took his bucket of soil full of wriggly worms, which were just loving life, and passed it up the aisles to the students in the lecture theatre. It was lunchtime, and many had food bags from fast-food chains, the air thick with that stale-oil-in-the-fryer smell. As many refused to grab the soil and feel/smell it, I realised how strange we are as humans in these disconnected modern times. Here these students were, eating processed takeaways whose fries can have up to 18 ingredients in them, depending on the country, and they were grossed out by soil?! When you learn about how magical soil is, teeming with life, giving life to other beings, and then learn about what goes into the average fast-food French fry, from what type of potato, to how it's grown, how far it travels and what strange ingredients are mixed with it to make it taste just so, you soon realise that we're grossed out by absolutely the wrong thing. It's understandable why, if you've never been shown just how special soil is.

Now you're about to see, if you haven't already, that the soil was the hero in that story, not the golden arches. Take it away, Costa …

Compost and worm farms: rethinking the waste and landfill legacy

by Costa Georgiadis, @costasworld

Because you already have Alexx Stuart in your world, it goes without saying that you've been exposed to a massive series of interconnected positive behaviours and decision-making that are engaging you with sustainability on a day-to-day basis. This is a wonderful thing, and it makes me happy to know that as a result of just one or two of these new behaviours you are now by default out there in the world as a change-making influence.

But all of this good work can be undone and in fact the scales can be rapidly tipped the other way if you have yet to engage with one particular day-to-day activity: waste. Output. Rubbish. Garbage. Food scraps. Landfill. Let's unpack this reality, because it's a world-wide habit, and once you start auditing its presence in your life you will really start to have a massive impact on the whole world. To quote a fantastic song created by my good friend Charlie Mgee from Formidable Vegetable (formidablevegetable.com): 'There is no such thing as waste, only things in the wrong place.'

I go further and say there is no such thing as waste, because that's an outdated word from a bygone era. We can now remove it from our vocabulary and replace it with the word 'resource'. When we start to look at waste as a resource, then it becomes a case of resource recovery, not rubbish removal. And resources have a value, so if there is a cost involved then you and I immediately have skin in the game.

Shifting your thinking from waste to resource is quite a mindset change, so I'll preface this section on compost by saying that when you start to separate your food scraps and you begin to break the

> **When we start to look at waste as a resource, then it becomes a case of resource recovery, not rubbish removal.**

cycle of those scraps going into landfill, this will elevate exponentially all the other good work that Alexx has inspired you to do. I can hear you saying, 'Yes, I've started to buy locally. Yes, I'm looking into the ethical realities of my food choices. Yes, I'm buying garments that don't support an industry where people are paid paltry wages and live in shocking conditions. Yes, I'm looking at nutrition and health in a new light. Yes, I'm looking into the benefits of regenerative agriculture and my sustainable food choices. But I feel bad: I still throw my locally grown, pasture-fed, organically nurtured food scraps and leftovers into landfill.'

My premise is that if you do nothing more than stop throwing food into landfill, not just at home but wherever you go, this impact is equal to if not far greater than all of those other transitions you're making, because you're not leaving a ticking timebomb known as landfill for the next generation. Of all the environmental challenges we face as individuals and as a collective generation, confronting our complicit participation in the long-term bequeathal of landfill to our children is one that we can change from the moment we finish reading this next sentence. We can take some very simple actions that will create new behaviours with massive environmental benefits. We can start *now*, it will not cost money, and once we've become participants there will be no turning back.

I have long been enticing and encouraging people to become compost connoisseurs and urban worm farmers, and every time the composting light bulb flickers on for someone, I get as much excitement and drive to share the story again as I did the very first time someone joined the dots. So let me help you join the dots with these simple steps.

How-to steps to becoming a compost rock star

In the kitchen

* **Separation and a container:** Separating your food scraps starts at your kitchen bench. All you need is a benchtop tidy or bin to put the food scraps into. It must have a secure lid so that you reduce the chance of little vinegar flies congregating. Better still, just find an old pot with a lid, because this has a kitchen theme and means you can repurpose an old one or even find a funky one at the op shop with perhaps some retro images or flower motifs.
* **Filling your benchtop tidy:** Line the bottom of the bin/saucepan with some newspaper or used paper towel. As you add your scraps, throw in any paper bags, paper wrapping, newspaper, ripped-up toilet rolls and hand towel rolls – even cardboard boxes and takeaway cardboard containers. This is all about getting your compost mix at the correct ratio. Ideally, you want 50 per cent food waste to 50 per cent brown waste or carbon, which is things like paper, cardboard, dead leaves, dried grass, etc. Get the ratio working at the start and it will make for better, faster compost-making in the long run. Getting the carbon material in as you go means that you don't need to add as much when you take it to your compost bin.
* **Hot tips:** The paper and cardboard also help to absorb any liquids that build up in the bucket, meaning it won't smell. If you do get vinegar flies buzzing around, keep the bucket in the fridge or empty it more frequently.

From the kitchen to compost

If you live in an apartment and don't have any space to start a worm farm or compost bin, there are still plenty of things you can do with food scraps. An easy option is to contact your local community garden, which will gladly accept your food-scrap deliveries. Alternatively, you can start to use a valuable app called ShareWaste (or whatever similar app is operating in your part of the world), which helps you find a compost host in your area. You can then deliver the resources to their place for them to compost.

If you do have some space in your garden, on your rooftop or even out on your street verge, you can always start a worm farm or a compost bin. In Australia at least, you can readily acquire them from most local councils, which run programs to provide subsidised bins and farms. Otherwise, you can purchase them. If you have the time you can even create a worm farm using old polystyrene boxes.

Starting a compost bin

1 **Choose your bin:** Compost bins come in all shapes, sizes and styles. There are domes like a Dalek, rotating bins, four-sided rectangular bins, rolling bins – the list goes on. For any bin, the process is fairly much the same. And it's all about balance and consistent observation and effort. Not a burden, just a little bit of consistency is the key.

2 **Set up your bin:** To kickstart your bin, position it on level ground. It's important to make it vermin-proof by sitting it on a sheet of aviary mesh. This will prevent any digging underneath and into the bin by unwanted visitors.

3 **Start your bin:** Begin with a layer of dry material, such as dried leaves, dried twigs or dried grass or newspaper. Next add a shovelful of garden soil or compost you already have, which helps to set up the microbial life in the bin. That soil has all sorts of living organisms already living in it, so it's a bit like a sourdough starter or soup stock.

4 **Get composting:** It's now a matter of adding your green material from the kitchen and garden as you go. If you put one container of food scraps or green waste into the bin, you must add at least one to one and a half containers of brown or carbon material, such as dried grass, leaves, straw, newspaper* or cardboard. Get this ratio right, and the compost will break down with more reliability and you won't be confronted with either a dry bin or the other extreme – a wet sludgy anaerobic smelly mess.

5 **Turn your bin regularly:** Once your bin is full, you need to turn it once a week for the next eight to 10 weeks or so. During this time you no longer add new material to the bin. You will see the waste breaking down into a beautiful rich brown material, which will not smell. If a bad smell is emanating from it, you need to add more brown waste and turn the contents to aerate them. You'll soon see

that composting actually requires two bins, so that while one bin is being broken down and matures you can continue loading the second bin with your newfound resources and daily habit.

*Shredded newspaper is readily available from your neighbourhood recycling bins, or ask your local cafe if you can have their used papers if you don't buy newspapers yourself. You can also use cardboard. Keep a ready supply of paper/cardboard in a container near your compost so you can actively get the ingredients ratio right every time you take your benchtop tidy to the compost bin.

THE KEY TO GOOD COMPOSTING IS THE ADAM PRINCIPLE

A is for **Aliveness** and how much nature's workers are hard at it, such as microbes and earthworms.

D is for **Diversity,** which is about adding a mix of ingredients beyond just your food scraps. That includes garden material, paper and cardboard, soil, egg shells and egg cartons, straw and manure, mulch, and so on.

A is for **Aeration**. This is like the turbocharger for the compost; with more air, the microbes and worms can do their work and break down the material. So it needs to be aerated and turned regularly.

M is for **Moisture**. Compost needs moisture, as the fuel that makes things happen. Your compost needs to be moist all the time. Again, consistency is the key.

Compost problem-solving FAQs

• • • • • •

Composting is easy once you get the hang of it, but in the meantime you might need to solve these common issues.

Q **Why does my bin stink so much that I want to gag when I open the lid?**

Your ratio is out. The food scraps and green material have broken down into a glue and forced all the air out, making the bin anaerobic – which comes with the side serve of strong smells. To solve this you simply need to turn/aerate the bin and add some coarse material, such as a shovelful of garden soil and some shredded paper and cardboard, to get oxygen back into the bin. The smell will then disappear. Don't let the smell turn you off; simply turn the smell off with your actions.

• • • • • •

Q **Why is my bin full of dry material that won't break down?**

When it's too dry, you need to add some more green material. If that's not food scraps, it can be grass clippings or garden clippings or chicken manure. Then you need to add at least one watering can full of water, bit by bit as you turn the compost with your compost aerator. Regular mixing of your pile will give you a good visual indication of how wet or dry your compost is.

• • • • • •

Q **What's the difference between a compost bin and a worm farm?**

The key thing to remember as far as worm farms and compost bins go is that worms break things down a lot slower but create a higher grade of finished material. Compost bins, on the other hand, can take larger volumes and break them down into a lot of good-quality material over a shorter period of time. My advice is to have both, because that way you get enough compost to continually build up the soil in your garden or your containers, and at the same time you get the higher quality of humus compost out of the worm farm, which you can also add to all your beds or pots. As an added bonus, you can turn worm compost into liquid fertiliser by mixing it into a bucket of water and pouring onto your plants.

Setting up a worm farm

Proprietary worm farms are available either through your local council's composting program or from local garden centres and nurseries. They are very clean and neat, and can be kept in a garage, on a balcony or rooftop, or even indoors. When operating correctly, they have absolutely no smell. You can also make your own using polystyrene boxes.

Worm farms usually come with three distinct layers. The bottom layer, into which the legs fit, catches the liquid or worm juice that drains from the upper layers. When the farm is up and running, you can drain this off periodically and use it to fertilise your plants. The second layer when setting it up is the bedroom. This is filled with the supplied coir fibre, and the worms will settle in here before moving to the next layer, which is the dining room. In this layer it's good to sprinkle a base of garden soil with shredded newspaper over the top. Water this layer in and then start adding food scraps underneath the newspaper.

Most worm farms will come with a container of about 1000 worms, which you can release into the moist coir fibre bedroom layer. They will then make their way up to the dining room when the food is introduced. Don't overfeed a worm farm, as the worms can only eat so much during any period of time. One valuable tip: the worms will chew through the food scraps a lot quicker if you chop them into smaller pieces. When feeding the farm, lay the scraps out across half the dining level and cover them with the shredded newspaper. It may take a week to ten days for the worms to eat through the equivalent of a couple of takeaway containers of food scraps. Observation is the key. Watch and see when the scraps have been consumed and then add some more. As they digest the food scraps and transform them into rich worm castings, the level in the dining room will slowly rise to the top.

When the dining layer is full, you can harvest and use the valuable compost castings in your vegie patch, pot plants and container gardens, and generally around any plants. The easiest way to harvest castings is to remove the lid and any cardboard or newspaper on top, and expose the surface to the sun. The worms will migrate deeper into the worm farm, so after 10 minutes you can start to scrape the castings off the top. Repeat this process every 10–15 minutes, until all the worms have moved down into the second layer. Return the worm farm to its usual position, and start filling the dining layer with food scraps again. Repeat this process over and over.

Becoming a master composter

Once you're a composter you become one for life. The best part about the habit change is that you will no longer throw food waste into a landfill bin. Whether you're at work, at home or out and about, throwing resources into the bin will no longer be an option. It's really quite a liberating reality to move into. But like any change, take it step by step, and don't put too much pressure on yourself until you find that the routine becomes the habit. And then there'll be no turning back.

What's more, you'll inspire others by taking your new habits with you everywhere you go, including carrying containers to bring the resources back home so you can transform them into valuable food for your garden, your family and your local landscape. Welcome to the World of Compost Contribution – a truly regenerative activity. Awesome to have you turning with us.

Don't hesitate to share your pictures of compost success on Insta @costasworld. I prefer happy snaps of worms and humus to fancy food. After a few weeks at this game, I reckon you will too.

Happy composting! Now I'll hand you back to Alexx.

GET BUSY REGENERATING THE EARTH

Are you inspired? Costa's passion for educating on the importance of compost and waste as a resource is infectious, and just what the world needs right now. Get composting, get a few pots of herbs going, get sprouting or a vegie patch or special raised bed or pod for a big balcony or a tiny backyard, and you're regenerating the planet, preventing methane from being trapped in landfill, and sequestering carbon. Suddenly, it isn't 'out there for the farmers to do', but one of the most important jobs you'll ever do.

Another important job? Cooking from scratch and sourcing food from regenerative producers. Let's move on to this exciting next part of the journey.

CHAPTER

3

Change starts
with us

What do we really need?

Remember me diligently seeking to avoid products with gluten in them? There I was, checking all the additive names and numbers, when perhaps the better questions would have been: What do I really *need*? What is essential for my nourishment and to me thriving? What are the building blocks that help us conceive, give birth to and raise the next generation healthily? What helps me preserve and build muscle mass and bone density as I get older, so I can age healthy and strong? Is it white chocolate? Is it root beer bubble gum? Is it 80 per cent dark-chocolate-coated honeycomb (okay, I actually wish it was for that one)? Is it jelly snakes? Is it lemonade? Is it chocolate milk with 16 teaspoons of sugar in it? Is it those gluten-free cheesy puffs? Nope.

Barely anything in a fair few of the middle supermarket 'food' aisles constitutes the kind of food we actually need to thrive. So many items we regularly put in our trolleys have no real reason to exist – we've just been trained to believe they're what we need to enjoy life, have fun, experience our tastebuds tingling ... It's all a lie and it has served to disconnect us from things that matter. They're distractions. Think of the emissions we could save by not buying them. Think of the huge areas of land dedicated to growing crops to produce these ultra-processed, unnecessary products sold as food. Think of the millions spent on electricity to power the manufacture of these products. Think of the petrol used to transport them. Think of the biodiversity those big farms could spearhead by transitioning from monoculture to multiculture farms with nuts, fruits, seeds, native grains, vegies and ethically raised, well-managed animals, and focusing on providing food for nourishing mealtimes.

We have more than enough space to grow food to feed the world, it's just that most of what we're feeding the world right now is trash – all volume and calories, little nutrition.

'We have more than enough space to grow food to feed the world, it's just that most of what we're feeding the world right now is trash – all volume and calories, little nutrition.

Change the world, one shopping trolley at a time

It can feel overwhelming, I get it, to imagine all that land used to grow corn for corn syrup for candy, or sugar cane or sugar beets to sweeten soft drinks ... How do we change this? What can we do? Well, the demand starts with us. If we drink that soft drink and eat that candy, then the automated stock-tracking/buying system in the store you bought it from triggers another unit to be ordered from the distributor or depot once the stocks fall to the minimum holding the store owner has set. Then, the distributor, who has a similar automated buying system, generates an order from the manufacturer, and that manufacturer places their orders of raw materials with their farmer suppliers ... We are all triggering an order to the next person in the chain for literally everything we purchase. This means that if want something 'out there' in the big picture to change, then we need to break the chain, starting with our own shopping basket, then impacting friends and family through changes in the way we entertain and in what we serve. (But forget the side of preachy. Just lead by example and enjoyment.) And voilà.

The crucial biggest step, as I suggested in Chapter 1, is moving from products to produce. Next, we need to source, as best as we can, produce grown using regenerative agricultural methods (and/or grow our own). If we do this more and more each week, while connecting to the seasons and to a greater variety of options over time, we're really starting to make a difference. While you and I are here together on this page now, someone somewhere is running a biodynamic farming webinar, a permaculture course, a silvopasture conference, a soil-health workshop, a holistic management course ... It's happening right now, all over the world. And our job? To keep expanding the market of happy produce-buying customers who support regenerative agricultural practices.

'Yes, great, Alexx,' you might say, 'but right now my shopping looks miles away from the utopian regen basket and more like a heaving snack trolley. Help!' I don't want to leave anyone behind, so if you're new not only to sourcing more regeneratively but to having a produce-focused diet, here's a little exercise to get you started.

Your impact

Simply by shifting from a processed-packet-heavy trolley to a produce-heavy trolley and getting your scratch-cook on, you're making a huge shift towards a regenerative diet and reducing carbon emissions. In the US, for example, around 60 per cent of items in the average shopping trolley are ultra-processed food and beverages. That's 60 per cent of items that we as humans do not need or thrive on, made from a very small range of ingredients sourced on the global market for best price, so they're often very high in transport emissions to boot. And it's not just the US – 50 per cent of Australia's diet comes from ultra-processed foods, too. Many products in this category contribute to our modern chronic disease epidemic, thanks not only to their excess sugar, sodium, ultra-processed fats and various additives, but also to their lack of micronutrients such as bioavailable vitamins, macro- and trace minerals, and polyphenols and enzymes that support vitality and digestion.

Rome wasn't built in a day, so in your early days of making change, please celebrate your wins rather than pining for perfection. And if you've already got to the stage of being a produce-eater for the most part, can you think of a friend who needs your help? Hook them up, teach them to make a snack bar or how to cook a casserole in different ways to keep things interesting ... Cooking together is such a beautiful way to connect and to build community and skills.

It can be a little daunting and the prospect might even seem downright boring when you don't yet know what to *do* with all that produce to make it sing. Trust me, I've been there, but if I could do it, so can you. By the time you finish this book, you'll have flexible recipes at your fingertips, your cooking repertoire will be rich, your confidence will have grown and, I hope, your enthusiasm for cooking from scratch will be unleashed.

The low tox way is all about incremental, empowered change. Any step forward is progress, and while we don't want to be lazy – we're working to reverse huge damage to the planet and its biodiversity, after all – we don't want to be so overwhelmed or paralysed by fear that we don't act at all. Let's take it one ingredient at a time, one meal at a time, one shopping basket at a time. We're doing this! We're going to start where we can.

Don't focus on what you can't change right now or don't have access to. We're going to start where we can.

EXERCISE: CHANGING THE WAY YOU SHOP FOR FOOD

1 Do a regular shop as you've always done and don't cheat by only putting produce in there for this exercise. We need tough love to create the big 'aha' realisation moment that will be your springboard.

2 Identify all the items in your trolley that aren't necessary for meals or that hinder thriving – ultra-processed foods such as soft drinks/sodas, junk lollies/candy, heavily packaged and sugary snacks, cereals or chips and crackers with additives, artificial flavours and the like.

3 Buy it as usual and take it home. Keep the receipt.

4 Write down in a journal what function each of those unnecessary items performs in your week (lunchbox treat, fun drink, treat snacks, junk 'in case the kids' friends come over', etc.).

5 Now write down potential substitutes for each item. This chapter's lists, Pinterest or my website lowtoxlife.com are great places for scouting out ideas and brainstorming. You're now making a plan for swapping each ultra-processed thing with a real food or, as a baby step, a better version of store-bought. For example, it could be as simple as replacing all soft drinks/sodas with home-filtered water (hello, savings in $$$ + packaging emissions + excess sugar), perhaps with the treat option of moving to a soda maker then adding a splash of juice or some pieces of fruit, or to kombucha or kefir or a home-made cordial for a party.

6 Now underline all the lines on the receipt for items that don't actually sustain or support the human body or that come in excessive packaging and plastics. Add up the total cost of those items (use the calculator on your phone): that becomes your long-term reinvestment budget for more nutritious meals, less vacuous snacks and, eventually, regeneratively sourced produce.

7 Get busy working through your list of ditch and switch. The ideas in the following pages will make this seem totally doable.

8 Remember, you've got this! Being aware and being on your way are what counts.

Three easy tactics to implement right now

If you're worried you can't go 'full regen' straight away, here are three ways you can make a huge contribution towards saving the planet.

1 **Become a no-food-waste ninja:** If you make the absolute most of every shopping trip and don't waste anything, you'll make a big difference. If global food waste was a country, it would be the third largest emitter behind China and the US. In the US, 40 per cent of all food produced is wasted. In Australia, about 20 per cent or 7.3 million tonnes of food is wasted each year – that's a lot of landfill. So focusing on reducing food waste to the absolute minimum is a huge step on the road to a regenerative diet. Here we have to get smart. We need tough love. Stop asking yourself 'What do I feel like' and start asking 'What could I rustle up with what I already have?' Focus on your gratitude for having food at your fingertips when many don't. Food isn't a whim or a fancy, it's a precious thing. Treating and using it like it's precious is the way forward, and this won't be the last time I drill this point home. So cook from the fridge and pantry, and use it all up before reaching for the takeout menu.

2 **Start composting:** If your scraps go in the bin, they end up in landfill, which is responsible for about 16 per cent of the methane released from the planet, as well as other harmful gases such as ammonia and sulfides. A rule of nature is that anything that was living dies to become new life, so let's not trap our surplus produce between dead things underground and prevent it from becoming something new and beautiful. The average household bin load is about one-quarter food scraps, so if you start a compost bin or worm farm (see page 92), not only will you be throwing away less rubbish in general, but you will be turning these scraps into rich fertile soil. And maybe you can use that to get some homegrown food happening, or to give some love to your house plants. Alternatively, you can use your kerbside green-waste bin or a local compost pick-up service. My favourite markets in Union Square, New York City, will take your week's compostable scraps and turn them into compost for local gardens and businesses or for you to buy.

3 **Think dirty dozen and clean 15:** With conventionally grown produce, focus on putting the dirty dozen (see page 110) at the very bottom of your list (or nowhere near it) and replacing them with your first regen ag swaps. Stick to the clean 15 for now, safe in the knowledge that you can work on them over time without stressing too much.

THE DIRTY DOZEN AND CLEAN 15 FRUIT AND VEG

If you can't afford or get hold of organic produce, this list will help you make the best choices when it comes to conventionally grown produce. The list is compiled by the US Environmental Working Group (EWG) each year after testing more than 30,000 samples. While some food technologists argue that the pesticide levels in these fruits and vegetables are well under the US Environmental Protection Agency's (EPA's) safety recommendation levels, many doctors and scientists believe that some pesticide residues may bioaccumulate in the body and lead to illness. The EWG uses six measures to determine pesticide contamination of produce:

* percentage of samples with detectable pesticides
* percentage of samples with two or more detectable pesticides
* average number of pesticides found on a single sample
* average amount of pesticides found
* maximum number of pesticides found on a single sample
* total number of pesticides found on the crop.

How relevant is this for Australians? The research shows that you want to prioritise organic apples, pears, berries and leafy dark greens, but a list as comprehensive as the one opposite, specific to Australia, is not yet available.

THE DIRTIEST DOZEN

- ✗ Strawberries
- ✗ Spinach
- ✗ Kale
- ✗ Nectarines
- ✗ Apples
- ✗ Grapes
- ✗ Cherries
- ✗ Peaches
- ✗ Pears
- ✗ Capsicum (peppers)
- ✗ Celery
- ✗ Tomatoes

THE CLEAN 15

- ✓ Avocados
- ✓ Sweet corn
- ✓ Pineapple
- ✓ Onion
- ✓ Papaya
- ✓ Frozen green peas
- ✓ Eggplant (aubergine)
- ✓ Asparagus
- ✓ Cauliflower
- ✓ Rockmelon (cantaloupe)
- ✓ Broccoli
- ✓ Mushrooms
- ✓ Cabbage
- ✓ Honeydew melon
- ✓ Kiwi fruit

 Many doctors believe that some pesticide residues may bioaccumulate in the body and lead to illness.

What NOT to buy

The best way to decide whether to buy produce or not is to consider the following:

1 **Provenance:** If you live in Australia and you see cherries in July or asparagus in March, step away! They're flown in (cherries usually from the US and asparagus usually from Mexico), and are anything but 'fresh', treated using various chemical processes in quarantine so that they're 'safe' and not a biosecurity threat. I fully appreciate we don't want pests from overseas, but we have to ask ourselves whether we *need* fresh produce from overseas. We must learn to fall in love with what is seasonally available on our doorstep. If you absolutely must, frozen berries from overseas are a better choice because they don't need these treatments. I'd be lying if I said that I don't indulge in these every now and then, but fresh produce from overseas is always a hard no.

2 **Packaging:** The produce has a fun product name and is packaged – 'Snack apples', for example, sold in a plastic tube of four apples; or 'Kids' snacking carrots' sold as small carrots in a plastic tub. Productising produce is a no. Buy an apple or a carrot, and if it's too big for a tiny person, cut it. We don't need to be conned into finding produce more fun or convenient because it's packaged to be. We're smarter than that!

3 **Proportions:** Let the alarm bells ring if it's all perfect and the same size. Have a look at a vegie garden or on a farm and you'll see it's darn near impossible to get uniformity. Nature is always about bioindividual magnificence, and while creating uniformity might be easier for barcoding, it usually means some serious chemicals were needed to avoid any spots or imperfections, and/or a ton of produce was wasted – the big operations reject anything that doesn't fit their system design for transporting and selling the product. Shop where the carrots have funny extra legs or baubles that look like privates, and have a giggle with your kids. Shop where you see an insect in the lettuce or a bit of dirt.

4 **Pre-cut with preservatives:** Pre-cut packaged fruit has generally been treated with some sort of preservative spray. Learning to chomp on whole fruits and vegies is an important thing for small people. My son as a toddler would easily take half an hour to get through a big carrot, but he got there in the end and it strengthened his jaw and improved his 'chomping' ability. Skip the preservatives and do something great for your child.

MY SEASONAL EATING
'AHA' MOMENT

———

Shopping at a farmer's market, growing some food of your own, or buying from a community supported agriculture (CSA) network or organic box delivery service will instantly plug you in to seasonal availability. I still remember the first time I realised I couldn't just look at a recipe I wanted to make and go out, get the ingredients and cook it.

It was a pear dessert of Maggie Beer's and we'd just decided to transition to eating local/organic, so I popped over to our new green grocer and couldn't find the pears anywhere. I asked innocently, 'Where are the pears?' and the answer came: 'It's December' (our summer here in Australia). I felt really silly at that moment as a bright-eyed 30-year-old city girl new to organics and still creating a deeper connection with produce and source. When the heck were pears even in season anyway? I had no idea.

My dinner party plan was foiled by the seasons, but it was a good lesson and I've tuned in to nature's magnificent marketing calendar ever since. The pear dessert became a peach one and was just as delicious, I'm sure. From then on, I simply started to adapt my favourite recipes to use what was in season or available. Full disclosure? Sometimes I crack and buy a bag of frozen organic berries because I just can't fork out the $12 a punnet for the fresh ones and my doctor wants me on lots of antioxidant-rich berries. No one needs to lie here. We're all just doing our best and, as I say, it's not what you do some of the time that matters but what you do most of the time. As long as you stick to like for like in texture and/or type of ingredient, swaps are what makes for easy, flexible work in the kitchen most of the time.

What if we have to shop for conventional produce?

When progressing along our low tox living goals, there is always something we can do, whatever our budget or situation constraints. If the areas you can focus on right now are waste reduction, composting, and reducing ultra-processed foods in the mix, these are huge gains not to be belittled for their significance. So, if conventional produce is where you have to keep sourcing for now, I am sharing the pyramid chart opposite, and I do so almost hesitantly. Why? I'm not a fan of how vulnerable charts like this are to being misunderstood, or interpreted to suit a particular group's interests, or how their general nature often doesn't allow for managing certain health conditions, or socioeconomic realities. In saying that, I also acknowledge that if you had to shop solely conventionally right now, you'd like a climate-forward conventional produce guide to help you do so. So, here is the guide for that.

However! If, for example, you are a type 2 diabetic, and have to shop conventionally, all the physicians I've interviewed over the years would say: ignore this chart, you're no good to anyone or the planet on dialysis – eat your protein, healthy fats, nuts, seeds, fruit, veg and legumes, and keep cereals and processed foods with high starch and grain to a minimum. Also, we must be mindful that this chart would have the ultra-processed food industry having a field day with 'cereals' being on there as one of the lower impact food groups, because they can market themselves as climate-friendly – despite the impact of their processing, shipping, storing, freezing, etc. Argh! See why I don't like charts? Reductionist, black and white, and this conversation is anything but. So proceed with awareness, focus on progress not perfection, and celebrate the gains along the way.

Beware food trends

We've already seen how increased avocado demand has led to land clearing and an abuse of human rights in Mexico. Who would have thought that a delicious brekkie in a cafe in Europe could lead to such destruction in a faraway place? We saw a few years ago, when quinoa took off around the world as a high-protein vegetarian option, the price of it in Bolivia and Peru became too high for many local people who depended on that food. How do we ensure that we're not doing more harm than good when we make our choices? Well, this isn't an exact science, and we're probably

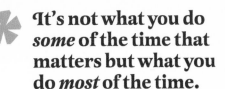

It's not what you do *some* of the time that matters but what you do *most* of the time.

going to screw up more than once – and if we do, I think it's important not to use it as an excuse for no longer trying, but to acknowledge it as a means to overall improvement and progress. One thing we can do is try to source locally and ethically, and whenever a new food trend pops up, look into it to ensure that the good we believe ourselves to be doing here isn't causing issues for communities elsewhere.

It's not what you do *some* of the time that matters but what you do *most* of the time. My motto is variety. Big-time variety. No big bend towards one 'hot new' trend. No more days of cereal for brekkie, a sandwich for lunch. It's all about growing our repertoire, embracing the full spectrum of produce available in our local area and from regenerative sources wherever possible. Work through the whole range of foods available, as local as possible, and from there make the most of what's seasonally available, with the odd stopgap tin, jar or emergency takeaway on the busy days that catch you out.

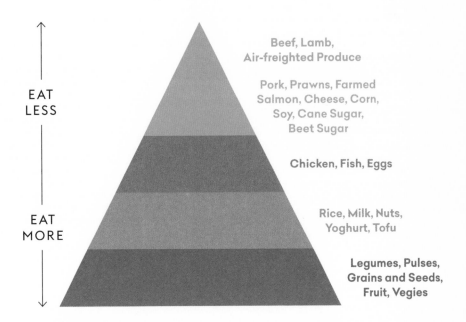

Get your real food here

As you start to source more produce from regenerative agriculture methods, here is a list of wholefoods to celebrate and enjoy.

Packaged pantry staple tactics

Once you start thinking about where your food comes from, you'll soon realise just how much plastic is involved in food packaging – which again is a huge emitter and polluter. What can we do to change that story? I have a list for that:

* Look for local, regeneratively produced as your top priority.
* If a food is from overseas, research its provenance – most of a product's carbon emissions happen before it leaves the farm gate, so while food miles aren't the biggest of all agricultural impacts, we have more transparency and connection when we source the majority of our food locally.
* Go for glass packaging that can be recycled.
* To reduce plastic waste, buy pantry staples from bulk stores or from online pantry staple stores that sell in recyclable paper or compostable packaging.
* Reserve tinned foods (most often lined with plastics of some kind) only as an emergency fallback rather than as a go-to.
* Over time, ask yourself whether you could make a big batch of certain things once a month yourself or when it's in season. Think chutneys, tomato passata/puréed tomatoes, pestos, made from fresh produce and preserved in your fridge, freezer or pantry.
* Ask yourself: If what I normally get comes in plastic, how can I still get that pantry staple without the plastic?

THE BASIC REAL FOOD LIST

Fresh seasonal local vegies

Fresh herbs

Fresh seasonal local fruits

Olives

Meat and eggs – with traceability to a regen ag source, to avoid your dinner contributing to land clearing or animal cruelty

Fish and seafood – responsibly caught, sustainably managed smaller fish, to avoid overfishing and bioaccumulated mercury; caught by sustainable fisheries as locally as possible. Our oceans need to rest and regenerate.

Fresh cheeses – goat's curd, haloumi, feta, cottage cheese, quark

Aged unprocessed cheeses

Whole milk and yoghurt

Nuts – fresh or in-house-made nut/oat/hemp milks, nut butter and nut cheeses – buy these or make your own

Seeds – pepitas (pumpkin seeds), sunflower seeds, hemp seeds, linseeds (flaxseeds), chia seeds

Various grains – whole, soaked and prepared with care

Unrefined sugars – local honey, maple syrup, yacón

Quinoa and buckwheat

Healthy fats for cooking – butter, ghee, coconut oil, organic grass-fed tallow (beef fat), organic pork lard, duck/goose fat and olive oil

Healthy fats to eat raw – olive oil, cold-pressed flaxseed oil, macadamia oil, avocado oil, coconut oil, hemp oil

Coconut – fresh baby coconuts if local, or desiccated or shredded

Pure chocolate and cocoa/cacao – made without additives, preferably organic and fair trade

Legumes – for digestibility and bioavailability of nutrients, soak for 12 hours in water with a splash of something acidic (e.g. apple cider vinegar, lemon juice), then drain, rinse and boil until tender

Healthy beverages – Fresh vegie juices, kefir water, kombucha, home-made

iced tea, smoothies, herbal teas, dandelion tea, black organic tea, organic coffee and Swiss-water-process decaffeinated coffee

Spices and dried herbs – push yourself to try some local to you if you haven't already. Are there indigenous herbs you could enjoy?

Soy – tempeh, organic tofu, natto, tamari – must be organic-certified to avoid GMO and ensure you're not contributing to land clearing

Sea vegetables – dulse flakes, arame, kombu, wakame, kelp. In our house we call dulse flakes 'purple sprinkles', and they're a special condiment and 'topper' for many soups, casseroles, gratins and stews.

Traditionally made vinegars – such as apple cider vinegar with 'mother'

Superfoods – such as maca powder, acai berries, goji berries, green powder blends from pure sources, lucuma powder, bee pollen

The real food rock stars: perennials

While all plants sequester carbon to varying degrees, some are grown and harvested once or twice a year – e.g. sugar cane, cereals/grains and soy – causing soil disturbance and carbon release from the soil. Farmers are finding methods for minimising till, so I don't want to label anything as 'wrong' here. Some, as we've seen with sugar, corn and soy, are grown by clearing forest lands in order to feed factory-farmed animals. Some are sprayed with nasties that poison waterways.

But some plants are perennial rock stars. Perennials are plants you can plant once and harvest for years, so there's far less tillage and therefore less soil disturbance, which means greater levels of carbon can be sequestered. They are deeper rooted than annuals, and therefore also hardier when there are periods of drought. Thanks to those deep roots, they draw up lots of nutrients and contain a higher level of trace minerals than most other plant foods. The high level of minerals also encourages bacteria, fungi, worms and animals, so they're a boon for biodiversity above and below the ground.

If we can prioritise these perennials, especially the ones that grow local to us or that we could have a go at growing ourselves, as things to add to meals or to build meals around when possible, we are sending tiny little no-till, deep-rooted ripples out into the atmosphere instead of carbon. You'll see in the recipes that I use a lot of fresh herbs, spring onions, nuts and olive oil to bolster the presence of perennials in the week's cooking. Every little thing helps.

Shall we do a bit of a perennial chart? I think so. It's time to meet your perennial rock stars. You'll never walk past and ignore them again, and if we can all add a few to our baskets each week and season, we're sending a powerful message of demand for plant foods that require less tillage. In a food forest, as we saw with agroforestry in the last chapter, perennial herbs and vegies form the lower herbaceous layer. As well as being great plants to eat, they are important ground cover and sometimes erosion control for slopes. They're also ready at different times from the annuals, so for the home-grower and farmer alike, they bring added harvest and bounty.

Perennials to prioritise

HERBS AND SPICES

Anise

Bay leaf

Chicory

Chives

Curry leaf

Dandelion

Fennel

Garlic

Ginger/galangal ginger

Greek basil

Horseradish

Hyssop

Lemon balm

Lemon verbena

Lemongrass

Lovage (looks like parsley, tastes like celery)

Marjoram

Mint

Moringa

Nettle

Oregano

Parsley

Rosemary

Sage

Sorrel

Tarragon

Thyme

FRUIT

Apple

Apricot

Avocado

Blackberries

Cherries

Currants

Dates

Figs

Goji berries

Grapes

Kiwi fruit

Lemon

Lime

Mango

Nectarine

Olives

Orange

Peach

Pear

Persimmon

Plum

Raspberries

VEGIES

Asparagus – that first sautéed asparagus in spring is the best

Collard greens

Dame's rocket

Globe artichoke

Good King Henry – once a British staple; steam the leaves like spinach, use the seeds like buckwheat and enjoy the flowers like broccoli. Bring it back, world!

Kailaan (Chinese broccoli)

Lamb's lettuce (corn salad)

Miner's lettuce/winter purslane

Perennial beans – most beans are annual, but some (e.g. scarlet runner beans) will resprout each year

Perennial broccoli varieties – e.g. nine star, purple cape

Radicchio

Red bunching onions or Egyptian onions – I've never seen or tasted the latter, have you?

Rhubarb – aha! Not a fruit? Nope.

Sea kale – a cross between kale and collard greens; sauté like kale or spinach

Silverbeet (Swiss chard)

Spring onions (scallions)

Sweet gourd (calabash)

Sylvetta rocket (arugula) – the peppery kind

Watercress

NUTS

Almonds

Chestnuts

Hazelnuts

Macadamias

Pecans

Pistachios

Walnuts

TREATS

Carob

Cocoa – yes, chocolate is on the list! (Hehe. Thought you'd be excited). But remember, traceable, ethical, regenerative farming practices.

Coconut

A practical guide to sourcing real food

At this point you might be wondering how you're going to go about sourcing better in a practical sense. You really want to try sourcing food grown using regenerative agriculture methods, or at least a few items to start with. But ... spray-free, free-range, pasture-fed, chemical-free, all natural – how the heck do you decipher all the labels? And what about packaged foods? Are they all out, and if not, how do you know what's okay and what's not? How do you learn what to do with leftovers, or how to save things before they go 'off' if you're having a busy week?

A lot of questions but also a lot of answers – and that's exactly what's going to happen for the rest of this chapter. I'm going to double down on lists and checklists to help you navigate everything:

1   lists to connect you to local, regeneratively farmed produce and stores that stock it
2   lists to help you with the biggest pain points: time and money
3   lists to help you feel inspired with what you've got, what's left over and what you might not normally have considered using
4   templates to help you start conversations to find more regeneratively farmed/sourced produce near you, and get more high-quality food into your schools, community centres and institutions.

So let's begin, shall we?

Your real food FAQs

· · · · · · ·

Q How can I find local produce and choose the best options?
Often the greatest motivation and encouragement comes from finding like minds to share the journey with, and from having in that mix people who have been at it longer than you have. How do we find them? Well, thanks to the magic of the internet, it's easy.

Here are ten online searches (use Ecosia if you want to plant trees every time you search the internet) to find regeneratively grown food near you. Say, for example, you lived in Vista, California:

1   Facebook groups for organic food Vista California
2   CSA [community supported agriculture] boxes Vista California
3   Regenerative farm Vista California
4   Biodynamics Vista California
5   Organic grocer Vista California
6   Sustainable seafood Vista California
7   Organic fruit and vegetables Vista California
8   Organic store or co-op Vista California
9   Organic produce Vista California
10 Organic produce markets Vista California

Just substitute your own town or city and you'll quickly start to find things around you that you can try. In testing the list above, I found CSAs, beautiful organic ranches, and organic food farmer's markets, grocers and farm tours. Now I want to go back to Vista, California, home of my favourite soap maker Dr Bronner's, which co-authored the regenerative organic ag certification (see page 67).

· · · · · · ·

Q What if I can't find any local produce?
The irony is that people closer to the farms out in regional areas often don't have access to a big choice of produce. One option in this case is to get growing your own, but when it comes to access and choice for everyone, you might just need to be a pioneer in your area. I gave a talk a few years ago in an Australian

town that was very remote, and yet it had a thriving community of families wanting to do their best to eat well and source produce from farms in their state. During the workshop we planned groups to organise and commit to certain quantities of produce, so that they could approach the local supermarket, butcher and grocer with a proposition: If you get in 20 organic chickens a month, we'll pre-order them from you so that you know they'll sell. Another group set up a co-op for pantry staples. Another volunteered to contact all the closed organic produce farms and secure a fortnightly visit if the town could commit to making it worth the farmer's while. Deals were struck and a path with access to more organic, regeneratively grown food was made – where there's a will, right?

· · · · · · ·

Q How can I make regeneratively farmed food more affordable?

* **Stay in season:** Nature has her very own marketing calendar to keep us from getting bored with eating the same thing over and over. We've got used to having a tiny variety of things available all year round, but we're tired of that now. We see the same things over and over again. So the next time you're tempted by the hot new chocolate bar or Korean barbecue prawn chips (seriously, I have actually seen this flavour before), step away and ask yourself 'What's in season?' The bonus is, things are cheaper and taste better in season, so lap it up while the sun's shining and then pine for it until you see it again next year. It makes everything so much more special.

* **Join a co-op:** Or start one, so you can order produce in bulk and split it with co-op members at a fraction of the retail price.

* **Focus on three high-nutrient meals and fewer snacks:** Or barely any snacks. Less money spent on snacks means more money for nutritious meals, which means winning. If you switch from toast and jam to eggs, toast and a bit of spinach, you'll be full for a lot longer and flooded with satisfying nutrients. So while the egg breakfast costs you more, you don't need the $4 muffin from the cafe or the 'baked not fried' chips at 10 am, and you're actually then saving money.

* **Switch to cheaper cuts:** If you eat meat, switching from expensive muscle meats to cheaper cuts not only saves you cash you can use to trade up to the good stuff, but also tends to diversify the nutrition in the meal, with even more nutritional variety when you go a bit more nose to tail. Your butcher may also do cow shares, which are very economical.

- **Stop wasting food:** More on that soon, but stretching what you have before you buy more is going to go a long way towards transforming your food mix without bloating your budget.
- **Grow your own:** Could you grow some veg yourself in pots or in the garden? Join a community garden or local council/county workshops to learn how to get going. There are lots of online courses, too.
- **Buy some things in bulk:** For something you go through a lot of, instead of getting a small amount each week, can you buy it in bulk? Often the 1 kg (2 lb 4 oz) or 5 kg (11 pound) packs are much more economical. So if, for example, you make lots of buckwheat-based things or lentil-based things and can get bulk pantry staples, you'll save money you can use to trade up to biodynamic and/or organic options. You'll also save on packaging.
- **Consider eating less:** There's a French saying when it comes to dessert – for example, when you're full and you don't 'need' more but you want a little something – 'Consider 50 per cent.' If you have half as much of that little something it will last twice as long. Trade up in quality and sourcing for your treats and eat half as much of them at a time.

· · · · · · ·

Q How can I tell if a producer is a good one?

Now remember, kindness and curiosity are the vibe here – no accusatory tones. I like to assume that everyone is simply doing their best with what they know or think customers want, and just because you may not end up buying from that stall or farm doesn't mean you need to be unkind – ever. All farmers, regardless, work harder than most humans ever experience in their lives, and no farmer is the enemy here – they're simply making what the market wants. If we change, eventually they too will change for us. With kindness and being repeatedly asked for synthetic-free and input-free produce, who knows, your farmer might just start experimenting with new methods, or RSVPing to that interesting biodynamics workshop that's coming up.

I've seen this many times and truly do believe that kindness unites and moves us forward. We have to remember that we all want access to good food, a well-paying job, the best for our kids, health, a house to call home … We're really not that different at all, right? If they have a couple of items that are grown regeneratively either by them or someone else but the whole stand isn't in that style, a powerful thing you could do is to purchase those regen items and not the others. When a business sees demand go up in an area, it will respond by providing more of it.

Here are a few questions to ask. Please don't ask them all! Be cool, assume goodness, and come from a good place yourself, and this might make for years-long conversations at the markets:

* Where's your farm?
* Are you new farmers or is it a family farm?
* Having a good season?
* Have you guys gone with any particular certifications?
* Can I ask which synthetic inputs, the sprays and the like, you use? We're trying to experiment with sourcing food grown using regenerative farming methods.
* If they label their product 'spray-free' but don't have organic or biodynamic certification, ask, 'How do you avoid pests? I can't grow a tomato with it being wolfed down by a critter!' (A bit of light humour makes everyone comfortable.)
* Has the produce been sprayed with a preservative for freshness?
* Does all the produce you sell here come from your farm or from others as well? Unfortunately, you can't always assume that the produce at a farmer's market is local. I've seen a farmer's market stall selling lemons from America! Reminder, I live in Sydney, so that is strange indeed. Sometimes, the 'farm fresh' experience you were after misses the mark big-time.

For things like sausages

* Do you make the sausages yourself using meat from your farm?
* Do they contain preservatives and/or sulfites (202, 220, 223, 224)?
* Do you use any synthetic flavours or yeast extracts?
* Do they contain gluten? (Only ask this of course if, like me, you need to avoid it.)

For smoked or preserved meats or fish

* Do these contain nitrates?
* Has caramel/synthetic colour been added? (This is often the case for smoked fish and smoked meats.)
* Do they contain sulfites (202, 220, 223, 224)?

For non-certified-organic vegetarian or vegan options

* Where does your soy ingredient come from?
* Do you know the ingredients of the vegie patties? I'd love to have a quick look.
* Who supplies your produce?
* Which farms do your eggs and dairy come from?

Q How can I organise produce switches?

Too much of one thing but not enough of another?

* Ask in your Facebook groups about local meet-ups.
* Do an internet search for '[your suburb/area] community garden/co-op/organic shop/composters/permaculture group.
* Ask at your local health food shop or organic grocer if they've heard of any growing/co-op catch-ups in the area.
* Check out the annual local council/county festival/events where there are stallholders – you'll probably find like minds there at a couple of the stalls.
* Check out all the stalls at the nearest farmer's market – same deal, you'll most probably find a couple of like minds or a regenerative farmer or two there.

· · · · · ·

Q How do I find online resources for growing my own food?

You'll want to connect with local resources to help you through your local seasons, but here are a few things you can pop on your to-do list if you've been wanting to get into growing your own food but haven't quite got there yet.

* Check your local council/county website for food-growing workshops.
* Read books and blogs with information on growing for your climate, seasons and type of space. If you're in a balcony-only situation, search for 'best tips for balcony gardens'; if you're on a quarter of an acre with a good garden space, search 'how to establish raised beds on a lawn garden'. Another useful thing to search is 'What can I grow as companion plants to avoid garden pests' or '10 ways to avoid common pests' or 'How to establish a vegie garden resistant to pests' or '10 natural things to protect from pests'. You want to know how to establish things with the least likelihood that you'll lose your food. We lost our first kale crop overnight to a group of very hungry caterpillars the first time we planted something, and it was super disheartening. The key is to get more knowledge than 'Oh, I'm going to put this in a plot and grow food', and then, if it fails, think you *can't* grow food. One isolated fail that wasn't setting you up for success in the first place doesn't mean it's impossible.
* Search for local permaculture and community garden Facebook groups and start helping out in local food gardens to learn the ropes. Experienced gardeners are so supportive to newer people giving it a go, because every great gardener wants other people to feel the joy they feel.

* See what TV shows are on to help inspire you – *Gardening Australia* has been motivating people to grow home vegie patches and verge gardens thanks to current host Costa Georgiadis and the many home gardeners he and other presenters have interviewed over the years.
* Check out popular tags on Instagram for growing food, and connect to people who post a lot on the subject. You might want to just grow a few things in something like a 'Vegepod', or go full permaculture garden either in a small garden or on half an acre. You'd be surprised how many people you can connect to online to do this. Popular food-growing tags include #permaculture #vegiepatch (or #veggiepatch or #vegepatch) #growfood #vegiegarden (etc.) #growyourfood #growfoodnotlawns #organicfood #permacultureliving #communitygarden #foodgarden.

. . . .

Q How can I thank my farmer/producer?
They need our support. Here are some suggestions:

* Leave a review on their website (and/or Tripadvisor if it's a destination farm people can visit).
* Write them an email.
* Share on your social media channels the great experience you've just had with someone's produce.
* Cook something delicious, share a pic and tag them or share a link to their farm and say why they're so special.
* Put up their flier (if they have one) on your school and/or office noticeboard.
* Like their social media posts and comment on them – it means more people will see their wonderful work (that's how the algorithm works).

. . . .

Q How can I connect to wild-foraged local foods?
Once we hit the recipes, you'll see they incorporate quite an internationally common array of ingredients. I want this book to mean something to people no matter where they pick it up in the world, and to unite us all in connecting to local resources and making staple, simple recipes very much our own. To that end, I want to encourage you to see what's around you that you can use as delicious, local substitutes for some of the ingredients in the recipes in this book. For example, here in Australia, we often use pepperberry as our 'pepper' spice or add lilly pillies or Davidson plums to casseroles or soups for tang. You might read that

in Virginia, USA, and say 'You use *what*?' but with a bit of digging you'll find some delicious local wild foods that you could use for the same effect.

Whenever you taste a recipe to make adjustments for sweet, sour, pepper and salt, ask yourself 'What wild and local foods have I perhaps not yet discovered that I could substitute for sugar, lemon, black pepper or sea salt? This is a great project with kids and willing teenagers, to get them on the detective case. Here are some good starting points:

* Look on your local council/county website for any indigenous, wild food tours that might be held in your area and take the family.
* Search for terms such as 'foraging tour [your town/city/region]' to see what local guided-foraging specialists are offering that you can join.
* Search 'native foods local to [your town/city/region]'.
* Search Instagram for any foragers or indigenous/native food guides to support your vocab expansion in this area.
* Buy a book on wild foods and foraging that focuses on where you live.

* * * * * *

Q **How can I tell good from bad packaged food?**

It would be extremely unrealistic for anyone to say that from this day forth they're going to go cold turkey and walk away from every type of packaged food. When we go 'all in on day one', we're not setting ourselves up for success. It's a steep learning curve, and while you can make a hero effort for two weeks, a week that's busy at work or a birthday party will be your undoing, which will make you feel ashamed and sad you 'couldn't do it' and all that usual self-denigration jazz. No thanks. Of course it's great for emissions reduction to buy as much of your weekly food as you can as wholefood, from regenerative sources if possible, but it's far better to have millions moving forward imperfectly than ten perfect zero-waste eaters. When you do find any packaged foods you're happy to bring into the fold, use this list to set you up for success:

* Join an additive-free and/or wholefood-focused Facebook group or our Low Tox Club, where like minds discuss and share wins and ask questions. Chances are someone there has been at things for longer than you and will be able to help steer you towards better local options.
* Be aware that 'Free from' is usually an alarm bell, not an asset. 'Free from' gives you one tiny piece of information, like 'dairy-free' or 'gluten-free' or 'meat-free',

but it doesn't give you the whole picture. Flip to the back, look at the ingredients and ask yourself: 'Is this the list of an ultra-processed food or is it a simple, great ingredients list I can easily understand?'

* And do the same with 'Low fat', which is usually code for chemical poop storm. Again, check out the full ingredients list. Have they added a host of thickeners based on gelatine, which is 99 per cent of the time going to be of animal-origin and from factory-farmed, unethical operations? Have they jacked up the sugar or, worse, synthetic sweeteners to make up for the blandness? A little fat from wholefood sources in our day helps us feel full and absorb the fat-soluble vitamins A, D, E and K. Enjoy that full-fat pot of yoghurt – vegan or milk-based from a great ethical company – top it with fresh fruits (perennial power) and enjoy the experience.

* If it has a fancy flavour name on the front, like 'Honey soy chicken' or 'Sweet chilli and sour cream', ask yourself: 'What does a food technologist have to manipulate in a lab to get those flavours onto a chip? Are there ingredients that say 'flavour', such as 'natural flavour' or 'flavour enhancer'? These aren't ideal, and often produce excitatory reactions in the brain. This can be a 'nice little high' for one person who's not sensitive, but to another, they can cause flushing, brain fog and hyperactivity. Step away from the flavoured chips, crackers and 'baked not fried' grain snacks, and make the switch to plain chips with delicious vegie-packed dips, so that reaching for your next treat is a more nourishing experience.

* Check for any preservatives from the sulfite family – 202, 220, 223, 224. These can cause a host of issues, including hives, exacerbation of skin conditions such as eczema and dermatitis, aggravated asthma, rapid heartbeat and mast cell activation.

* Switch from the supermarket crumpets, pikelets and grated cheese rolls to a local baker, or teach yourself how to make them at home, or, for the love of nature, just grate the cheese yourself and melt it on. We can do it!

* Look for products that are certified organic. This will give you confidence that the food was at least produced using no sprays that contribute to polluted waterways and soil degradation. But take care – it might be certified organic but it can still be processed junk that's high in sugar.

Q How can I avoid genetically modified foods?

Genetically modified (GM) foods are foods grown from seeds that don't occur naturally, which means a farmer needs to buy patented seed from a corporate manufacturer each year, rather than follow the age-old tradition of saving seeds. I covered the health concerns this raises in my first book, but there's also a food sovereignty issue with the increased dependency of farmers on corporations, and a risk of contamination by GM seeds on neighbouring non-GM farms. Here are five clues there might be GM ingredients in a product:

1 It's from a big multinational brand – they tend to use global markets for cheapest ingredient sourcing to save on costs, so if it contains an ingredient that's one of the world's principal GM crops, it's always worth checking. There's no guarantee it will or won't contain GM ingredients. Email the manufacturer and ask if you're not sure.

2 It contains corn, soy, sugar (from sugar beet), canola, cottonseed, potato, peas or golden rice. These are all potentially crops that have been genetically modified, so it's always worth checking for products that aren't certified organic. Cotton, soy, corn and canola are the big four to watch out for, though.

3 The packet says 'Made from local and imported ingredients', meaning that even if your country doesn't grow GM foods, they could have been used in making this product being sold locally.

4 The product contains ingredients made from these crops – such as oil, textured vegetable protein (TVP) from soy, sugar from sugar beet, high fructose corn syrup or glucose from corn, protein powder or starch. These ingredients can also be made using great-quality crops that aren't GM, so investigate, ask for guarantees that it's GM-free, or buy certified organic.

5 The product contains animal ingredients such as meat itself, or gelatine or stock/broth made from animals that have eaten GM crops. For example, when cows, pigs and chickens are factory-farmed or non-organic/pasture-fed, their feed may contain GM soybeans and corn.

Q 'What do packaging claims really mean?

Keep your wits about you and remember the following:

* 'All natural' means absolutely nothing.
* 'Made with' means that while there might be organic cocoa in that chocolate biscuit, there's a whole bunch of other stuff you might not want in there too.
* 'Free from' only tells you what's not in there, not what is.
* 'Made with the goodness of [enter wholefood sounding ingredient here]' doesn't tell you everything it's made with.
* 'Great for growing little bodies' – says who? You decide for yourself.
* 'Perfect for snacking on the go' – says who? What's in it? Usually a cucumber is perfect for snacking on the go, rather than a strange array of ingredients pressed neatly into square shapes. Again, you decide what's perfect, not them.
* 'Contains important vitamins for growing children'. Often these are synthetic vitamins and often, depending on individual genetics and some basic human biochemistry, those vitamins won't be as bioavailable as if we were to get them from a diet rich in great wholefoods. 'Enriching' with folic acid, for example, isn't the same as consuming naturally occurring folate in leafy greens and legumes.
* 'Farm fresh' – is it though? I've seen this label on UHT milk, which is ultra-pasteurised and has a shelf life of over two years. Be strict and discerning.
* 'Now with 120 g/4 oz more value – for free!' Ask yourself a) Is this something I even need? b) What are the ingredients like? c) When a company sacrifices quality to drive prices down and volume up, how does that affect the farm, or workers' rights on farms and in logistics?
* 'Everything you need for a balanced meal'. Again, the ingredients list will tell you if that's true. If there's more than herbs, spices, meat, fish, eggs, vegies, fruit, whole grains, legumes, nuts or seeds in there, then it has things you don't need for a balanced meal.

TIP FOR REMOTE COMMUNITIES

———

If there's no regenerative farm right near you but there is one a couple of hours away, why not try this? Get your community together, find ten families who want to commit to a weekly order of regeneratively farmed produce, then write to the farm two hours away and say: I have ten families who'd make a weekly order of $80–150 of seasonal fruit and veg from you if you could justify that for one delivery a week to us. One low tox community member has even offered to meet them halfway to pick it all up and distribute, for the cost of fuel plus $50 for her time. Another woman started a co-op and slowly, over time, got a huge range of pantry staples and produce into a remote town in my home state. I've been to some extremely remote areas in Australia to give talks, and when we all put our heads together, it's amazing what we can make happen.

Start small before you go big, and celebrate gains along the way. Don't focus on or feel sad about your big supermarket shop. Feel excited that you've found a way to order one new thing that doesn't come from the supermarket or isn't conventionally grown. If you really want to change what you buy and set your dollars working to their full power, there's almost always a way to make things happen. If this is you, check out the template scripts at the end of this section to help you get the party started.

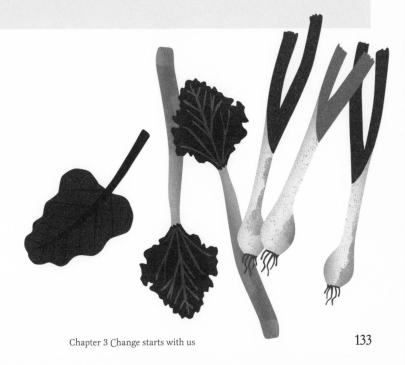

How to get the most out of every last bit of produce

The lists coming up are all about broadening the possibilities when it comes to produce. Half the time we're not bored with produce-driven meals, we're bored with what we do with produce. So here's a ton of inspiration on how to use some common produce items. It's really about making produce the star and starting to feel more excited about all the things you can do with it.

Seven quick-prep no-watch meals

As well as using the ideas below, start Pinterest boards or a browser bookmarks folder and search these types of recipes online. Remember to check the recipe section in the next chapter or lowtoxlife.com too, of course.

1 **Slow-cooker meals:** Whack it all in, switch the slow-cooker on. Set and forget.

2 **Soups:** Chop, sauté and add liquids, then – pro tip – cook in the oven in a cast-iron casserole dish with the lid on without having to worry if it's catching and having to stir it. An hour in a 170°C (325°F) oven, then either blend or serve chunky. This is one of the easiest and least stressful ways to ensure everyone in the family gets a couple of their favourite things in there. It's just perfect for lazy summer evenings.

3 **Tray bake meals:** Pop it all in the tray. Bake it. Check out my Roasted Garlic, Herb and Apricot Chicken Tray Bake (page 255). Use left-overs for a salad (see page 208).

4 **Gratins:** Try my Mauritian Pumpkin au Gratin (page 224) or cauliflower cheese (page 158). So good!

5 **Pot roasts:** Check out my chicken curry pot roast and next-day soup idea over at lowtoxlife.com – so ridiculously simple and yummy.

6 **Crustless quiche:** If you want a nourishing meal on the table fast, you can prep the filling, bake it as is, serve it with a salad and done. Probably a good idea to line your pie dish with unbleached baking paper first. (Sponge down the baking paper afterwards and save it for next time.)

7 **Frittata:** A cousin of the quiche. As long as you have left-over roast veg, this is a very quick assemble-then-bake situation.

Seven produce-driven 10-minute meal styles

1   **Taco wraps with left-over protein food:** Get your soft tacos or wraps, grate your cheese, mash some avocado, chop/shred some seasonal vegies and serve with organic legumes of choice or left-over meat. I find just mixing some taco seasoning into the avocado or dusting it on the meat turns it into a Mexican meal in a flash.

2   **Tasting plates:** Chop raw vegies, grab cheeses, left-over protein foods, a dip, some olives and sliced seasonal fruit, and serve with bread, crispbread, pitas or seed crackers.

3   **Omelette:** Mastering the art of a good omelette means you're only ever 10 minutes away from a nutritious, easy meal. Throw a few salad leaves and cherry tomatoes on the side, and voilà. If you don't think your omelettes are very nice, try one of the many YouTube instructional videos from chefs.

4   **Fish and salad:** Fish cooks fast, so one way to simple dinner perfection is getting a sustainably sourced fish option from near you, pan-frying it and prepping a quick salad to serve alongside it. Take it from plain to punchy by melting a couple of tablespoons of salted butter and the juice of ¼ lemon in the pan after the fish is on the plates for a super-fast sauce.

5   **Stir-fry:** So darn fast to get a meal on the table. See my Adaptable Stir-fry (page 202) to make one from just about anything.

6   **Cheat's soup:** If you have some prepped, cooked legumes and broth or a good broth powder, soup is scarily fast to prepare with a sautéed onion or two, enough lentils to fill you up, a splash of tomato passata (puréed tomatoes) and broth with salt and pepper to taste – *boom*!

7   **Chopped salad in a food processor:** Pile it all in, pulse for 6 seconds, pop a protein food on top, toss in dressing. Done.

15 simple non-packaged snacks

We need to stop thinking of packaged foods or baked goods as a snack
to 'get us through'. If you have a well-stocked fridge with a few leftovers, an
abundant crisper and a full fruit basket on the bench, then a good snack
is always seconds away. Think produce, keep the variety going, and move
through a simple list like this through the week. A lot of them a five-year-old
or older can make for themselves, and quite a few could be prepped on
a cruisy day ready to go in containers in the fridge.

1   Vegie chips such as kale or beetroot
2   Single-ingredient mango, banana or berry sorbet – For an easy and
    fast 'instant ice cream', blend frozen fruit pieces until they're creamy.
    You may need to blend for a few seconds, scrape down the sides with
    a spatula, and blend again. A tablespoon or two of coconut milk or
    yoghurt for each 2 cups of fruit adds to the creaminess.
3   Apple wedges dripping with nut butter
4   Cucumber 'crackers' (i.e. slices) with mashed avocado on top
5   Popped corn with butter or extra virgin olive oil and sea salt
6   Strawberries dipped in honey and yoghurt
7   Celery peanut butter boats
8   Cup o'berries
9   Roasted chickpeas with extra virgin olive oil and sea salt
10 Boiled egg with salt and pepper
11 Left-over roast sweet potato (or is it only my son who could eat
    a million pieces of this cold?)
12 A banana
13 A couple of slices of left-over roast meats with some relish
14 Beef jerky
15 Cheese and pear

Vegie chips such as
kale or beetroot

Apple wedges dripping
with nut butter

Popped corn with
butter or extra virgin
olive oil and sea salt

Strawberries dipped
in honey and yoghurt

Cup o'berries

Boiled egg with
salt and pepper

Left-over roast
sweet potato

Beef jerky

Cheese and pear

20 ways to jazz up your greens and love them

1 Steam or sauté them and squeeze fresh lemon juice over.

2 Combine spinach and zucchini (courgette) in a frying pan with eggs for a healthy green-egg scramble.

3 Add some crispy pan-fried nitrate-free bacon for a delicious flavour and crunch burst.

4 Throw left-over herbs and wilted greens into a blender with lots of olive oil, garlic, lemon juice and pine nuts to make a delicious pesto to drizzle over your meals.

5 Sauté them and scatter chilli flakes over the top for some heat.

6 Sprinkle with some dulse flakes for a nutrient boost and an umami flavour.

7 Roast broccoli with olive oil, lemon juice and sea salt for a crunchy change.

8 Add a garlicky flavour with fresh crushed garlic or ground garlic powder.

9 Bake kale into chips and season with lemon juice, chilli, salt, vinegar or a fancy spice blend.

10 Add fresh herbs like sage, parsley, coriander (cilantro), dill or basil for pops of flavour.

11 Turn a basic zucchini (courgette) into zucchini fritters (page 204).

12 Scatter fresh goat's cheese or blobs of nut cheese on top for a cheesy change.

13 Sauté them and add pine nuts and currants for a Middle Eastern side dish.

14 Cook spinach, silverbeet (Swiss chard) or collard greens until wilted, then add garlic, onion and a few splashes of cream or coconut cream to make a creamy green side dish. Season to taste.

15 Coat green beans in olive oil and pan-fry them with fresh garlic and lemon.

16 Mash up or blitz an avocado with tahini, olive oil, lemon juice, salt and pepper until quite smooth. Stir kale or greens through for a delicious side dish.

17 Wrap cooked mince, chicken or tempeh in large lettuce cups rather than bread.

18 Roast brussels sprouts with olive or coconut oil, and top with a dressing of miso paste, sesame oil and tamari for an Asian side dish. Just mix 1 tablespoon each of miso paste, sesame oil and tamari in a bowl, adding 1 tablespoon maple syrup if you want a sweet kick too, and toss the roasted brussels sprouts through before serving.

19 Sauté zucchini (courgettes) or brussels sprouts with leafy greens and red onion in olive oil in a frying pan and top with a sprinkling of nuts and seeds, a drizzle of olive oil, a blob of hummus, if you like, and a squeeze of citrus juice or drop of your favourite vinegar.

20 Steam or pan-fry leafy Asian greens such as bok choy. Drizzle with sesame oil, scatter with some sesame seeds and mix in a teaspoon of miso paste.

Steam or sauté and
squeeze lemon juice over

Make a healthy
green-egg scramble

Add some crispy pan-fried
nitrate-free bacon

Turn left-over herbs and
wilted greens into pesto

Scatter fresh goat's
cheese on top

Sprinkle with some
dulse flakes

Sauté and scatter with
chilli flakes

Sauté and top with nuts

Bake kale into chips

Seven ways with asparagus (perennial power)

Local and in season is especially important here, as a lot of asparagus is flown around the world out of season. According to research, the airfreight necessary for produce makes it 50 times higher in carbon emissions than something shipped by sea. Asparagus is in season in spring–summer, so wherever you are, be sure to watch out for the switcheroo to imports that happens when the season is over – it usually comes in the form of an enticing 'special'.

1   Thinly slice it raw and add to a leafy green salad for crunch. You can get chef-fancy and cut it at diagonal, or you can use a vegetable peeler to make ribbons instead.

2   Pan-fry with a little olive oil or butter to accompany any meal – breakfast, lunch or dinner (bottom right). I find this takes just 3–4 minutes on medium heat.

3   Add roughly chopped to a frittata (top). For a basic frittata, you can crack 10 eggs into a mixing bowl and whisk. Pour into a pie dish and throw in some finely chopped purple onion, small chunks of left-over cold roasted vegies, some chopped asparagus, baby spinach and diced pasture-raised ham or bacon if you eat meat. Dot some fresh goat's cheese or feta cheese through it. Bake until there's barely a wobble in the middle – 25–30 minutes on 180°C (350°F). And voilà: you have a simple grab-and-go snack or lunch on hand for the next couple of days.

4   Drizzle with extra virgin olive oil and roast at 180°C (350°F) for 15 minutes. Serve on top of a salad or as a side at lunch or dinner.

5   Add to a stir-fry (page 202).

6   Add to a soup (page 198) or casserole (page 200) 2–3 minutes before serving for a touch of green freshness at the end. I find the woody end bits that we usually chop off are great for adding fibre (and that great asparagus flavour) to a blended soup, so there's definitely no need to waste those.

7   Make a simple salad with pan-fried or roasted asparagus (point 2 or 4 above) by adding cooked and cooled peas, fresh goat's cheese blobs, baby spinach and thinly sliced raw onion. Drizzle with the Lemony Herb Blitzed Dressing (page 194) or the Cuban Kicker (page 195) for a simple and delicious side dish or lunch.

10 ways with carrots

1 Steam then add butter and sea salt.

2 Cut into ½ cm (¼ inch) slices and fry with a little coconut or peanut oil, garlic, ginger and bok choy as a side dish.

3 Steam 1 kg (2 lb 4 oz) until soft, then purée with 2 tablespoons sour cream, 1½ tablespoons extra virgin olive oil, ½ teaspoon ground cumin, ⅓ teaspoon sea salt for a tasty purée. Replace the cumin with lemon pepper for variation.

4 Add well cooked to potato before mashing.

5 For a salad, grate carrots, stir in mashed avocado and add sea salt to taste.

6 For another salad, grate carrots, dress with lemon juice and extra virgin olive oil, and add salt and pepper to taste. Makes a great digestion enhancer.

7 Raw with a dip.

8 With a honey thyme glaze. Cut 6 carrots into quarters lengthways, cook in boiling water in a large low-sided frying pan with 3 sprigs thyme. Drain away the water, melt 30 g (1 oz) butter into them and arrange flat on a baking tray. Drizzle 2 tablespoons honey over the top and crack over some black pepper to taste. Bake in a 180°C (350°F) oven for 35 minutes.

9 For carrot fritters, whisk together 1 cup flour of your choice, 2 organic, pasture-raised eggs, ½ cup (125 ml) milk of your choice and 1 teaspoon baking powder. Stir in 2 cups (300 g) grated carrot, 1 cup (200 g) corn kernels and 1 handful chopped herbs (optional), and cook for 3 minutes each side. Voilà! Easy fritters.

10 Use your vegie peeler to cut long ribbons from 4 carrots. Mix in a bowl with ½ cup (125 g) yoghurt, 1 tablespoon tahini, 1 tablespoon lemon juice, 1 handful finely chopped fresh herb of your choice, and salt and pepper to taste. Serve as a side, or add lettuce and chickpeas or a few slices of fried haloumi = main event.

10 ways to extend a whole roast chook

How many delicious, easy meals does one chicken make? Maybe more than you think. Here's how you can stretch one regeneratively farmed roast chicken into 10 different recipes. By the way, if you compare the price per kilo/pound of that famous tinned ham to the price of a whole regen ag chook, the chook is cheaper. Can you believe it? So often we think of something as expensive when if we look at it more closely we can be surprised. And we can be pretty sure that tinned ham doesn't come from pigs who enjoyed a great quality of life on a beautiful farm, rolling around in the mud, right? Now, back to the chicken …

1. Turn the carcass into a broth by cooking it in water with carrot, celery, onion, thyme and parsley. Sip on it as a nourishing elixir or add it to meals as stock.
2. Turn chicken broth (point 1 above) into a soup with a few extra vegies and herbs.
3. Shred chicken breast and toss into a healthy salad.
4. Stir juicy chopped chicken thigh through flavourful curries.
5. Top your favourite pizza base with chopped chicken breast, vegies and cheese.
6. Throw into a wok with vegies for an instant stir-fry. You can use the Adaptable Stir-fry recipe on page 202.
7. Freeze chicken broth (point 1 above) into ice cubes and add to smoothies for a nutrient hit of amino acids.
8. Make crispy chicken-skin chips. Take any skins you're not using, pat dry completely, stretch out on a stainless-steel baking tray and roast for 20 minutes in a preheated 200°C (400°F) oven.
9. Toss through cooked pasta with a creamy, tomato or pesto-based sauce.
10. Add to a wrap with salad and a yummy sauce from the flavour makers section (pages 177–95).

Five ways with a protein food + sautéed onion base

Stop boring yourself to tears with your meals! Here are five ways to turn your standard protein food and onion base into yummy and varied meals.

1 **Slow-cooked casserole:** Sauté your protein food of choice, onions, zucchini (courgette) and carrot in a flameproof casserole dish until browned and softened. Add some stock to just cover the protein food, zucchini and carrot. Put the lid on and cook in a 160°C (315°F) oven for 2–3 hours, until done to your liking or the meat (if using) is falling apart.

2 **Asian stir-fry:** Brown off the protein food and soften the onions, then remove from the wok. Fry vegies of your choice, along with garlic, ginger and spring onions, for a minute or two, then return the protein food and onions to the wok with your choice of sauce. Serve with noodles, quinoa or rice, or eat as is without grains.

3 **Soup:** Cook the protein food and onions and set aside. Sauté chopped carrot, celery and zucchini (courgette) until soft then top it off with 4 cups (1 litre) broth or stock. When cooked to your liking, stir in the protein food and onion mixture and heat through. Add ½ cup (125 ml) coconut cream and 1 tablespoon curry paste for a curried soup version; or simply add some fresh thyme and parsley for a Euro version, with a good squeeze of lemon juice for zing.

4 **Mexican mince:** Cook the onions and protein food, season generously with Mexican spices like cumin, paprika, cayenne pepper, chilli and pepper, or a pre-mixed organic spiced taco blend. Add 2 cups (400 g) diced tomatoes (as local as possible) or some tomato passata (puréed tomatoes) and simmer away. Serve in tortillas or lettuce boats.

5 **Fragrant curry:** Brown meat or button mushrooms or chunky cubed eggplant (aubergine) until sealed and golden. Remove from the pan. Sweat some onion until soft. Add curry spices like garam masala, ras el hanout, cumin, cinnamon, chilli and turmeric – 1½ tablespoons curry spice mix for each 1 kg (2 lb 4 oz) meat, mushrooms or eggplant. Add ⅓ cup (80 ml) coconut cream and ¼ cup (50 g) diced tomatoes for an Indian blend. Stir in the meat, mushrooms or eggplant and simmer to let the flavours develop. You can use Malaysian or Thai curry pastes instead of Indian spice mix. I love to add 1 teaspoon honey to soften the curry.

STRESS-FREE COOKING TIPS

Keep your stress levels down when cooking by remembering a few key facts:

* If a good cook doesn't follow a recipe, that doesn't mean they have the exact recipe in their head. Instead, they feel free to add whatever they come across in their kitchen, in whatever combinations and amounts they think might taste good. If they're not sure, they taste and assess: what does this need? More sweet or sour, less intensity (add a splash of water)? Become a thinker in the kitchen.

* If you don't have limes, don't jump in the car and scour the supermarket for $2 limes. Look for lemons instead. Or ask around your neighbourhood if someone has a citrus tree. Some trees are heavy croppers and most people won't get through them all on their own. If there are only imported lemons in the shop at that time, maybe instead you could use a vinegar for a sour element – especially for dressings and savoury dishes.

* Unless it's a cake or bread, don't worry too much about super-precise quantities. You want to get the basic ratios right to balance the flavours, but if an adaptable recipe (pages 197–217) says 200 g (7 oz) meat and you only have 175 g (6 oz), you don't have to go out and buy more meat. I'm spelling this out because I genuinely didn't know this and used to be stressed by not having exactly what was needed – I don't want you to feel the same way. As the suggestions in this chapter show, I hope, quantities are very often flexible.

* If cooking for one, make enough to feed two or more and keep the leftovers for the next day – less work in the kitchen = greater chance of increasing scratch-cooking habits in the long term.

* If a quantity in a recipe doesn't seem quite right to you or your tastes, experiment until it suits you. You'll get to the stage where you do this without thinking about it.

* Adjust any recipe by halving or doubling, but don't be too crazy about exact double or half quantities, especially if it's a soup, stew, casserole or other savoury dish. Baking is where you need to be more exact.

Five meals with minced (ground) meat

Mince is a super-economical protein source and very versatile. When you're trading up to ethical, regenerative meat it will be more expensive per kilo, so mince is a good plan. Here's one way to stretch 1 kg (2 lb 4 oz) minced (ground) meat over five meals and keep it interesting while you do it.

1 **Korean bibimbap for one:** This is essentially a bowl of julienned vegies, so just use whatever you have. Fry 100 g (3½ oz) mince with ½ garlic clove, ⅓ teaspoon Asian spices like Chinese five spice and a couple of pinches of salt. Add to the vegies. Top with a fried egg, cooked sunny side up for dramatic effect, and a drizzle of your favourite chilli sauce. Easy, quick and packed with nutrients to keep you going all afternoon without reaching for packaged snacks. **Total mince used = 100 g (3½ oz)**

2 **Burger patties for four:** Mix 400 g (14 oz) mince with finely diced onion or onion powder, garlic, herbs and paprika. Form into eight patties and refrigerate or freeze until ready to cook. Break cooked patties up into salad bowls for a healthy protein hit. **Total mince used = 400 g (14 oz)**

3 **Mexican mince tacos for three or four:** Cook up 300 g (10½ oz) mince with chopped red onion, 2 tablespoons Mexican spices and ⅓ cup (80 ml) tomato passata (puréed tomatoes) or 2 chopped tomatoes. While the mince simmers down, add 1 cup (120 g) cooked black beans. Prepare bowls of chopped cucumber, capsicum (pepper) and coriander (cilantro), and mash up some avocado if they're local to you. A simple meal ready in 15 minutes. **Total mince used = 300 g (10½ oz)**

4 **Turkish mince flatbread for one:** Cook 100 g (3½ oz) mince with 1 small red onion, and ½ teaspoon mixed Turkish spices like cumin, sumac and cinnamon. Top a slice of toasted flatbread (page 274) with olive oil and the flavoured mince. Drizzle with some yoghurt and scatter some toasted pine nuts on top. Top with loads of fresh perennial herbs and spring onion. Delish! **Total mince used = 100 g (3½ oz)**

5 **English jacket potato with mushy peas:** Bake an unpeeled potato in the oven until soft all the way through. Top with 100 g (3½ oz) cooked mince seasoned with garlic. Cook ⅔ cup (100 g) frozen peas and mash to a purée with olive oil. Dollop on top of the hot mince and potato with 1 tablespoon sour cream. Serve with a side of greens for a balanced meal. **Total mince used = 100 g (3 ½ oz)**

Six high-protein plant meals

1 **Tofu and greens soup for two:** Fry the green part of 4 spring onions
   (scallions). Add 3 cups (750 ml) vegie broth, 2 teaspoons miso paste,
   200 g (7 oz) firm tofu cut into small cubes, 1 crushed garlic clove and
   2 cups chopped greens of your choice (e.g. Chinese broccoli, baby
   spinach, bok choy). Simmer for 2 minutes. Done.

2 **Build your own 'bowl':** Fill communal bowls with cooked beans,
   chickpeas and/or tempeh, grated carrot, nuts (e.g. chopped peanuts
   or cashews), diced cucumber, finely chopped spring onions (scallions),
   finely chopped leafy greens, cooked and cooled quinoa or brown rice,
   sliced avocado and some sort of a dip like hummus or tzatziki. Place in
   the middle of the table with a jar of zingy dressing (see pages 190–95).
   Give everyone a bowl to fill however they wish.

3 **Tasty quinoa or lentils:** Cook up enough quinoa or brown lentils for
   two. Fry a large red onion in 3 tablespoons olive oil or ghee until very
   brown and well cooked. Toss the onion through the lentils or quinoa
   with chopped parsley and a squeeze of fresh lemon juice. Season with
   salt and pepper to taste. Sauté some zucchini (courgette) and silverbeet
   (Swiss chard) in olive oil and serve with the quinoa or lentils.

4 **Simple bean stew:** Fry an onion. Add 2 chopped garlic cloves, 4 thyme
   sprigs and 1 handful chopped parsley stems, 1 cup (120 g) cooked
   kidney or black beans per person, 1 cup (250 ml) tomato passata (puréed
   tomatoes) and 1 cup (250 ml) vegie stock. Cook over medium heat
   for 15 minutes. Serve with flatbreads (page 274) or a slice of toasted
   sourdough, or over quinoa (point 3 above) to complete the plant protein.

5 **Smoothie:** Make a hemp-based protein smoothie with 3 tablespoons
   hemp seeds or ground hemp, ½ banana (maybe even skin and
   all – see page 160), ¼ avocado, 1 handful baby spinach, 1 teaspoon
   ground cinnamon, 1 cup (250 ml) milk of your choice, 5 ice cubes and
   1 tablespoon local honey (optional). Blend on high and sip slowly.

6 **Easy-peasy stir-fry for two:** Sauté an onion in 3 tablespoons sesame or
   peanut oil over high heat, then add, in order, 3 roughly chopped garlic
   cloves, a crushed 2.5 cm (1 inch) piece fresh ginger, 2 sliced carrots,
   1–2 handfuls roughly chopped Chinese broccoli, 1 teaspoon honey,
   2 tablespoons tamari, ¼ cup stock or broth, 100 g (3½ oz) organic
   edamame and 100 g (½ cup) diced firm tofu or tempeh. Stir-fry over high
   heat for about 3 minutes and serve as is or with noodles, rice or quinoa.

Inspo lists for eliminating food waste

We love a baddie to fight or a someone we can think of as worse than us, don't we? I wish we didn't. I'm a big fan of uniting around the issues and tackling them with good prioritisation together, all doing the best we can from where we can. As a first-generation Aussie who feels deeply connected to four different places in the world, I'm not going to stop visiting my family members overseas, but does that mean I can't significantly contribute to caring for this planet in other ways?

We've got to stop cancelling out other people's good efforts by pinpointing a couple of things as their failures. I promise we'll get a whole lot more done if we quit the put-downs or saying 'You mustn't care that much about climate change because lookie what we have here – a boarding pass!' We're all starting to be terrified to share anything we're progressing with or taking a stand on, because it might leave us open to a witch hunt for the one thing we're not doing perfectly and that supposedly therefore gives us 'no right' to comment/advocate/organise around an issue. It's actually a bit nuts.

The emissions from the aviation industry have attracted a lot of negative climate change press. While it's absolutely true that a large amount of emissions come from flying (at least the pre-COVID level of flying, anyway), here's something whose carbon emissions have three times the impact on global warming: food waste. Yep, read it again if you need to, but food waste is a monstrous contributor, and one well worth a loud voice and collective action. It's absolutely brilliant that the world realised we could hold meetings on the internet instead of taking a wasteful short-haul flight, but please, rather than getting mad at your plastic oceans or food waste activist friend for going backpacking in Chile, get excited about the work she's doing as an imperfect human. And maybe consider joining her imperfectly with a few of the following ideas to cut food waste.

If my 'approximate' recipes stress you out and you're at an earlier stage of cooking know-how, feel free to use them as inspiration and then look up a more detailed version online. If you're feeling brave though, become a master approximator like me.

Three 'fridge-scrap' meals in four steps

Waste-free savoury brekkie bowl

1 Start with the woodier or bulkier veg (e.g. diced mushroom, silverbeet/Swiss chard stalks). Sauté until SOFTENED.

2 Add a flavour punch (e.g. garlic cloves, onion slices, chilli offcuts).

3 Toss in any left-over green veg (e.g. silverbeet/Swiss chard leaves, spinach leaves, herbs, broccoli, zucchini/courgette).

4 Add a protein food (e.g. crack in a few eggs, toss in some bacon bits or scramble in some organic tofu).

Waste-free stir-fry

1 Add a grain of choice (left-over quinoa, rice, noodles, buckwheat) to oil in a wok or large frying pan.

2 Toss in any vegie scraps (e.g. carrot bits, broccoli stems, cauliflower stalks, limp greens, old zucchini/courgette. I like to blitz these less inviting bits into tiny pieces in my food processor for a few seconds before adding).

3 Add a flavour punch (e.g. the last bit of a fresh chilli, the last nub of ginger, a few old garlic cloves, the ¼ onion in the fridge, any sauces in the pantry).

4 Toss left-over herbs through and add some crunch (e.g. coriander/cilantro stems, those last few cashews or roasted almonds).

Waste-free cottage pie

1 Start with your mash – boil up any left-over root vegies (e.g. potato, carrot, swede, sweet potato, celeriac) until soft. Mash with your choice of fat (e.g. oil, coconut cream, butter) and set aside.

2 Cook up some left-over minced (ground) meat. Bulk it out with some lentils if necessary and toss in any left-over veg (e.g. silverbeet/Swiss chard leaves, spinach leaves, herbs, carrots, celery).

3 Add your flavours – keep it traditional with garlic, onion powder and sage, or mix it up with an international 149 blend.

4 Turn it into a pie – put the mince in a baking dish or individual ramekins and top with the mash. Bake in a 190°C (375°F) oven until golden and warmed through.

Waste-free
cottage pie
PAGE 149

Waste-free
stir-fry
PAGE 149

Waste-free
savoury brekkie
bowl
PAGE 149

Five meals to turn into a chunky soup the next day

Yep, you'd better believe the hype. Gone are the days of leaving leftovers at the back of your fridge to go off. These are the types of meals you can make up and repurpose the next day into something entirely different and delicious.

1   **Roast vegies:** For a sweet chunky soup, add vegie or chicken broth, and 400 g (14 oz) cooked legumes (e.g. lentils, chickpeas) or shredded chicken. Simmer until warmed through and you're good to go.
2   **Mashed potatoes:** Make a rich and creamy soup by adding enough vegie or chicken stock to reach your desired consistency and simmering until warmed through. Add some fragrant herbs like thyme, rosemary or sage for an authentic hearty flavour. For a protein hit, toss in some shredded left-over chicken.
3   **Vegie curry:** Simply thin out the curry base with a stock of your choice, add some more spices like chilli or ginger to keep the soup filled with that curry-like heat, and finish with a squeeze of lemon or lime juice.
4   **Lentil or grain salad:** Don't toss left-over grains or legumes. Combine them with stock of your choice, some chopped vegies and some fresh herbs.
5   **Pasta:** Make a minestrone by adding left-over cooked pasta to 4 cups (800 g) diced tomatoes, frozen peas and diced vegies. Add a little stock if needed.

Three ways to use nearly gone apples

1   **Humble apple crumble:** Dice the apples and cook in a pan with ground cinnamon and a splash of water until softened and thick. Combine oats (or quinoa flakes for gluten-free peeps), rapadura sugar, buckwheat flour, coconut oil and ground ginger in a bowl. Top the apples with this crumble mixture and bake for 10–15 minutes in a 180°C (350°F) oven until golden.
2   **Sweet slaw:** Grate an apple into a bowl with shredded red and white cabbage, chopped parsley and sliced spring onions (scallions). Make it creamy with 1 tablespoon organic yoghurt or make it zingy with a dash of apple cider vinegar.
3   **Porridge (oats) lifter:** Cook rolled (porridge) oats as you usually would for porridge, but add grated apple to cook at the same time. You'll be left with a beautiful apple-y breakfast.

10 ways to use left-over roast lamb or beef

1   Make a tasting plate with sliced meat, crudités, olives, a dip, a chutney
    or relish, and flatbreads (page 274) or crackers.
2   Pop into a wrap with salad bits you have lying around and some
    hummus, avocado or beetroot dip.
3   Mince (grind) in a food processor, cook with onion, a little tomato
    passata (puréed tomatoes) and chicken stock, and thicken with
    1–2 teaspoons tapioca flour or arrowroot until no longer watery. Use as
    a pasta sauce or pop it in a baking dish and top with rice, quinoa, vegie
    mash (see Waste-free Cottage Pie, page 149), grated cheese or blobs of
    nut cheese, and bake in a 190°C (375°F) oven until golden brown.
4   Brush with a tikka or tandoori paste and reheat gently in a frying pan.
    Serve with sautéed green vegies and raita (finely diced cucumber and
    finely chopped mint stirred into yoghurt) for an Indian plot twist.
5   Finely dice and pop in an omelette. This is not at all appealing to me,
    but my husband and son love it. Up to you.
6   Use to make a simple tangy lamb and lentil left-over soup. Chop a couple
    of left-over roast lamb slices. Pop 1 cup (250 ml) per person of vegie
    stock in a saucepan, add lemon juice until tangy, then add cooked lentils,
    chopped zucchini (courgette) and a couple of handfuls of baby spinach
    or silverbeet (Swiss chard) or collard greens (for perennial bonus points).
    Bring to the boil and simmer for a couple of minutes. Season to taste.
7   Make a ragu for pasta. Sauté a chopped onion, add a few slices of lamb –
    say, around 100 g (3½ oz) per person – 1½ cups (375 ml) broth and
    ½ cup (125 ml) tomato passata (puréed tomatoes) and cook over low heat
    for 20 minutes with the lid on. In the last couple of minutes add 1 cup
    (65 g) chopped collard greens or spinach and cook until wilted. Serve
    with pasta, zoodles (zucchini/courgette noodles) or biodynamic rice.
8   Make a pilaf with a local whole grain (e.g. biodynamic rice or quinoa)
    and add lamb, spices of your choice, and lots of chopped parsley and
    other fresh herbs you like. Make lamb, hummus and mini flatbreads
    (page 274), with chopped tomato and a squeeze of lemon.
9   Try a baby spinach, lamb, mint and pea salad dressed with a balsamic
    vinegar and maple sugar vinaigrette.
10 Finely dice, sauté with silverbeet (Swiss chard) or collard greens,
    and serve with left-over roast vegies or a fresh herb, rocket and spring
    onion salad.

Five ways to use left-over cooked potatoes, sweet potatoes or yams

1   Turn the peels into crispy potato skin chips. Toss in olive oil, sea salt and rosemary, then bake in a 200°C (400°F) oven until crispy.

2   Mix left-over roast potatoes into a frittata mixture for a filling lunch or dinner.

3   Toss cooked potato into a soup and heat through. Potato acts as a thickening agent too, to make your soup delicious and creamy.

4   Make salmon patties. Mash left-over potato with a tin of sustainably caught tuna or salmon, an egg, fresh herbs and enough buckwheat flour to bring it all together so it's not 'wet mush'. You want it to hold together. Shape into patties and fry lightly in olive oil until crispy and golden.

5   Toss cooked and cooled potatoes through a salad with 1-2 handfuls cooked beans, chickpeas or lentils (for some healthy resistant starch to feed your gut microbiome).

Five things to do with pan juices

You can't compost pan fats, whether it's olive oil or animal fats, and tossing in the bin with lots of kitchen paper is a thing of the past. We digest fats more effectively than the environment does, and good fats help us assimilate our fat-soluble vitamins A, D, E, K from foods, so it's best we eat them up rather than bin them. We have a few random sealed jars in the fridge with left-over pan juices from the roasting tin or frying pan that we save for the next week's cooking. Here are some of the things we do with them:

1   Pour over roast or sautéed vegies for a nutrient-packed and satiating sauce.
2   Spread (warm from the pan or solidified from the fridge) onto crusty bread. YUM!
3   Spoon over freshly popped popcorn. It'll melt and you'll be left with a rich flavour-packed MSG-free snack quite unlike those microwave bag versions. (PS: the bags are coated in PFAS, which will never break down in the environment. True story.)
4   Turn into a salad dressing by whizzing in a blender with some lemon juice, apple cider vinegar and a touch of dijon mustard.
5   Add them to a cold-meat sandwich filling, for moisture and added flavour.

Five clever ways to use broccoli stems

Gram for gram, the stems contain slightly more calcium, iron and vitamin C than the florets, so don't chuck them.

1   **Broccoli rice:** Using a peeler or paring knife, peel the tough outer woody layer of the stem. Throw the rest into a high-powered blender and blitz to rice-sized bits. Cook lightly in a pan with a drizzle of olive oil. Don't have a blender? Use a box grater.
2   **Broccoli stem soup:** Add stems to a basic green soup recipe with all of your vegie offcuts, 4 cups (1 litre) vegie or chicken stock and a few potatoes. Cook and blitz into a soup.
3   **Broccoli chips:** Use a mandoline to cut very thin slices of stem. Put them in a roasting tin and drizzle with plenty of good-quality olive oil. Roast in a 190°C (375°F) oven for 20 minutes, until crispy and golden. Sprinkle with sea salt to taste.
4   **Broccoli stem pickles:** Chop up the stems, put them in a sterilised 350 ml (12 fl oz) jar and add a sweetened brine solution: ½ cup (125 ml) white wine vinegar and ½ cup (125 ml) water with 1 tablespoon sugar and 2 teaspoons sea salt. Seal the jar and pickle at room temperature for at least 24 hours before digging in.
5   **Broccoli stem pesto:** Add broccoli stems to the basil when making pesto (page 178), with some extra olive oil to reach the right consistency.

Quick cauliflower cheese made with left-over cauliflower

Chocolate drop cookies using left-over nut pulp and chocolate ganache

Quick soup using left-over broth, miso paste and spring onions (scallions)

Lentil and chickpea burgers with left-over herbs

Left-over custard with added chia seeds, topped with left-over rhubarb compote

Chilled vegie tray bake tossed with left-over salad veg

Five things you just don't need to toss or compost

1 **Broccoli and cauliflower leaves:** They roast up beautifully with crispy edges. Rub with olive oil, add a dusting of dried herbs or spices and give them 20 minutes in a 180°C (350°F) oven. Delicious!

2 **Carrot and onion ends, and celery leaves:** Toss all endy bits of veg (as long as they're not mouldy) into a compartment in the freezer. We have a little section that's just for this – no lid, nothing fancy to 'shelter' them, they're just in that little section. When it's time to make stock, we've got all the ends to use and make it for free, saving money on store-bought stocks and emissions on packaging ... Stock is then just all these offcuts, plus thyme, parsley and filtered water in a pot, boiled well for an hour. Strain and keep in jars in the freezer, leaving a good couple of centimetres or an inch empty at the top and not sealing the lid too tightly before you freeze them – you don't want broken jars in there.

3 **Bones:** If you eat meat and you have leftovers, or you don't eat from the bones of a roast – we do both – add those to your stock compartment in the freezer and make the most of them when it's stock-making time. After that, what can you do with them? David from the Grow Network, who's a composting aficionado, fertilises his soil with bones and any left-over meats by digging a narrow hole 60–90 cm (2–3 feet) deep and burying them.

4 **Banana skins:** These are loaded with gut-bug-loving resistant starch. As long as they've been grown on a spray-free farm, you're good to blend the skins up in a smoothie to make it luscious and thick, or to pop into cake mixes. When I make a smoothie for two people, I add half a banana with its skin on and just the end stalk cut off.

5 **Nut pulp:** If you make your own nut milks you'll have leftovers you may have been composting. Nut pulp is another great one to chuck in the stock-making section of your freezer. Or pop a couple of tablespoons into soups and stews for extra fibre. Almond pulp can be frozen in a jar and used as a sub for a quarter of your flour mix for a cake or biscuits/cookies (page 158), blended into a smoothie, or added to a granola mix (it will dry out properly as it bakes). With nuts, try to find some that are local to you so you can know how they're produced.

13 WAYS LOW TOX LIFE COMMUNITY MEMBERS REDUCE FOOD WASTE

1. **Sammantha G:** 'Soak banana skins in boiling water for a day then pour onto tomato plants ... never had such a bounty crop of tomatoes.'

2. **Annette S:** 'After you've squeezed the juice from lemon pieces/halves, put them in a jar and cover with vinegar – leave on the bench for a couple of weeks or more (add more when you have them). Strain into half a spray bottle, top the rest with water and use for all cleaning.'

3. **Lucy B:** 'Zest lemons before you use the juice and freeze the zest for when lemons are out of season.'

4. **Mmsie:** 'Chop the offcuts of citrus fruits, pop them in ice cube trays then top up with water and freeze. Great in a G & T or kids' drinks.'

5. **Kristen W:** 'I soak the remaining lemon that's had the juice and rind saved or used in water overnight and drink two glasses on rising.'

6. **Carol D:** 'I save all my eggshells then blitz to a fine powder before spreading on the garden to enrich soil.'

7. **Mon L:** 'Add the pulp from juicing fruit and vegetables to meatloaf or rissoles to boost fibre, nutrients and yum.'

8. **Sonia D:** 'Egg yolks are great hair conditioners – rinse out in cold water! Egg white makes a good facial mask. Both are a nice doggy treat.'

9. **Robyn C:** 'All of the above and any scraps can also go into our worm farm and composters. Nothing vegetable leaves our block.'

10. **Karan W:** 'All dog-friendly vegie scraps go in the freezer. When there's enough, I make a big batch of broth for the dogs, which they have daily. Bread scraps blitzed to fresh breadcrumbs for cauliflower schnitzel.'

11. **Claire K:** 'Any scraps go to the chooks, which they are ecstatic about and come back in lovely fresh eggs.'

12. **Emma:** 'Bacon rinds are tastier than salt for flavouring soups and bolognese sauce. Slow-cook tomatoes that have gone soft with herbs, garlic and onion on low all day – for pasta sauce. Used coffee grinds can also fertilise the garden – they keep snails and cats away, too.'

13. **Nardia:** 'Left-over vegies are always a treat in a frittata the next day.'

Inspo lists for reducing food packaging

Five ways to avoid buying tins

Legumes, which are packed with fibre, are fantastic food for our good gut bugs. They also contain a good dose of protein to help you feel full for longer. They grow in plenty of wonderful places in the world, but after buying imported tinned ones, then dried ones, for years, I found we had biodynamically grown legumes right here in Australia. You'll do some digging and no doubt start to find these sorts of treasures soon, too. While I'm not one to judge you for having a couple of tins of legumes in the pantry for an emergency 'there's nothing for dinner' budget/speed option, they undergo laborious packaging and processing, and the tins often have plastic/epoxy coatings I'd rather not have my food next to for months on end. Banish the tins as much as possible, and make legume prep a part of your week. This is the kind of thing you can do while a kettle's boiling or you're hands-free on hold to make an appointment. And let's face it, if you're on hold with a telecommunications company, you actually have time for the whole week's food prep …

Here's how to prepare your own legumes, and avoid buying tinned versions of other things:

1   **Chickpeas and dried beans:** Soak for 24 hours in a bowl of water (I used filtered water) with the juice of ½ lemon or lime. Strain and cook in plenty of fresh filtered water until tender, then set aside in the fridge in glass containers. I do one to two meals' worth at the start of the week so they're cooked and ready to use for patties, curries, falafel, salads, stews and soups … I soak 500 g (1 lb 2 oz) and that usually makes, for our family of three, a large enough curry for a lunchbox hotpot the next day, and two little tubs of hummus.

2   **Lentils:** Brown lentils don't need to soak as long as beans or chickpeas, just on the day. So while you're boiling the kettle for morning tea, fill a bowl with water and pop the lentils in it with the juice of a lemon or lime or a tablespoon of yoghurt. When you get home that evening you can strain them and cook them. If you're making soup, you can add an extra cup of liquid and cook them straight in there from raw-soaked. If you're

making fritters, patties, burgers or salads, you'll need to cook them in fresh filtered water until tender before adding to those recipes. Red lentils don't need soaking at all and cook up really quickly.

3 **Coconut milk:** Making your own isn't hard, although I do slip here, especially when I want a thick creamy coconut sauce. It's actually super easy. Bring 4 cups (1 litre) water to the boil, then switch off the heat and add 2 cups (180 g) desiccated (shredded) coconut. Set aside to cool, then pop in the blender and blend on high for 1½–2 minutes. Strain through cheesecloth or a nut milk bag, keeping the coconut solids to use in your next cake or batch of muffins – just add ⅓ cup (80 ml) to future recipes so as not to waste it. I quite like adding it to smoothies for extra fibre, too. Store in a glass jar (see, you *do* need all those jars) and use within 3–4 days in smoothies, soups, curries, frozen popsicles or iced/hot chocolate – just give it a shake before you use it, as it can separate being a fresh DIY product. Some people add coconut milk to their coffee, but I'm afraid if you do that I can't be your friend. I don't understand you ...

4 **Tomatoes:** Ah, the ol' chestnut that 50 per cent of recipes in every cookbook and online call for. Why transition away from these, you ask? Tomatoes are acidic. The interior of tins is either steel or plastic of some kind, and these tomatoes are in there for a long time before getting to you. The acid can cause the lining to leach into the tomatoes, to which I say no thank you. Become a 'passata day' host if you're a grower, or a reveller if you have a community passata day, and go make tons of the stuff while tomatoes are in season to use in the wintertime. When you run out? Two options: either buy some tomato passata (puréed tomatoes) or chunky tomatoes in glass jars or bottles, or consider mixing things up and not doing much tomato-based stuff in the winter–spring when it's not their season. It's a hard choice, but an interesting one if you're truly on that connection journey to seasons and land.

5 **Corn:** Fresh. In season. Sliced off the cob, creamed, on the cob with butter. No contest from the canned stuff here. No packaging.

Five treats you can make easily with produce and avoiding packets

1   **Popcorn:** Easiest thing ever. Heat 2 tablespoons extra virgin olive oil
    or coconut oil in a big steel saucepan over high heat. As soon as you see
    the smoke point, turn down to medium–high and pour in ¼ cup (50 g)
    organic corn kernels. Put the lid on straight away. Give it a good shake
    with the lid on a couple of times during cooking, taking care not to burn
    yourself, and in about 3 minutes the popping will slow down. At that
    point turn the heat off, add a drizzle of olive oil or 1 tablespoon butter
    and melt through with salt to taste.

2   **Instant caramel sauce:** Processed caramel sauce is laced with colouring
    and flavouring agents in the processed world. Even when it's organic,
    there's still a grey area because of the additives allowed into packaged foods
    (remember my earlier example of organic gluten-free cheesy puffs? No
    matter how organic, that stuff is still ultra-processed). For a quick caramel
    sauce, put ¼ cup (40 g) roasted macadamia nuts, 15 pitted medjool dates,
    2 pinches sea salt, ½ teaspoon vanilla bean paste or powder if you have it
    and about ¾ cup (185 ml) water in a blender. Whiz on high for 1 minute.
    So simple and delicious.

Low Tox Life Food

3   **Choc top:** Love a good choc top at the movies? Heat 3 tablespoons coconut oil in a small saucepan over low heat. Add 2–3 tablespoons Dutch-processed, unsweetened cocoa powder, 1 pinch salt and 2 tablespoons maple syrup or honey. Once it's all melted in together, remove from the heat and cool. Spoon over bowls of ice cream.

4   **Simple chocolate ganache icing/frosting:** Store-bought icings are quite frightening when you look at the ingredients. Heat 1 cup (250 ml) organic cream or coconut cream in a saucepan. Once it bubbles and is just hot, pour into a bowl and add 210 g (7½ oz) dark chocolate (very important to get it off the heat and out of the hot pan before melting the chocolate to avoid curdling). Let it cool until it starts to thicken and then pour over your cake and spread with a knife. You could also make ganache balls/chocolate truffles with this recipe by setting it in the fridge then using a melon baller to make the balls and dusting them in Dutch-processed, unsweetened cocoa powder or desiccated (shredded) coconut.

5   **Jelly (gelatine dessert):** How simple is it to make a home-made jelly treat? Freshly squeeze 2 cups (500 ml) juice of your choice. Warm half of it in a saucepan on the stovetop. Remove from the heat and whisk in 1 tablespoon grass-fed, ethical gelatine, then mix into the other cup of cold juice. Pop into bowls, add a few pieces of whole fruit and set in the fridge for about 3 hours. Enjoy! Need a vegan version? Agar-agar from algae is your friend, and you need less of it than you would gelatine. Stir 1½ teaspoons agar-agar into 2 cups (500 ml) fruit juice, then heat gently until just hot to activate it. Pour into bowls or moulds with a few pieces of fresh fruit in each and set. Enjoy 2–3 hours later.

And now it's time for recipes

To be honest, I could have written another 100 pages of lists, so head to lowtoxlife.com for more repertoire-expanding lists. For now, though, let's get stuck into some more recipes and something I think you're really going to love: my flavour makers – the easiest way I know to keep cooking from scratch delicious and exciting without having to learn countless lengthy recipes with 20 ingredients. (Heck, I would order so much takeout if I had to follow complicated recipes line by line to create delicious meals.) Chapter 4 and all its deliciousness is literally on the next page. Let's go, shall we?

CHAPTER

4

Let's cook!

Check your cooking attitude

While I've shared a bit of kitchen inspiration so far, in this chapter I'm going to teach you some of my go-to recipes, so you're never, ever stuck as long as you have some produce and staple pantry items lying around. I'm also including some of the Low Tox Life community's all-time favourites among my recipes over the years, and new recipes I've loved dreaming up just for this book, some of which you can enjoy in the form of 'feasts'. Each feast is centred around inspiring farms that are doing wonderful things to regenerate topsoil, sequester carbon and give us the most nutritious, beautiful produce for our home table.

No whole food is excluded here except gluten. Sorry about that, but given that I can't test gluten-containing recipes, if you're cooking with me you're cooking gluten-free. (Grab some sourdough at any time if that makes you wanna cry.) But as all our dinner guests have discovered over the years, gluten-free definitely doesn't mean an absence of deliciousness. Likewise, I've offered mushrooms as substitutes in some of the recipes because they are absolute powerhouses, but unfortunately they are like kryptonite for me, so I don't cook with them.

I've suggested some recipe combinations to eat as 'feasts', but feel free to chop, change, cut and shuffle however you fancy, using whatever is available to you and in season at the time. If you're anything like me, you see rules and want to break them, so go for it.

I'll also share tips for expanding your cooking repertoire in order to use produce, reduce waste and repurpose leftovers. In these recipes we'll be going to Asia, France, Greece, the Middle East and Mexico. Why? Well, because my goal is to show you how a bit of good globally inspired food vocab mastery can make you happier to cook. If we know it's going to taste exciting and yummy at the end, we're less likely to reach for the engineered excitement of ultra-processed foods or to overdo takeaways whose ingredients we can't trace. Am I saying I never eat takeaway? Absolutely not. Am I saying it's only once or twice a month for us now? Absolutely yes.

Are there exceptions over the holidays when we just go with the flow? Yep. This isn't a race to 100 per cent home cooking and traceable ingredients this year. It's the beginning of imperfectly creating ripples of change as and when we can learn, and incorporating more and more home-cooked meals over time.

The more we focus on what we can control, which is what we do every time we cook from scratch using ingredients sourced from farms that are regenerating the landscape, the greater our ability to reshape the food system into something that will continue to feed us and the planet's creatures for many years to come.

But first, let's do a quick check of our cooking mental health and attitudes. It's all well and good for me to pack this book with a million ways to create yummy things, but if you're harbouring some kitchen blocks, we need to address them. Right now!

Why don't we love to cook?

First of all, I'll acknowledge here that some people just won't ever love cooking and that's okay. It's a means to an end. Sometimes, I really don't feel like cooking either, and then I love nothing more than a good outsource. One perk of being a city-dweller is the infinite choice on those nights, *but* we as a society have normalised takeaways to the point that they've become a huge source of waste, either from the packaging or from left-over food. It's also extremely damaging to the restaurant industry's already small profit margins. Enjoy a meal out sometimes, but support your local businesses rather than the tech-giant apps. These multinationals don't just charge you $5 for delivery, they clip the restaurant ticket by 30 per cent on average.

If you resent cooking or feel it's beneath you or a chore, then we can and must work on that, because cultural conditioning is at play here. Where do these feelings come from? The food industry, largely, which has told us repeatedly that you don't 'have to' cook. 'You shouldn't have to cook, we'll do it for you.' 'You're too busy to cook.' 'You're too smart to cook.' Hear something often enough and it becomes true.

How about we flip this and turn cooking into a gratitude practice? Imagine if every day you said, 'I get to cook and prepare food to love my body and the people around me.' Say it often enough and we believe it, right? So let's change the story, understand the incredible bounty that access to produce represents, and develop the smarts to gather it all up and turn it into deliciousness.

What to do if the kids refuse your food

This is a big one. Again, I could teach you everything you want to know about cooking and share all these recipes, but if carrying plates to the dinner table gives you anxiety, and you're just waiting for the barrage of 'I don't want it' and 'I hate that' to start, then Houston, we have a problem that needs addressing, now. Head to the Further Information section (page 292) for a bundle of fussy-eating resources I've put together with a dear friend and talented coach, Brenda. These will step you through every aspect of how this epidemic of fussy came about. In the meantime, you can start with these simple strategies:

* **Stop asking children what they want to eat or their opinions on foods.** Saying, 'Would you like a bit of broccoli, sweetie?' to a three-year-old who's just seen a fellow three-year-old at kindy say 'yuck' when offered broccoli, could well start them on the path to thinking they get to object to food and reject it. We're bringing kids into this world, not the other way around, and I'm a big fan of showing them the way when it comes to food. If you want to give them a choice, give it to them within the context of a couple of options: 'Which green vegie should we have with dinner tonight, snow peas or crunchy salad leaves?' Then affirm their choice at the table: 'Oh, these snow peas are yummy, sweetheart, great choice.'
* **Check your tone and food marketing.** Are you saying, 'Who wants a delicious cupcake?' like it's the best, most amazing thing in the world and then, when you talk about broccoli, sounding like your kids are in a food prison being reprimanded: 'Eat your broccoli, NOW!' If the broccoli gets the same sexy marketing campaign as the cupcakes do, and perhaps even more positive emphasis, then guess what? Perceptions change fast. I've seen this thousands of times. You've got this.
* **Stop taking kids to the supermarket.** I'm not going to say you're no longer allowed to shop there – baby steps after all – but if you do, go alone, or shop online for supermarket items if that's an option, and choose the plastic-free delivery. The only place they get to go food shopping with you is a farmer's market or mom-and-pop grocer, so that their understanding of food is actually food, not ultra-processed eye-level temptations that tell you life is more fun because of *enter groovily branded snack here*. They're still going to be exposed at friends' houses or on TV/online, but you're working to ensure it's not the norm when it

comes to meals and family shopping. Introduce them to their farmers, and when you sit to eat that night, talk about the farmers they met and how clever they are for growing such delicious food. You'll be surprised by how this can help.

* **Get them in the kitchen –** *not* **just for licking the chocolate-cake bowl.** Chopping things, peeling things, learning how to make complete meals – starting with some basics like scrambled eggs and toast, then on to one-pot/tray wonders. It's incredibly empowering. A twelve-year-old should be able to do dinner from start to finish – we have to remember we're training kids to be self-sufficient adults. If we don't impart cooking skills as they grow up, we can't be surprised when they end up eating frozen meals and breakfast poppers because they only know how to mix a cake.

* **Don't talk in terms of healthy versus unhealthy** or real versus fake, and certainly don't judge others for eating or drinking things you wouldn't, as it can set up shame and secrecy patterns in kids as they seek to explore and have more freedom when they're older. Focus on the magic of produce, how different foods support different parts of the body, and how they all work together to make us feel our best. Explain that while other foods might be fun at a party, they really do more to hurt both our bodies, through their high sugar and/or fat content, and the planet, through their processing/packaging, so for the most part we don't bother with them. No one is a bad person for eating the candy bar, but it's a bad thing that manufacturers are allowed to include nasty ingredients that lots of people don't know about. The people who eat the junk aren't bad, but the system that enabled its creation isn't great.

Ditch: 'I feel like'

This is possibly the biggest psychological shift we need to make. Just as we need to stop giving our toddlers free rein over what they eat, we've got to stop acting like we can eat whatever we feel like, on a whim. That's not how nature works. If we're going to deepen our connection to nature, and to how farms produce food, we're going to have to quit this 'I feel like' culture.

We are the first people in history with infinite choice when it comes to food, among other things, and it's hurting us and our planet. It hurts us because we eat more takeaway than ever before, which often involves more highly processed vegetable oils, deep-frying, high salt and processed carbohydrates. It hurts the planet because we buy food in all sorts of extra packaging a home-cooked produce-based meal doesn't have. And it hurts us because it forces the food industry to keep everything available all year round, which affects food procurement and production. This, in turn, perpetuates the myth that we can extract whatever we want and feel like, whenever we want and feel like it, instead of listening to and partnering with nature to see what she's providing on a farm near us, at that time and in that season. It also creates a huge amount of waste, because when we browse the fridge or think about how we 'just don't want to cook tonight', instead of using perfectly good produce before it goes bad at home, we get something new, and our home supplies edge another day towards the compost or bin graveyard. Wasted money and nourishment opportunities abound if we keep thinking 'I feel like'.

The remedy? We need to consider what we already have in a more positive, exciting light, and be grateful that we have food to work with and eat. Instead of saying, 'I don't feel like any of this,' try asking yourself, 'What can I make from all this good stuff?' Then you can get creative or simply lean in to a simple, nourishing 'something'. We need to let go of the pressure to make everything into a winning *MasterChef* pressure-test meal and sometimes have a boiled egg and soldiers with a few carrot and celery sticks and call it dinner. We've elevated ourselves above food preparation as well as above 'simple food', to the point where every meal is extraordinary, exciting and a taste sensation. We need to start appreciating the simplicity of good produce, respecting availability and applauding how smart we are to always know how to rustle something up. The inspo lists in Chapter 3 should help you a little if this is a challenge for you and you need to expand your repertoire. The basic adaptable recipes in this chapter (pages 197–217) will help too.

'But I'm not a good cook . . .'

This is just a vocab issue. Many of us weren't taught the language of cooking growing up, and many of us were disconnected from produce, from food seasons and from knowing our farmers by name. It's really quite amazing how things can change when we do get to know our farmers and learn a few cooking basics. Then we can get excited about what produce is available at different times of the year, and about each new seasonal launch. I eat pumpkin to the point of it being almost too much in late autumn and winter, so that I just can't do another pumpkin soup. But when it comes back around the following year? BOOM! Pumpkin au gratin for everyone, and we lap it up, excited for pumpkin season. Or in spring it's 'Yay, all-you-can-eat asparagus.' Connect to farmers and seasons. Get some basic skills so you can rustle up great meals. Watch out, world!

Nature's marketing calendar is the hottest launch calendar in the world. No ultra-processed food company on the planet can compete, so move over, 'BBQ Hoisin Chicken Flavoured Crackers – Baked Not Fried', and say hello to the hot new summer sensation: cherries. What's cool about following the seasons? We cycle through a huge variety of nutrients over the course of the year at a macro and micro level. For example, healthy sun exposure to ensure good vitamin D levels helps us process fructose more effectively, and when are the sweetest natural foods available? Summer, when we can enjoy all the delicious stone fruits and mangoes. Nature doesn't tend to make accidents, but we do, in thinking that chocolate-coated peanuts can be eaten all year round. Remove the seasons, dive into the ultra-processed food industry's hands, and we are literally defying the laws of biology. But we're not going to do that, right?

We started to see in Chapter 3 how a cooking approach based on 'I have this . . . what can I do with it?' is essential not only for wholefood, produce-focused, no-waste eating in the long term, but also for feeling more confident, willing and connected to 'why' it matters. In this chapter, I want to ensure a couple of things before I send you on your way:

1   **You'll always be able to make an easy and exciting no-fuss, produce-driven lunch or dinner – using a tried-and-true adaptable recipe and its variations, or a sauce, dressing or marinade.**
2   **You'll feel the inspiration of regeneratively farmed produce leap out from the page and onto your next feasting table with family and friends.**

None of my recipes are particularly groundbreaking or 'funky' – I haven't invented a hot new technique for making a negative-carbon-impact foaming-gel tart filling made out of soap nut extract, and nor will I be the next ultra-famous Instagrammer spending a whole day getting a dish to look award-winning (even though I swoon at those perfect images and the technical skill required to achieve them). I can tell you this: I've learnt to make simple, good cooking delicious, and it's something I absolutely love inspiring you to do. I also love inspiring the odd 'cooking project', as you'll see in the pages that follow. For the most part, though, I want to show you the kind of food whose recipe you won't need any more after you've made it a couple of times, thus giving you greater confidence to just throw things together.

I wonder whether part of the reason we watch chefs on TV and line our kitchens with cookbooks we barely touch is that we simply don't understand the basics. What we do know is protein plus veg in some sort of boring combo, but following an extensive recipe from scratch or one that a chef tells us is a 20 minute meal, only to find ourselves just pulling the final touches together an hour later, is a daunting idea indeed. Stick with me, as I make seasonal, produce-driven eating empowering and delicious. Get as much of your produce as you can from regenerative agriculture or grow a few key things yourself, and move forward from there, doing better every day.

So can we cook yet?

Yes! First, we start with some dollops, salsas, marinades and dressings. These cornerstones of a produce-driven kitchen will keep things exciting. I call them the 'flavour makers'. If you're going to get into a long-term relationship with produce, never to be tempted by cheap and nasty ultra-processed foods again, you gotta make it exciting, right? We want to get to the point where we can think, 'Hmm, I really fancy a . . .' and respond by using a season-dependent zingy dressing or salsa to take things in the direction of our hankering. That way we're unlikely to get bored.

Next, we'll move on to a few simple adaptable recipes for our arsenal, to take us in all manner of directions. And finally, we're going to prepare six delicious feasts featuring inspiring regenerative farms. I've offered vegan options for those who prefer it or who can't get access to regen ag meats straight away. This also means there are lots of friendly options for common allergies. I hope you enjoy making these feasts part of your weekly life.

Meet your
flavour makers

—

Fast flavour anyone can make

Here's my pro tip. On a Sunday, or whichever day of the week is quieter for you, invest an hour in food prep and whip up two to four of these sauces, dressings and marinades, along with a few other bits and pieces for the week ahead. Pop them in jars or containers, ready to make your meals delicious and varied as the week rolls on.

In the week I'm writing this, I prepped the Garlicky Tahini Parsley Sauce (page 184), the Greek Salad Salsa and its dressing (page 181) and the Sweet Honey Tamari Lime Sauce (page 180), and popped them all in the fridge on Sunday. For dinner one night I made the Falafel (page 272) and served them with salad bits and pieces, and the delicious tahini and Greek sauces for dipping the falafel into or mixing with the salad ingredients on the plate. So good. For lunch the next day I made a stir-fry (page 202) and used the sweet tamari sauce as a booster. Flavour crisis averted, with very minimal extra effort on the day.

My hope with these flavour makers is that they will:

* stave off boredom
* cut cooking time overall during your busier midweek meal-making
* reduce takeaways and the waste that comes with them
* motivate you to fill a produce-focused shopping basket

The more produce we buy and cook with, the more transparent our food provenance. We can then focus on taking it to the next level by finding regeneratively farmed produce. Sound like a plan?

Nine exciting add-a-blob sauces

Add exciting flavour to your meals, either by beefing up the flavours as you cook or toss together a salad, or by popping the sauce on the table for people to help themselves. Everyone will be coming back for more.

My go-to pesto (vegan or cheesy)

Makes one 440 ml (1 pint) jar*

1 cup roasted nuts of your choice*
⅔ cup (40 g) nutritional yeast or ⅔ cup (70 g) finely grated parmesan cheese
1 garlic clove (optional)*
1 large handful fresh basil leaves*
½ teaspoon salt
1 teaspoon dulse flakes*
½ cup (125 ml) good-quality olive oil, plus extra as needed

Pop the nuts, cheese (if using) and garlic in a food processor and pulse until chunky (not until they form a fine meal). Add the basil, nutritional yeast (if using), salt and dulse flakes. Blend for a further 2–3 seconds. Add the olive oil and blend for 3 seconds more. Taste. Add more salt if needed.

Transfer to a jar,* pressing down well to remove any air pockets, and top with a good drizzle of extra olive oil to prevent the top from oxidising (i.e. turning brown). It will keep in the fridge for 2–3 weeks.

*Notes: I actually prefer to use two small (220 ml/½ pint) jars rather than one bigger one, for greater flexibility and better shelf life. For the nuts, I most often use half pine nuts and half almonds. You can omit the garlic if it doesn't agree with you. Make sure you save the basil stalks for your next stir-fry or soup. Dulse flakes are dried sea vegies that add seasoning and extra minerals.

Pro time-saving tip: Double or triple this recipe to make a whole summer's worth. With a good 2 cm (¾ inch) layer of olive oil on top it will keep well, provided you've removed all air bubbles.

How to enjoy your pesto
* Top cucumber slices with it for a delicious snack.
* Go traditional and smother pasta or zucchini noodles with it.
* Add a tablespoon to a basic vinaigrette (see page 193) .
* Dollop it over a variety of protein foods, salads or nourishing bowls.
* Use it as a dip for vegies.
* Add it to wraps.

Peanut sauce

Makes one 2 cup (500 ml) jar

¾ cup (215 g) peanut butter
½ cup (125 ml) coconut milk
1 garlic clove, roughly chopped
2 tablespoons honey
2 tablespoons tamari or soy sauce
3 teaspoons rice vinegar or fresh lime juice
3 teaspoons sesame oil
1 teaspoon crushed or grated ginger

Blitz all the ingredients in a blender or food processor* until smooth. Taste and add a little more tamari or coconut milk if you fancy. Job done. Store in a sealed jar in the fridge for up to 1 month.

*Note: If using a hand-held blender, place the ingredients in a large deep jar or jug first – you'll thank me!

How to enjoy your peanut sauce

* For a big barbecue, serve the whole jar with firm tofu or chicken skewers (chicken pieces threaded on a skewer and barbecued).
* Eat it as a snack with celery or cucumber sticks (so good!).
* Mix a little through the Adaptable Stir-fry (page 202).

Mango coriander lime salsa

Serves 3–6*

2 mangoes, flesh roughly chopped into small cubes or thinly sliced
½ small red onion, finely chopped
1 small handful coriander (cilantro), leaves finely chopped, stalks roughly chopped
3 teaspoons fresh lime juice

Combine all the ingredients in a serving bowl and voilà: done. Eat it the same day or the next, storing it in a sealed jar in the fridge in the meantime.

*Note: This recipe will serve 4–6 people with small portions. We love it so much in our family it serves 3.

How to enjoy your salsa

* Include it as an option in a taco dinner 'spread'.
* Add it as a flavour injection into a summer cos (romaine) lettuce salad. Simply chop a cos lettuce and add this salsa. Maybe drizzle some olive oil over. Big salad done.
* Serve it as a topping on your protein food, be it tempeh, chicken or locally caught wild fish, served with a leafy salad.

179

Sweet honey tamari lime sauce

Makes ⅔ cup (170 ml)

1 large spring onion (scallion), finely chopped
½ cup (25 g) finely chopped coriander (cilantro)
    leaves
3 tablespoons finely chopped mint leaves
2 tablespoons toasted sesame seeds
1½ tablespoons tamari
1½ tablespoons peanut or sesame oil
1½ tablespoons macadamia or avocado oil
1½ tablespoons fresh lime juice
3 teaspoons honey

Place all the ingredients in a 440 ml (1 pint) jar, seal tightly with the lid, and shake until combined. Store in the fridge for up to 4 days.

How to enjoy your honey sauce

* Stir it through some cold cooked quinoa, soba noodles or Asian slaw as a dressing.
* Spoon it over fish, tempeh, tofu, chicken, cooked adzuki beans or beef.
* Toss it through a stir-fry of vegies once it comes off the heat then serve immediately.
* Use it as a sauce with dumplings.

Greek salad salsa

Serves 4–6*

3 tomatoes, finely chopped

1½ small cucumbers, finely chopped

½ red onion, finely chopped

⅓ cup (55 g) pitted kalamata olives, finely chopped

⅓ cup (20 g) finely chopped parsley stalks

Dressing

⅔ cup (110 g) pitted kalamata olives

¼ cup (15 g) chopped parsley

½ cup (125 ml) olive oil

1½ tablespoons red wine vinegar

1 tablespoon fresh lemon juice

1 teaspoon chopped fresh or dried oregano

½ teaspoon chopped fresh or dried rosemary

¼ teaspoon salt

Place all but the dressing ingredients in a medium bowl.

Combine all the dressing ingredients in a jug or tall jar, and blitz with a hand-held blender until smooth and thick.

Combine half the dressing with the chopped ingredients and it's ready to serve. Store the left-over dressing in a sealed jar in the fridge and use within 1 week to jazz up some simple salad leaves or sliced tomatoes and feta cheese.

*Note: Serves 4–6 as a generous salsa on a meal plate, with leftovers for two more family salads.

How to enjoy your Greek salad salsa and dressing

* Include it as part of a barbecue spread.
* Add it to a green leafy salad with chicken or lamb strips.
* Serve it with added chickpeas, feta or nut cheese and rocket (arugula) leaves.
* Pop it in a school lunch wrap with avocado, feta and green leaves.

Fennel cucumber pickle

Makes one 700 ml (24 fl oz) jar

1 fennel bulb (about 150 g/5 oz)
½ teaspoon salt
4 cups (1 litre) water
3 tablespoons honey or maple
    syrup
300 ml (10½ fl oz) apple cider
    vinegar
1 teaspoon coriander seeds
1 teaspoon fennel seeds
1 small cucumber, halved
    lengthways and seeds
    scooped out, then thickly
    sliced

Cut off and set aside 2–4 of the fennel fronds. Remove the tough outer layer, cut the bulb and stalks into smaller pieces, then slice roughly, or cut into thick slices using a mandoline. Add the salt to the water and soak the sliced fennel in it overnight. The next morning, drain, retaining 1 cup (250 ml) of the soaking water, and set aside.

Combine the honey, vinegar and spices in a small saucepan. Place over low heat and simmer for 15 minutes. Remove from the heat and add the cucumber and drained fennel pieces and the reserved soaking water. Set aside to cool.

Decant the cooled mixture into a sterilised jar* and add the reserved fennel fronds. It will keep in the fridge, unused, for 3 months with a good layer of extra virgin olive oil, or 1 month without.

*Note: To sterilise a jar, wash in hot soapy water, dry in a 160°C (315°F) oven for 20 minutes, then remove from the oven to cool.

How to enjoy your cucumber pickles
* Add them to sandwiches.
* Include them on tasting plates with cheeses, dips, chutneys, tomatoes, cold roast meats and flatbreads.
* Bring some zing to your next tofu-, fish- or chicken-based lunch or dinner.

Smoked chipotle mayonnaise

Makes 150 ml (5 fl oz)

Don't mean to brag, but this is so yummy. You'll never buy mayo again. The memory of my Mauritian grandmère making mayo, and how easy it looked, had me trying to make it in my late 20s – by memory and 'feel'. Whoa there, young fledgling, not so fast. It was a disaster. The result? Abandoning all attempts due to the abject failure that it was, until I was 41 – but I've more than made up for lost time, shall we say? When you know how to make your own, you're in control of the life led by the chooks who produced the eggs, you're in control of the oils used, and you can favour styles that work better for the human body.

4 organic pasture-raised egg yolks*

1 tablespoon fresh lime juice

¼ teaspoon salt, or to taste

¼ cup (60 ml) extra virgin olive oil

¼ cup (60 ml) avocado oil

¼ cup (60 ml) macadamia or MCT oil*

2 teaspoons maple syrup or honey (if you like a sweet kick)

1 tablespoon smoked chipotle hot sauce* (omit for plain mayonnaise)

Pop the egg yolks in a narrow jug and add the lime juice and salt. Blend for 30 seconds using hand-held blender.* Add each of the oils in turn, drizzling in a few teaspoonfuls at a time *while* blending on high, and blending each addition for 20 seconds before drizzling in the next.

Add your sweetener of choice and the smoked chipotle (if using), and do a final blend for 5 seconds. You now have a delicious thick mayonnaise for spreading on bread, serving with meats or falafel, or dipping into with crudités. Store in a sealed jar in the fridge for 4–5 days – if it lasts that long.

*Note: Keep the egg whites for making macaroons – why not? If you don't have macadamia or MCT oil, simply add an extra 3 teaspoons each of the extra virgin olive oil and avocado oil. (MCT stands for medium-chain triglycerides, in case you were wondering. It's a component of coconut oil.) I use Tabasco brand chipotle hot sauce, but you could use ½ teaspoon smoked chipotle powder instead. If you don't have a hand-held blender, you can whisk by hand or use a food processor.

For a thinner, creamy salad dressing: Add an extra 3 teaspoons of each of the oils, 2 pinches of salt and 3 teaspoons fresh lime juice, then blend for a further 10 seconds until combined (or use these adjusted quantities from the beginning).

Garlicky tahini parsley sauce

Makes 1 cup (250 ml)

1 garlic clove, roughly chopped
zest of 1 lemon
1 small handful parsley
100 ml (3½ fl oz) extra virgin olive oil
¼ cup (60 ml) fresh lemon juice
2½ tablespoons tahini
½ teaspoon salt

Place all the ingredients in a large tall jug or jar. Using a hand-held blender, blend until smooth, thick and creamy. Store in a sealed jar in the fridge and use within 1 week.

How to enjoy your parsley sauce

* Mix it into cooked and cooled legumes as a creamy sauce, then serve on quinoa and garnish with fresh parsley and spring onions (scallions).
* Use it as a thick, tangy and creamy salad dressing, for example for a leafy green salad for eight people, with chopped nuts and cold roasted vegies added.
* Drizzle it over roasted broccoli, cauliflower or brussels sprouts.
* Serve it as a dip for carrot and celery sticks.

Chimichurri

Makes one 440 ml (1 pint) jar

8 spring onions (scallions)
5–7 garlic cloves
2 large tomatoes, cut into quarters
5 lightly packed cups (100 g) chopped flat-leaf parsley leaves
3 lightly packed cups (90 g) chopped coriander (cilantro) leaves and stalks
¼ cup (60 ml) white wine vinegar*
1 teaspoon dried oregano
½–1 teaspoon salt
½ cup (125 ml) extra virgin olive oil

Preheat the oven to 200°C (400°F).

Arrange the spring onions, two of the garlic cloves and the tomatoes on a small roasting tray. Roast for 20 minutes, then remove from the oven and set aside to cool.

Meanwhile, place all the other ingredients except the oil in a food processor, adding the garlic and salt to taste.* Cut the tails off the cooled spring onions and add them, with the cooled tomatoes and garlic, to the processor. Pulse until combined. At low speed, drizzle in the olive oil until well combined.*

Use on the day or within 48 hours. Store in the fridge in a sealed glass container, with a sheet of unbleached paper pressed onto the sauce surface to prevent oxidation.

*Notes: If you don't have white wine vinegar, substitute fresh lemon or lime juice. If you're using a hand-held blender, place the ingredients in a large deep jar.

Pro tip: Rather than drizzle the oil in slowly, I just chuck the lot in and give it a few seconds to combine.

How to enjoy your chimichurri

* Use it to add a flavour kick to basically anything: legumes, meats, responsibly fished seafoods.
* Turn a salad into 'salsa' by mixing it in with your hands to coat everything, then adding a little olive oil or salt to taste if needed.
* Add a blob of it to a green or tomato soup as a garnish.
* Serve it as a dippy salsa for potato wedges or purple sweet potato fries.
* Mix it into plain cooked rice or pasta for a delicious quick meal.

Five marinades to make simple meals exciting

Marinades can be used to, erm, marinate any type of protein food for a minimum of an hour, or overnight for a deeper flavour. These are perfect for the Adaptable Stir-fry (page 202), where you can throw in the drained-off marinade as the sauce – a true and simple one-pot wonder, a 10 minute dinner with a few different flavour options. For food health and safety reasons, you *must* either cook or ditch left-over marinades, and not just serve them cold. That's why I love tossing them into stir-fries.

Once you've mixed a marinade, pour it into a dish large enough to add your protein food of choice, while ensuring it's well covered. Marinate tempeh, tofu or legumes for 30–40 minutes. Marinate meats for 1–12 hours (which means you can whip one up before work in the morning and it will be ready and waiting to use when you get home from work). Always leave to marinate in the fridge.

Lemon honey
rosemary marinade
PAGE 189

Garlic maple
miso marinade
PAGE 188

Drain your marinated protein food, retaining the marinade. Cook your protein food and only add the marinade about a minute before you've finished cooking – otherwise the sweet ingredients in the marinade will burn, and eating burnt food isn't great for your heart. If you're doing a barbecue, you can quickly heat up the marinade in a saucepan.

Here's a tip for 'making in advance and having on hand'. You can prepare any of these marinades, pop them in a glass container or jar, leaving at least an inch empty at the top, label it and freeze it for up to 3 months. It's great to do up a big batch in advance and then have lots of exciting options on hand when you fancy them.

**Korean bulgogi
marinade**
PAGE 189

**Pineapple mint
marinade**
PAGE 189

**Jamaican jerk
marinade**
PAGE 188

Garlic maple miso marinade

Makes about 1 cup (250 ml)

1 spring onion (scallion), finely chopped
1 x 2.5 cm (1 inch) piece ginger, grated or finely chopped
2 tablespoons miso paste*
⅓ cup (80 ml) tamari
2½ tablespoons sesame oil*
2 tablespoons sesame seeds
2 tablespoons maple syrup
1 tablespoon mirin*

Combine all the ingredients in a jar. Seal the lid firmly and shake well to mix.

Store in the fridge for 4 days. Alternatively, make up without the spring onions and it will keep in the fridge for up to 2 weeks. Add the spring onions when ready to serve.

*Notes: I love brown rice miso paste, and toasted sesame oil is best if you can find it. Mirin is a Japanese sweet rice wine. If you can't get hold of any, rice vinegar is a good substitute.

Jamaican jerk marinade

Makes about 1½ cups (375 ml)

There are lots of different twists to a jerk marinade. This is where I've landed. Approximately. My husband will attest to the fact that I rarely do exactly the same thing twice in the kitchen – which means I find it very hard to write recipes down. Hehe! I hope you'll consider yourself lucky that this one is so super tasty the recipe is frozen in time. It's worth the multiple ingredient haul needed to create it.

4 spring onions (scallions), finely chopped
3 garlic cloves, crushed
1–4 scotch bonnet or habañero chillies*
1 x 2.5 cm (1 inch) piece ginger, crushed
½ cup (125 ml) extra virgin olive oil, macadamia oil or avocado oil
¼ cup (60 ml) fresh lime juice*
¼ cup (60 ml) fresh orange juice
2 tablespoons white wine vinegar
1 tablespoon maple syrup or honey
2 teaspoons ground allspice
1 teaspoon salt
½ teaspoon ground cinnamon
¼ teaspoon ground or freshly grated nutmeg
¼ teaspoon black pepper

Combine all the ingredients in a food processor and blitz until smooth. Store in the fridge and use within 48 hours.

*Note: Before you go all in with chillies you don't know, test a tiny amount on your lip. About 3 limes will give you ¼ cup (60 ml) juice.

Pineapple mint marinade

Makes about 1¼ cups (310 ml)

10 mint leaves, roughly chopped
2 garlic cloves, finely chopped
1 cup (190 g) finely chopped pineapple
¼ cup (60 ml) apple cider vinegar
1 tablespoon honey
¼ teaspoon salt
¼ teaspoon ground allspice (optional)*

Combine all the ingredients in a jar, seal firmly with the lid and shake until well combined and the pineapple has released some of its juice. Store in the fridge and use within 48 hours.

*Note: Although the allspice is optional, it does give a lovely depth of flavour.

Lemon honey rosemary marinade

Makes about 1 cup (250 ml)

2 garlic cloves, crushed
zest of 1 lemon
½ cup (125 ml) fresh lemon juice
⅓ cup (80 ml) extra virgin olive oil
¼ cup (15 g) dried or fresh rosemary
1 tablespoon honey
½ teaspoon salt
black pepper, to taste

Combine all the ingredients in a jar. Seal the lid firmly and shake well to combine. Store in a sealed jar in the fridge for up to 2 weeks.

Korean bulgogi marinade

Makes about 1 cup (250 ml)

2 spring onions (scallions), thinly sliced
2 garlic cloves, crushed or finely chopped
½ cup (125 ml) tamari or soy sauce
¼ cup (60 ml) sesame oil
¼ cup (40 g) sesame seeds*
2 tablespoons coconut sugar or maple sugar
½ teaspoon black pepper

Combine all the ingredients in a jar, seal firmly with the lid and shake until well combined. Store in the fridge and use within 48 hours.

*Note: Toasted sesame seeds always taste more exciting to me. If you have a few minutes, toss them in a dry frying pan over medium heat until just golden.

Pro tip: Try filling a lettuce cup with a spoonful of the cooked-off marinade, some cooked quinoa or biodynamic rice, grated carrot and a long piece of spring onion.

Eight delicious dressings to splash, mix and drizzle over whatever you fancy

Carrot ginger tamari dressing
PAGE 195

Watermelon mint dressing
PAGE 192

Creamy coconut zing dressing
PAGE 193

Mum's
vinaigrette
PAGE 193

Probiotic
kefir 'ranch'
PAGE 194

'I can't believe it's
not slaw' dressing
PAGE 192

Cuban
kicker
PAGE 195

Lemony
herb blitzed
dresssing
PAGE 194

'I can't believe it's not slaw' dressing

Makes about 1 cup (250 ml)

Bye-bye, cheap additive-fuelled, plastic-squeezy-bottled slaw dressings from the supermarket using cheap seed oils and extra sugar. *Blergh!* My slaw dressing is just so easy. This recipe does a simple family slaw of 4–6 cups grated cabbage and carrot for six people, but you can double or triple if doing a bigger slaw for a party.

1 large avocado, roughly chopped
¼ cup (60 ml) fresh lemon juice
2 tablespoons macadamia oil*
2 tablespoons maple syrup or rice malt syrup
2 pinches of salt
black pepper, to taste

Combine all the ingredients in a deep wide-mouthed jar and blitz using a hand-held blender until smooth and creamy. Taste and adjust the sweetness, sourness or seasoning. It's ready to mix into your slaw.

It will keep for 2 days in the fridge, so if hosting guests you can make it the day before. If you're hosting about 10 people, I suggest doubling the recipe.

*Note: You can use any cold-pressed mild-tasting oil instead of the macadamia oil.

Watermelon mint dressing

Makes about 1½ cups (375 ml)

I love this delicious fresh-tasting dressing with a rocket (arugula), basil, mint and fresh goat's cheese or feta salad for added vibrant, fruity deliciousness.

1½ cups (250 g) finely diced watermelon,
    seeds removed
20 mint leaves
2½ tablespoons extra virgin olive oil or
    macadamia oil
1½ tablespoons red wine or balsamic vinegar
    or the juice of 1 lime
¼ teaspoon salt or to taste

Pop all ingredients in a blender or a deep jar. Pulse on high or blend using a hand-held blender until everything is combined.

This is best used within 48 hours, so if you're not making a big party salad, do a half batch and use for 2 days' worth of salads.

Mum's vinaigrette (and Grandmère's egg variation)

Makes about 1¼ cups (310 ml)

Mum's version is a 'batch' vinaigrette that lives at room temp for up to a month. You *must*, however, use the egg variation the same day. My grandmère always used to serve the latter with lobster or prawns at Christmas or with cooled steamed vegies like choko or squash. Because it's hot in Mauritius over the summer, we often ate cooked vegies cold out of the fridge. It's still one of my ultimate comfort foods.

1 cup (250 ml) extra virgin olive oil
100 ml (3½ fl oz) white wine vinegar
2 teaspoons dijon mustard
1 teaspoon honey
¼ teaspoon salt or to taste
2 pinches of black pepper

OR Grandmère's egg variation
½ cup (125 ml) extra virgin olive oil
2½ tablespoons white wine vinegar
1 teaspoon dijon mustard
½ teaspoon honey
1 pinch of salt or to taste
1 pinch of black pepper
2 crushed hard-boiled organic pasture-raised eggs
½ cup (25 g) finely chopped chives or parsley

Combine all the ingredients, except the egg and herbs for Grandmère's variation, in a jar. Seal firmly with the lid and shake until emulsified. Keep as directed in the intro above.

For Grandmère's variation, add the egg and herbs then shake just before using. Use the same day.

Creamy coconut zing dressing

Makes about 2 cups (500 ml)

I love this for a cold zoodle (zucchini/courgette noodle) salad with mint, grated carrot, kelp noodles, biodynamic rice and tempeh/tofu or cooled chicken strips. It works equally well as a stir-fry sauce, come to think of it, or added to 4 cups (1 litre) of a simple broth-based soup for an exciting east Asian kick.

2 spring onions (scallions), finely chopped
½ cup (25 g) finely chopped coriander (cilantro) leaves
2 tablespoons black sesame seeds
½ cup (125 ml) tamari, soy sauce or coconut aminos
½ cup (125 ml) coconut milk
⅓ cup (80 ml) fresh lime or lemon juice
2–4 tablespoons maple syrup or honey
2½ tablespoons fish sauce

Combine all the ingredients in a jar. Seal firmly with the lid and shake until well combined. Store in the fridge for up to 1 week.

Probiotic kefir 'ranch'

Makes about 1 cup (250 ml)

This is such a lovely creamy dressing for chopped salads, slaws and crunchier greens.

1 garlic clove, crushed
⅓ cup (80 ml) finely chopped chives or the green part of spring onions (scallions)
2 tablespoons finely chopped parsley
½ cup (125 ml) goat's milk kefir*
¼ cup (65 g) sour cream
1 tablespoon apple cider or white wine vinegar
1½ teaspoons dried onion powder
¼ teaspoon salt

Place all the ingredients in a bowl and whisk until well combined. Alternatively, pulse in a blender for a couple of seconds. Store in a sealed jar in the fridge for up to 5 days.

*Note: Instead of kefir you can use yoghurt or an extra ½ cup (125 g) sour cream.

Lemony herb blitzed dressing

Makes about 1¼ cups (310 ml)

I love this dressing so much. Simple. Vibrant. Thick. Coat your favourite salad leaves with it and enjoy.

¾ cup (15 g) parsley leaves
1½ tablespoons finely chopped chives
zest of 1 lemon
⅔ cup (170 ml) extra virgin olive oil
2½ tablespoons fresh lemon juice
2½ tablespoons fresh orange juice
1 teaspoon maple syrup (optional)
1½ tablespoons thinly sliced spring onions (scallions)

Place all the ingredients except the spring onion in a food processor. Blend until well combined. Pour the dressing into a jar and then add the spring onion. Store in the fridge for up to 1 week.

Carrot ginger tamari dressing

Makes about 1⅓ cups (330 ml)

This is great for dressing shaved cabbage, fennel and carrot salads. When I make this I do it with left-over cooked carrot. Roasted is especially delicious. If you do this, omit the first paragraph of the method. If you're a sweet potato fan, try cooked and cooled roasted sweet potato instead.

1 large carrot, thickly sliced
½ cup (125 ml) filtered water
1 x 2.5 cm (1 inch) piece ginger, peeled
¼ cup (60 ml) mirin* or rice vinegar or 2 tablespoons fresh lime juice
2 teaspoons sesame or peanut oil
1 teaspoon honey
2 teaspoons tamari
1 small handful fresh coriander (cilantro)

Put the carrot in a small saucepan with enough water to cover in a small saucepan and boil over medium heat until soft. Set aside to cool while you assemble the rest of the ingredients.

Put the carrot, the ½ cup water and the remaining ingredients in a blender or food processor. Blend on high until well combined and smooth.

*Note: See the note about mirin on page 188.

Cuban kicker

Makes about 1 cup (250 ml)

This delicious rich-yet-fresh-and-zingy dressing is full of flavour and works super well in a salad with chickpeas. You can either cook the garlic or use it raw. Cooked tends to be easier on the tummy and create a richer flavour, while the raw is fresher and bitier. Try both. If you're doing raw garlic, it's just a matter of placing all ingredients in a small food processor and blitzing.

⅓ cup (80 ml) extra virgin olive oil
3 garlic cloves*
2 tablespoons finely chopped parsley
⅓ cup (80 ml) fresh orange juice
2 tablespoons fresh lemon or lime juice
½ teaspoon ground cumin
½ teaspoon salt
1 pinch of chilli flakes*

If cooking the garlic, heat 2 tablespoons of the olive oil in a small frying pan over medium heat. Add the garlic and cook for 1–2 minutes to release the sweetness. Set aside to cool in the pan, retaining the oil.

Combine the remaining ingredients in a deep jar. Add the cooled garlic and oil, and blend, using a hand-held blender, until smooth. Store in a sealed jar in the fridge for up to 1 week.

*Note: The garlic can be cooked or raw. Raw makes it extra zingy and super fresh. Omit the chilli flakes if you have any no-spice peeps in your family.

Adaptable recipes for any ingredient

—

Let's look at some adaptable recipes for kitchen basics – simple meals for simple, nourishing pleasures. They'll help you feel like you're always ready to rustle something up.

Learning these adaptables is one of the most important things you can do to become a great low-stress cook. By adaptable I mean the bare bones of a recipe that you can take in a few different flavour directions without having to learn a new recipe each time. One of the greatest mistakes we make, in my humble opinion, as we try to build kitchen prowess, is always trying to make a different recipe and always feeling like we need someone else's 'creation' to guide us. Get good at a few adaptable basics and you'll quickly see the patterns emerge from the ratios of different ingredients used – vegies to liquid, flours to butter, spices to volume of overall dish.

These staple meals, desserts and snacks ensure I never feel stressed in the kitchen, knowing I can always create something delicious. They might seem a bit daunting at first, but I promise you'll get really fast at these. You'll only need to think or follow the first couple of times.

Cooking from scratch and excelling in the kitchen with confidence is the single biggest way we can impact the food system. Dramatically reducing ultra-processed foods and cooking from produce and single, traceable ingredients means full transparency as to where our food comes from, and thus we can start to make better choices.

It's a brilliant way to reduce plastic packaging while eliminating all those long-shelf-life additives and preservatives from your diet. It's also cheaper. Winning!

Adaptable quick soup

Serves 4, or 6 as a small starter ✴ **Makes** 1.75 litres (7 cups)

This is so easy to make, and there are infinite ways to jazz it up and create your own variations over time. Use these approximate basic ratios, and remember to check the fridge for your oldest limp and undesirable vegies or wilted fresh herbs you could hide in here.

2 tablespoons extra virgin olive oil
1 large onion, roughly chopped
100 g (3½ oz) carrot, finely chopped
100g (3½ oz) celery, finely chopped
500 g (1 lb 2 oz) protein food (e.g. cooked lentils, chickpeas, pasture-fed meat, organic chicken),* cut into bite-sized pieces if necessary*
2 tablespoons* herbs and spices (e.g. finely chopped garlic, Italian herbs, bay leaves, turmeric, ginger)
700 g (1 lb 9 oz) additional vegies (especially cruciferous veg, zucchini/courgettes, fennel; pumpkin or sweet potato)
1.25 litres (5 cups) organic stock (e.g. chicken, vegetable, beef)
salt and black pepper, to taste

Heat the olive oil in a large stockpot over medium heat. Sauté the onion, carrot and celery, leaving the lid on to sweat them for about 5 minutes, until tender, taking care they don't stick or burn, and adding a splash of water if you need.

Add the protein food and, if using meat, cook until lightly browned and just cooked through. Add the herbs and spices and cook for 2–3 minutes, until fragrant. Add the additional vegies and the stock. Bring to the boil, then reduce the heat and simmer, covered, for 20–35 minutes.

When ready to serve, adjust the seasoning as needed.

Options to jazz it up

✴ **Spicy:** Add 2 tablespoons curry paste with the protein food, then ½ cup (125 ml) coconut cream. For the photo I used legumes and vegetables, topped with fried Tuscan cabbage (cavolo nero) and buckwheat kernels.

✴ **Creamy:** Stir through ½ cup (125 ml) organic thin (pouring) cream at the end.

✴ **Minestrone:** Add ½ cup (125 ml) tomato passata (puréed tomatoes) with the stock, and use greens and carrot as your additional vegies. Add 1 cup (90 g) organic pasta to the cooked soup, then simmer, covered, until the pasta is al dente.

✴ **Creamy tang:** Garnish with crumbled goat's cheese.

✴ **Gut-healing:** Omit legumes; choose a slow-cooker cut of meat, bring to the boil, then place in a 140°C (275°F) oven until the meat falls apart (3–4 hours).

✴ **Aussie bush spices:** Add ¼ teaspoon each of ground lemon myrtle and ground coriander with ½ teaspoon ground saltbush.

*Notes: I love doing 200 g (7 oz) finely diced beef with 1⅓ cups (300 g) cooked cannellini beans for the protein food, as the starchy beans make for thick chunky soup. Obviously, if one of your spices is chilli powder or flakes, you won't want 2 tablespoons!
If you're using a herb or spice for the first time, add a little, do a taste test, then add more if necessary. You can't take something out again once you've put it in!

Adaptable casserole

Serves 4–6

It was a happy day indeed – and boy, did I feel clever – when I realised you could pop a few things in a pan, close the lid, open it four hours later and it would be guaranteed delicious. How did I not know this before I was 35? I kick myself for painstakingly following recipe after recipe to prepare a meal, when really, true freedom in the kitchen comes from not needing one at all, knowing the basic adaptable recipe and applying it to what you have on hand. This is when you really start to save money and reduce waste, too. Enjoy the freedom you'll find with my adaptable casserole recipe to make it your own and take it in different flavour directions.

Whatever your variation, serve this with cooked quinoa, biodynamic rice, polenta, grits or mashed potatoes, or – my favourite – over a bed of sautéed in-season greens.

2 tablespoons extra virgin olive oil
1 large onion, roughly diced
300 g (10½ oz) base vegetables (e.g. onion, carrot, zucchini/courgettes, celery), cut into chunks
1 kg (2 lb 4 oz) diced protein food (e.g. pasture-fed beef chuck steak, lamb shoulder, pork shoulder, or cooked beans or chickpeas)
1 teaspoon salt
1 tablespoon tapioca flour
2 garlic cloves, finely chopped
1 cup (250 ml) tomato passata (puréed tomatoes)
2 cups (500 ml) organic stock (e.g. chicken, vegetable, beef, fish)
4 cups (150 g) loosely packed chopped dark leafy greens
1 large handful freshly chopped parsley or coriander (cilantro)
black pepper, to taste

Preheat the oven to 160°C (315°F).

Heat the olive oil in a large flameproof casserole dish over medium heat. Sauté the onion and base vegetables, leaving the lid on to sweat them for 2–3 minutes, until tender. Add the protein food. If using meat, cook for 2–3 minutes, until lightly browned. Sprinkle with the salt and tapioca flour, and add the garlic. Cook for a minute, until the protein food is coated and the garlic is fragrant. Add the tomato passata, stock, leafy greens and half the herbs (along with any flavour accents from the list opposite).

Bring to the boil, then pop the lid on and transfer to the oven for 2–3 hours, until the meat is tender; or, for beans or chickpeas, for 1 hour. When ready to serve, adjust the seasoning as needed and top with the remaining herbs.

Options to jazz it up

* **Australian bush:** Add ½ teaspoon each of ground coriander, akudjura (bush tomato), wattleseed and mountain pepperleaf.
* **Moroccan:** Add 2 teaspoons grated fresh or ground ginger, 1½ teaspoons ground cumin, ½ teaspoon ground coriander and 10 halved dried apricots.
* **Local:** Add 1½ tablespoons dried herb mix local and/or native to your area.

* **Creamy:** Stir through 1 cup (250 ml) organic thin (pouring) cream at the end of cooking.
* **Hearty:** Add 2 cups diced starchy vegetables and 1½ cups (375 ml) extra stock.
* **English stew:** Add ¼–⅓ cup (60–90 g) dijon mustard.
* **Freshness:** Add the juice of 1 lemon or lime at the end.
* **Greek:** Add 2 rosemary sprigs and 1 teaspoon dried oregano.

* **French:** Add 1 tablespoon dried herbes de provence mix and ⅓ cup (80 ml) red wine with the passata.
* **Mexican:** Add ⅔ cup (100 g) chopped red capsicum (pepper) strips and 2 tablespoons taco seasoning.
* **Indian:** Add 2 tablespoons curry powder with the salt, then use half the passata with ½ cup (125 ml) coconut cream.

Adaptable stir-fry

Serves 4 with rice or noodles (3 without)

As stir-fry 'laypeople' we often have nowhere near enough sauce and so the flavour is thin. Or we overcook it. *Blergh!* Add whatever you fancy, depending on what's in your fridge or in season. Bonus points if you use perennials, such as leafy greens, broccoli varieties like nine star or purple cape, or scarlet runner beans. Serve on its own, or with rice, noodles or quinoa.

400 g (14 oz) protein food (e.g. organic chicken or grass-fed beef strips; OR bite-sized pieces of firm tofu or tempeh)

¼ cup (60 ml) peanut or macadamia oil, for shallow frying (tofu or tempeh only)

about 1 cup (250 ml) marinade (see pages 186–89 or the suggestions opposite)

2 tablespoons peanut or coconut oil

1 teaspoon sesame oil

650 g (1 lb 7 oz) mixed stir-fry vegetables, chopped roughly into slices and/or strips (e.g. carrot, broccoli, green beans, capsicums/peppers, snow peas/mangetout, water chestnuts)

2 garlic cloves, crushed

1 tablespoon finely grated ginger

2 spring onions (scallions), thinly sliced

1 large chilli, chopped (optional)*

If using meat, place in a medium container and add the marinade. Seal and leave to marinate in the fridge for up to 12 hours.*

If using tempeh or tofu, heat the peanut or macadamia oil in a medium frying pan, then add the tempeh or tofu and fry gently for 2 minutes per side or until browned. Set aside and add a quarter of the marinade, so they can soak in the flavour while the vegies are cooking.

Heat the oils in a large wok or frying pan over high heat. Drain the meat, if using, retaining the marinade, and cook for 1–2 minutes, tossing it around. Remove and set aside. Return the pan to the heat and add the vegetables, garlic and ginger. Cook for 3 minutes, or until lightly softened but still vibrant. Return the meat, if using, to the wok and add the spring onions and chilli, along with reserved or remaining marinade (add only half if serving without noodles or rice). Cook until well combined and fragrant.

If using tempeh or firm tofu, drain and place on top of each serve.

*Notes: Only add the chilli, of course, if you want some heat – it's hotter with the seeds. For tender meat, try using a tenderiser to flatten it before cutting into strips. Ideally, you want to start marinating meat in the morning for a lunch or dinner stir-fry, so it develops a nice deep flavour.

Got leftovers? For a solo lunch the next day: boil 1½ cups (375 ml) stock, toss in any left-over stir-fry, add ½ teaspoon miso paste and heat for a minute or two. Garnish with sliced spring onion (scallion).

Other marinade options

* **Teriyaki:** Combine ⅓ cup (80 ml) tamari, ⅓ cup (80 ml) mirin, 2 tablespoons rice malt syrup or honey and 2 teaspoons sesame oil.

* **Sesame ginger:** Combine ⅓ cup (80 ml) tamari, ⅓ cup (80 ml) mirin, 1 tablespoon sesame oil and 1 tablespoon finely grated ginger. Sprinkle toasted sesame seeds on top to finish.

* **Satay:** Combine 1 crushed garlic clove, ½ cup (125 ml) natural peanut butter, ¼ cup (60 ml) water, ¼ cup (60 ml) coconut milk, 2 tablespoons tamari and ¼ teaspoon chilli flakes.

Adaptable fritters

Makes 18 fritters about 10 cm (4 inches) in diameter • **Serves** 4–6

Fritters: a reliable crowd-pleaser, right? Most of them are rather high on the empty starches and low on the nutrient density though, so these are designed to pack in the nutrients – to nourish the soul with delicious comfort food vibes and keep you going for hours. Serve these with a salad (page 208) and everyone's a winner.

butter or extra virgin olive oil, for shallow-frying

Fritter base

2 organic pasture-raised eggs
⅔ cup (90 g) tapioca flour or arrowroot
⅔ cup (170 ml) milk of your choice
¼ cup (30 g) coconut flour
1 heaped teaspoon baking powder
½ teaspoon salt

Fritter 'core' additions

1–1⅓ cups (150–200 g)* sweet potato, potato, carrot or zucchini (courgette),* grated
¾–1 cup (150–200 g)* fresh corn kernels
½ cup chopped fresh herbs (e.g. parsley, coriander/cilantro)
⅓ cup (40 g) chopped spring onions (scallions)

Added fibre or protein options (optional)*

½ cup (90 g) chopped naturally smoked nitrate-free ham
½ cup (100 g) mashed cooked lentils or chickpeas
½ cup (100 g) finely diced firm tofu or tempeh
½ cup (70 g) finely diced haloumi cheese

Preheat the oven to 180°C (350°F).

Combine the fritter base ingredients in a large mixing bowl, stirring until thick, gloopy and wet. Stir in core additions and any added fibre or protein options you're using. The mixture should be wet, but not so wet that if you spooned it into the pan, the liquid would 'run away' from the edges. Too dry? Add an extra splash of milk. Too wet? Add another ½ cup grated vegies and 1 tablespoon tapioca flour.

Heat 1 tablespoon butter or olive oil in a large nonstick frying pan over medium heat. Working in batches, drop in heaped tablespoonfuls of the fritter mixture. Cook for 3–4 minutes, until golden brown on each side, turning once, then transfer to an oven tray and bake for 10 minutes or until heated through.

*Notes: Stick to the lower weight suggestion for corn, zucchini or sweet potato if you're adding one or two of the fibre or protein options. If using zucchini, you must squeeze the gratings in a clean tea towel (dish towel) to remove any excess water. Watery fritters? No thanks!

Adaptable pie

This simple adaptable recipe will help you bring pies into your family meal mainstream, with a delicious helping of vegies to go with it.

2 tablespoons extra virgin olive oil

500 g (1 lb 2 oz) base vegetables (e.g. onion, carrot, zucchini/courgettes, celery), finely diced

500 g (1 lb 2 oz) protein food* (e.g. pasture-fed beef chuck steak, lamb shoulder, organic boneless pork roast, organic chicken thigh, grass-fed beef or lamb mince), diced as needed; OR 450 g (10½ oz) cooked brown lentils, 150 g (3½ oz) brown mushrooms, roughly chopped and 150 g (5½ oz) Swiss chard or collard greens, roughly chopped)

2 tablespoons tapioca flour or arrowroot

2 tablespoons spices and dried herbs (e.g. crushed garlic, Italian herbs, herbes de provence, paprika)*

400 ml (14 fl oz) organic stock (e.g. chicken, vegetable, beef)

½ cup fresh herbs, finely chopped, to serve (e.g. parsley, coriander/cilantro, thyme, basil, oregano, curry leaves)

salt and black pepper, to taste

1 sheet (24 cm/9½ inch square) puff pastry or shortcrust (pie) pastry*

1 organic pasture-raised egg (optional), whisked

Heat the olive oil in a large stockpot over medium heat. Sauté the base vegetables, leaving the lid on to sweat them for about 5 minutes, until tender, taking care they don't stick or burn, and adding a splash of water if you need.

Add the protein food and cook until lightly browned and just cooked through. Sprinkle with the tapioca flour and stir for a minute or two. Add the spices and dried herbs and cook for 1 minute, until fragrance bursts out of the pan and into your face – so delicious, that smell! Add the stock and season to taste. Bring to the boil, then reduce the heat and simmer, covered, for 2–3 hours for slow-cooker cuts of red meat, 45 minutes for chicken or non-meat options. Remove from the heat, then stir the fresh herbs through and adjust the seasoning if necessary.

Meanwhile, preheat the oven to 200°C (400°F). In the last 20 minutes of cooking the filling, remove the pastry sheet from the freezer to thaw.

Transfer the filling to a 23 x 29 cm (9 x 11½ inch) pie dish. Top with the pastry sheet, gently pressing it around the rim of the pie dish to seal and trimming away any excess with a knife. Using a sharp knife, make a small vent in the centre of the pastry for steam to escape during cooking. If you want to get cheffy and create a golden glow, glaze the pastry by brushing with the whisked egg.

Bake for 20–30 minutes or until the pastry is golden, puffy and cooked through. Serve with vegie sides aplenty or a nice salad (page 208).

*Notes: For meat that stays tender, choose slow-cooker cuts for red meat or thigh for chicken. Perhaps try some indigenous herbs and spices. The first time, add half the suggested quantity – you can add more, but you can't take it out again. If no nearby stores offer fresh ready-made pastry sheets, the better store-bought option is definitely shortcrust. You can also make your own – I have a recipe on lowtoxlife.com.

Options to jazz it up

* **With a kick:** Stir through 2–3 tablespoons wholegrain mustard before filling the pie dish.
* **Earthy:** Before simmering, add 1 cup (90 g) chopped brown mushrooms and 2 tablespoons fresh thyme leaves.
* **Sweet:** Add 1 cup (150 g) diced pumpkin (squash) before simmering.
* **Textured:** After glazing, sprinkle 1 tablespoon sesame seeds over the top for a lovely crunchy crust.

* **For Australians:** Stir 2 tablespoons tomato paste (concentrated purée) and 1 teaspoon honey through a beef mince filling before simmering, for a rich pastry-free spin on the Four'N Twenty pie.
* **Curried:** For the herbs and spices, use 3 garlic cloves, a finely grated 4 cm (1½ inch) piece ginger and 2 tablespoons mild curry powder. Bask in the admiration for your masterpiece.

Epic adaptable salad

Main * **Serves** as many as you like

When people invite us over, they often ask me to bring a salad, saying, 'I just never seem to be able to make it exciting.' Honestly, this is the easiest fix in the world. Here's my secret: contrasting flavours and textures, and a cracking good dressing. That's it. That's the secret.

Here are some options you could consider to make your salads exciting. And on the next page, I bring these ideas together in my sample Roast Chicken Salad.

Crunch
* Buckwheat kernels or 'buckinis' – a great crouton replacement
* Baked seeds
* Fennel – for extra crunch, try dicing it finely rather than shaving
* Raw asparagus – slice thinly for little bits of crunch
* Kale or beetroot leaf chips on top
* Finely chopped celery
* Roasted nuts
* Roasted salty chickpeas

A sweet kick
* Lower-sugar dried fruits like currants or finely chopped prunes or figs
* Sweet left-over veg – sweet potato, roasted beetroot, etc.
* Grated apple
* Fresh mint
* Grated raw beetroot
* 1 teaspoon honey, maple syrup or rice malt syrup in the dressing
* The amazing spicy maple pecans from my first book, *Low Tox Life*

Softness
* Mixed leaves
* Shaved fennel or beetroot (cut using a mandoline)
* Grated carrot
* Cooked and cooled quinoa or cooked puy lentils

Spice
* Onion
* Spring onions (scallions)
* Large chillies with soft heat
* Spices in the dressing – black pepper, a hint of cumin or turmeric

Freshness
* Fresh herbs – mint, basil, coriander (cilantro), parsley, native herbs. We vastly underutilise these leaves *and their stalks*. There's no excuse for leaving herbs to rot away in the fridge. Get them into a salad in abundance – half in the salad, half in the dressing. Done!

Pantry and fridge randoms

* Kelp noodles – amazing for a good hit of iodine (although note that after the Fukushima disaster, I prefer to avoid sea vegies packed in Japan)
* Left-over cooked quinoa
* Left-over steamed vegies – lightly steamed broccoli is delicious cold through a salad the next day
* Things you've got lurking that need using

'Meaty' vegetarian options

* Cooked and cooled chickpeas or beans
* A few strips of grilled haloumi
* Chunks of feta or goat's cheese
* Pieces of gruyère cheese
* Roast veg – I love, love, love cold roasted eggplant (aubergine) for this
* Tempeh – it's not my favourite, but if it's yours, knock yourself out
* Shaved parmesan
* Tahini

Something tangy

* Pomegranate arils – they're amazing for little acidic punches of flavour
* 1 tablespoon dried cranberries, roughly chopped
* Chunks of orange, grapefruit or, if in season and available, blood limes or finger limes or a local citrus unique to your area
* Cherry tomatoes
* Fresh goat's cheese
* Greek-style yoghurt
* Mustard

Note There are a million other things you could add. These adaptable concepts are all about you taking the basic idea and running with it to use what's available in your neck of the woods.

Roast chicken salad using the Adaptable Salad template

Serves 4

I often make this simple epic salad when we have left-over roast chicken. Make sure you save some pan juices – that's my secret ingredient. I vary the dressing according to my mood and what I have on hand, but this salad is delicious with the 'I Can't Believe It's Not Slaw' Dressing (page 192) for a creamy vibe, or the Lemony Herb Blitzed Dressing (page 194). I do a double batch of the dressing so I have some left for a couple of solo salads over the week.

3 cups (450 g) chopped left-over roast chicken and 2–3 tablespoons pan juices

10–12 asparagus spears, thinly sliced*

2 spring onions (scallions), roughly chopped

1 small red onion, thinly sliced

1 cup (125 g) thinly sliced* fennel bulb

4 handfuls mixed locally grown green leaves

1 large handful mint, rough chopped, without stalks – keep those for putting in herbal tea

1 handful parsley, roughly chopped, stalks and all

1 handful coriander (cilantro), roughly chopped, stalks and all

½ cup (70 g) toasted nuts and/or seeds

¼ cup (40 g) dried currants (optional)

Pop all the ingredients in a large salad bowl. Add your dressing of choice and toss. Job done. Four people served and satisfied.

*Notes: Freeze the woody bottom 5 cm (2 inches) of the asparagus spears for soups – they're too fibrous for eating raw. You could shave the fennel bulb using a mandoline, if you prefer.

Adaptable lunchbox snack bar

Makes 6*

This great snack bar has good nutrient variety and is perfect for lunchboxes or to feed sporty kids when ferrying them around. The yummy variations let you keep it exciting without having to learn five different snack bar recipes.

½ cup (75 g) sunflower seeds or any favourite nut or buckwheat kernels*

½ cup (75 g) pepitas (pumpkin seeds)*

45 g (1½ oz) butter or ghee, melted and cooled

3 tablespoons rice malt syrup*

1 tablespoon buckwheat flour, tapioca flour or arrowroot

1 teaspoon ground cinnamon

½ teaspoon vanilla bean powder or vanilla bean paste (optional)

Preheat the oven to 180°C (350°F). Line a 12 x 20 cm (4½ x 8 inch) loaf (bar) tin with unbleached baking paper.

Pop the sunflower seeds and pepitas in a blender or food processor and pulse for a couple of seconds until roughly ground. (If we're being very specific, think a quarter of a sunflower seed.)

Combine the butter and rice malt syrup in a medium bowl. Add the seeds, flour and spices, then mix until everything is well combined. In a food processor this takes about 5 seconds.

Transfer the mixture to the prepared baking tin and spread out evenly, pressing down with your hands.

Bake for 20 minutes or until golden. Remove from the oven and use a sharp knife to make score lines for the bar shapes you want – but don't 'cut' them yet. Cool to room temperature on a wire rack, then gently break into bars using your hands. They will keep in an airtight container for up to a week.

***Notes:** Do a double or triple batch for a large family and use a larger baking tin. You can replace the sunflower seeds and pepitas with any favourite seed or nut – the point is to have a couple of different nuts or seeds to make up 1 cup for variety and taste. You could replace the rice malt syrup with maple syrup or honey, but their higher glucose content means they won't harden the bars in the same way.

Variations

* At the end, fold in ¼ cup (30 g) roughly chopped dark chocolate or ¼ cup (45 g) finely chopped dried fruit (e.g. cranberries, prunes, apricots, dates) when available.
* Replace the cinnamon with 1 heaped teaspoon Dutch-processed unsweetened cocoa powder for a hint of chocolate.
* Add 1 tablespoon nut butter of your choice.

Adaptable fruit crumble

Serves 6

Who doesn't love a good crumble, right? It's just such a delicious way to get the party finished on a simple Friday night family meal.

Fruit mixture

7 cups seasonal fruit (apples, pears, plums, peaches or berries), roughly chopped if necessary into 1–2 cm (½–¾ inch) chunks
⅓ cup (80 ml) filtered water
1–2 tablespoons honey
1 teaspoon your choice of sweet spices*
1 tablespoon tapioca flour or arrowroot (optional)*

Crumble topping

160 g (5¾ oz) plain (all-purpose) flour*
110 g (3¾ oz) chilled butter, cut into cubes, or chilled coconut oil
½ cup (60 g) finely chopped hazelnuts or hazelnut meal*
⅓ cup (65 g) coconut or maple sugar
1 pinch of salt
½ teaspoon vanilla bean powder or paste*

Preheat the oven to 180°C (350°F).

Combine the fruit, water, honey and spices in a medium saucepan. Cook, covered, over medium heat for 5–10 minutes, until the fruit has softened but chunks still remain. Taste carefully (it will be hot!), and add more sweetness and spices as needed. If it's watery (it depends on the fruit), add the tapioca flour and stir until thickened. Transfer the fruit mixture to a 23 cm (9 inch) pie dish. Set aside.

To make the crumble topping, pop the flour in a large mixing bowl and, using your hands, rub the butter through until the mixture resembles breadcrumbs or coarse sand. Stir through the hazelnuts, sugar, salt and vanilla. If you have the luxury of time, refrigerate the mixture for half an hour before baking (remember that time you said you wanted to meditate more? This is your sign.). Top the fruit with the crumble mixture.

Bake for 30 minutes, or until the crumble is golden and fragrant.

*Note You're free to add whichever spices to the fruit you wish. I often do ½ teaspoon each of vanilla bean paste or powder and cinnamon. In the crumble, use vanilla if available, or try another sweet baking spice. You'll only need the tapioca flour or arrowroot if there's a lot of thin watery liquid before baking. For the crumble topping, I usually substitute buckwheat flour; gluten-free 1:1 baker's flour; or half tapioca flour and a quarter each of almond meal and buckwheat flour. If you're allergic to nuts, try ground sunflower seeds or similar.

Spice or herb combos to try

* **Autumn spices:** 1 teaspoon ground cinnamon, ¼ teaspoon ground or grated nutmeg, ¼ teaspoon ground cardamom
* **Basil and strawberry:** With strawberry as your fruit of choice, cook with 1 small handful fresh basil for a delicious summery twist
* **Vanilla and ginger:** 2 teaspoons ground ginger, 1 teaspoon vanilla bean powder
* **Aussie spices:** ½ teaspoon ground strawberry gum, which tastes a little like passionfruit, and 1 pinch of ground lemon myrtle

Adaptable cake

Serves 6 (single small cake)

This is the first gluten-free cake I ever created, so this baby is 17 years old now. I wanted a simple recipe you could take in several directions so you could get really good at it. It's a sturdy number, so you could bake several batches for a birthday cake. For the photo, I've done two and stacked them up, with whipped cream and blended fresh strawberries between and on top, to serve 10.

3 organic pasture-raised eggs
½ cup (175 g) maple syrup, rice malt syrup or honey
2 teaspoons vanilla extract or 1 teaspoon vanilla bean powder
2½ tablespoons coconut flour*
⅓ cup (50 g) buckwheat flour*
⅓ cup (45 g) tapioca flour*
½ cup (125 ml) melted butter, ghee or coconut oil, cooled
1 heaped teaspoon baking powder
1 teaspoon lemon juice

To jazz it up (optional)
＊ 1–2 overripe bananas, finely chopped (but use only ⅓ cup/115 g maple syrup)
＊ 80 g (2¾ oz) frozen berries
＊ 80 g (2¾ oz) super-finely chopped sweet red apple and 1 teaspoon ground cinnamon
＊ ¼ cup (40 g) dried cranberries
＊ 8 sulfur-free dried apricots, finely chopped
＊ 80 g (2¾ oz) dark chocolate (85% cacao), roughly chopped (and replace 1½ tablespoons of the buckwheat or tapioca flour with 1½ tablespoons Dutch-processed unsweetened cocoa powder)

Preheat the oven to 170°C (325°F). Line a 20 cm (8 inch) round cake tin with unbleached baking paper (or do nonstick the old-fashioned way by coating the tin with melted butter or olive oil, then dusting it with flour and shaking off any excess).

Combine the eggs and maple syrup in a large bowl. If using liquid vanilla extract, add now. Beat using a blender, food processor or hand-held electric mixer until you can see lots of air bubbles.

Sift the flours into the egg mixture, then add the vanilla powder (if using), butter, baking powder, lemon juice and your chosen adventure from the list, if using. Stir gently until just combined.

Set aside to stand for 1 minute. The mixture will thicken.

Pour or spoon into the prepared tin and bake for 22–25 minutes, until a skewer inserted in the centre comes out clean. A double batch in a single larger tin will take longer, 35–40 minutes.

*Notes: Why three different flours and not just one of them? I've found that for perfectly textured gluten-free cakes and pastry, you need a blend of a few different light and heavy flours and nut meals. Feel free, instead of the three flours listed, to add the same total volume of a gluten-free all-purpose flour if that's easier for you. If one of the flours you use is coconut flour, add an extra third of the total volume used here.

Feasts of well-farmed plenty

—

Celebrate great produce

Here are six sets of dishes I love to serve together, inspired by the produce from a few wonderful examples of regenerative farms around the world. I discovered them as I was researching the farming methods that will help us repair our planet and regain the deep nutrition we've lost in moving away from farm-fresh foods. I hope you find fun and discovery as you decide what to cook from the following pages, and I can't wait for you to share the fruits of your labours with me on socials, #lowtoxfoodbook.

Do you have to cook all the recipes together or at the same time? Not at all! Sometimes I love pulling out all the stops and making lots of things, and sometimes I just do one dish and I serve it with something different. I also replace ingredients all the time, based on what I have to hand. At the end of the day: you do you.

Along the way I've added efficiency tips, ideas for other ingredients to expand the possibilities if you have a surplus of produce and are only just starting to explore what to do with it. I've also penned a few leftover ideas so that all the good stuff gets used up and you save time and stress (see pages 280–83).

These feasts are about celebrating local produce, grown in the best conditions you have access to, regeneratively where possible, so you can ditch all that processed and packaged food and become a food-waste ninja. This is where we can really move the needle and repair our landscapes, our food system and our health from the ground up.

I hope you enjoy these recipes as much as I've enjoyed creating them for you and for the people I love.

A BOUNTIFUL
Vegetarian feast

Inspired by Rodale Farm, Kutztown, Pennsylvania, USA

Rodale Farm, created by Bob Rodale, is, as you know, the birthplace of the term 'regenerative agriculture'. It's also the site of the Rodale Institute, where the longest-running trials of organic versus conventional produce are run. Its Vegetable Systems Trial, for example, examining the impact of management practices on vegetable nutrient quality and soil health, includes butternut pumpkin (squash), potatoes, lettuce, green beans and sweet corn. What better way to honour the Rodale Institute than a vegetarian feast using these beautiful ingredients? Bob's daughter Maria says:

'My father coined the term regenerative agriculture by observing nature. Our job is to tap into and support the many natural processes that exist, to heal ourselves and the land by farming and living regeneratively.'

A BOUNTIFUL
Vegetarian feast

MENU FOR 6

Starter
Mauritian pumpkin au gratin

Main
Roasted brussels sprouts
and fennel with tahini cream
and fresh herbs

Sides
Chopped kohlrabi, apple
and rocket salad with
roasted hazelnuts and
honey herb pesto

Corn, spring onion and
broccoli fritters

Dessert
Spiced pumpkin pie with an
almond and ginger crust

**Roasted brussels sprouts
and fennel with tahini
cream and fresh herbs**
PAGE 226

Corn, spring onion
and broccoli fritters
PAGE 229

Chopped kohlrabi,
apple and rocket salad
with roasted hazelnuts
and honey herb pesto
PAGE 228

223

Mauritian pumpkin au gratin

Starter • **Serves 8** • **Prep time** 15 minutes • **Cooking time** 40 minutes

This dish will forever bring my grandmother back to life in my mind. We have big lunches in Mauritius, so often Grandmère would do a gratin with bread and a leafy greens salad as a simple dinner. It might seem weird to mix cheese with ginger, but trust me it's great. It's a Mauritian thing. You can serve it as a simple meal on its own, but it also works as an autumnal starter when pumpkins are in season. Warm comfort in a bowl.

This is really easy – yes, you do have to check on it and stir the pumpkin to ensure even cooking ... but I do this when I'm also cooking another dish or two. That way, when you're chopping and organising other bits, you just take little breaks to stir the pumpkin.

40 g (1½ oz) butter or ghee, or coconut oil or macadamia oil*

1 large red onion, finely chopped

1 x 2.5 cm (1 inch) piece ginger, crushed, grated or finely chopped

2 garlic cloves, crushed

1.5–2 kg (3 lb 5 oz – 4 lb 8 oz) butternut or kent pumpkin (squash), roughly chopped into smallish chunks

1 small handful parsley, finely chopped, plus extra to serve

4 thyme sprigs

4 spring onions (scallions), green part only, roughly chopped

½ teaspoon salt or to taste

1 cup (250 ml) chicken or vegetable stock or filtered water

2 cups (200 g) grated cheese or 1 cup (60 g) nutritional yeast*

Heat the butter or ghee in a large heavy-based saucepan* over medium heat. Fry the onion for 6–7 minutes, until well softened and golden. Add the ginger, garlic, pumpkin, parsley, thyme, spring onion, salt and stock. Reduce the heat to medium–low and cook, covered, for 15–25 minutes, stirring every 5–8 minutes, until the pumpkin is well cooked. The last time you stir, leave the lid off until most of the liquid evaporates.

Preheat the oven to 180°C (350°F).

Remove the pumpkin from the heat and mash it roughly into a very chunky mash rather than a purée. Transfer to a 20 x 30 cm (4 x 12 inch) enamel, glass or ceramic baking dish and scatter the grated cheese over the top.

Bake until golden brown, garnish with the extra parsley and serve immediately.

*Notes: Use coconut or macadamia oil and nutritional yeast options for dairy-free. You don't want the pumpkin to stick to the bottom of the pan and burn before it cooks, so you'll need a heavy-based saucepan or stockpot or a flameproof casserole dish. I use an enamelled cast-iron casserole dish.

Roasted brussels sprouts and fennel with tahini cream and fresh herbs

Main • Serves 6

¼ cup (60 ml) filtered water
600 g (1 lb 5 oz) brussels sprouts, halved lengthways
1 large red onion, cut in half then wedges
3 fennel bulbs, tough outer layer removed, cut into 1 cm (½ inch) slices
¼ cup (60 ml) extra virgin olive oil
1 small handful mint, roughly chopped
1 small handful parsley, roughly chopped
4 spring onions (scallions), green part only, thinly sliced

Tahini, macadamia and lemon cream

100 g (3½ oz) tahini
¼ cup (60 ml) extra virgin olive oil
¼ cup (60 ml) fresh lemon juice
½ cup (130 g) plain yoghurt*
1 teaspoon local honey or maple syrup
½ teaspoon ground cumin
½ teaspoon salt
black pepper, to taste
140 g (5 oz) roasted* macadamia nuts, roughly chopped

Preheat the oven to 200°C (400°F).

Heat the water in a large frying pan over high heat. Add the brussels sprouts and cook until the water evaporates.* Transfer the brussels sprouts to a roasting tin and add the onion, fennel and olive oil, stirring or shaking well to coat. Roast for 30 minutes, until the sprouts are well-browned.

Meanwhile, pop all the tahini cream ingredients except the macadamias in a blender and whiz on high for 1 minute, or until smooth. If it's not creamy enough, add 2–3 tablespoons water and blend again. Taste and adjust the seasoning.

To serve, spoon the tahini cream onto a large platter, spreading it out evenly, then scatter the macadamias over the top. Remove the vegies from the oven, cool for a minute or two, then pile them over the creamy base. Top with the fresh herbs and spring onions.

*Notes: To roast macadamia nuts, spread them on a baking tray and roast in a 170°C (325°F) in oven for 15 minutes. For dairy-free, substitute coconut yoghurt for the plain yoghurt. Pre-cooking the brussels sprouts in a frying pan will prevent them drying out and burning in the oven.

Chopped kohlrabi, apple and rocket salad with roasted hazelnuts and honey herb pesto

Side • Serves 6

1 kohlrabi, thinly sliced using a
    mandoline or finely chopped
2 apples, cut into matchsticks*
2¾ cups (100 g) rocket (arugula)*
⅔ cup (100 g) hazelnuts,
    roasted*

Pesto dressing
1 tablespoon honey
2 tablespoons fresh lemon juice
20 mint leaves
1 cup basil or parsley leaves*
½ cup (125 ml) extra virgin olive
    oil
⅓ cup (50 g) hazelnuts, roasted*
¼ teaspoon salt
⅓ cup (35 g) grated parmesan
    cheese or ¼ cup (15 g)
    nutritional yeast
black pepper, to taste

Pop kohlrabi, apple, rocket and hazelnuts in a salad bowl.

To make the pesto dressing, whiz all the ingredients in a blender on high for 5 seconds, or until combined. You could also pound them together using a large mortar and pestle. Whatever works for you.

Mix the pesto into the salad using your hands – get in there and coat everything thoroughly.

You are ready to rock.

*Notes: To cut an apple into matchsticks, cut the four cheeks away from the core and chop into slices, then matchsticks. If you're familiar with local wild greens, challenge yourself to find an unsprayed section of 'weeds' or park and collect some chickweed, amaranth, dandelion greens or another one you know about. Replace 1 cup of the rocket measurement with these local wild greens. If you don't know what's out there, why not take a foraging tour with a local expert? You can make the pesto dressing with whichever of the two herbs is available at the time. To roast hazelnuts, spread them on a baking tray and roast in a 170°C (325°F) oven for 10 minutes. To remove the bitter skins, rub the hot nuts gently in a clean tea towel (dish towel). You'll see that both the salad and the pesto dressing contain roasted hazelnuts, so roast them all together.

Corn, spring onion and broccoli fritters

Side ∗ **Serves** 6 ∗ Makes about 16

Who doesn't love a good fritter? You can fry these the day before and reheat them in the oven on the day. Another alternative is to get someone cooking them on the barbecue while you get the rest of the feast together for serving. You can also bake this as a 'fritter block' in the oven and cut into squares, which works brilliantly for easy lunchbox meals.

olive oil, for greasing

2 organic pasture-raised eggs

½ cup (125 ml) milk of your choice*

½ cup (70 g) buckwheat flour

½ cup (65 g) tapioca flour or arrowroot

1 heaped teaspoon aluminium-free baking powder

⅓ teaspoon salt

1 cup (200 g) fresh corn kernels

½ cup chopped fresh herbs (e.g. parsley, coriander/cilantro)

½ cup (60 g) chopped spring onions (scallions)

1½ cups (185 g) grated sweet potato

1 cup (90 g) finely chopped broccoli

Preheat the oven to 200°C (400°F).* Line a baking tray with unbleached baking paper.

In a large mixing bowl, combine all the ingredients and stir until the mixture is thick, gloopy and wet. You should be able to make a blob of it without all the liquid running off, but it shouldn't be so dry that you can form it into a shape (how's that for specific, right?). Too dry? Add an extra splash of milk. Too wet? Add another ½ cup grated vegies and 1 tablespoon tapioca flour or protein powder.

Heat a generous drizzle of olive oil in two large frying pans* over medium–high heat and drop in heaped tablespoons of the fritter mixture. Fry for 3–4 minutes on each side, until golden brown, turning once. Cook them in batches and place on a baking tray. Pop them in the oven shortly before serving, to make sure they're hot.

*Note: I use organic almond milk or oat milk. If you're roasting brussels sprouts, the oven will already be on. You will already have used one of the frying pans to pre-cook the brussels sprouts – no need to wash it.

Fritter dipping sauce: I made a quick tahini yoghurt for the photo (page 223) by whisking together ½ cup (130 g) plain yoghurt (use coconut yoghurt for dairy-free), 2 tablespoons tahini, 1 tablespoon lemon juice, 1 teaspoon salt and ½ teaspoon black pepper. An easy one to use at a moment's notice.

Spiced pumpkin pie with an almond and ginger crust

Dessert ◆ **Serves** 8–10 ◆ **Cooking time** 55 minutes total

You can make the filling ahead of time and have it in the fridge ready to go. You can also make the whole pie in advance - it keeps in the fridge for 3 days.

Filling

2 cups (400 g) roasted and cooled butternut or kent pumpkin (squash)
5 organic pasture-raised eggs
120 ml (4 fl oz) maple syrup or honey
½ cup (125 ml) coconut cream or organic thin (pouring) cream
½ cup (125 ml) milk of your choice
2 tablespoons tapioca flour, arrowroot or cornflour (cornstarch)
⅛ teaspoon ground or grated nutmeg, plus extra to serve
2 teaspoons ground ginger
2 teaspoons ground cinnamon
⅛ teaspoon ground cloves
⅛ teaspoon salt

Spiced pastry and/or cookies

200 g (7 oz) frozen or chilled butter
½ cup (60 g) quinoa flakes or rolled (porridge) oats
1½ cups (190 g) tapioca flour or arrowroot
120 g (4¼ oz) hazelnut or almond meal
100 g (3½ oz) buckwheat flour, plus extra for dusting
2 heaped teaspoons ground ginger
1 teaspoon ground cinnamon
¼ teaspoon ground cardamom
½ teaspoon vanilla bean powder
⅓ cup (115 g) maple syrup or honey, at room temperature

To make the filling, blend all the ingredients on high for 30 seconds. Cover the bowl and set aside at room temperature while you prepare the pastry.

Preheat the oven to 190°C (375°F). Lightly grease a round 20–23 cm (8–9 inch) pie dish or tin.

To make the pastry, pop all the ingredients except the maple syrup or honey in a food processor and pulse three or four times, for 3–4 seconds at a time, until the mixture resembles moist sand or breadcrumbs. On low, gradually add the maple syrup or honey over a few seconds, until the mixture forms a dough. If it's a bit crumbly, add 1 tablespoon olive oil.

Dust a clean work surface generously with flour. Transfer the dough to the work surface and shape it into a ball. Place ball of dough in the prepared pie dish and, using clean fingers, press into the bottom and sides to cover evenly, to about 5 mm (¼ inch) thickness. Break off any that comes up over the edges and set aside for making decorative cookies, as in the photo.

Using a fork, gently prick the pastry bottom all over, about 10 times. Place a sheet of baking paper over the pastry and cover with baking weights or uncooked legumes.

Reduce the oven temperature to 160°C (315°F). Add the filling to the pastry and bake for 40–50 minutes, until the centre barely wobbles. Sprinkle with extra nutmeg and serve warm or at room temperature.

To make cookies: Roll dough to about 5 mm (¼ inch) thick. Cut using a cookie-cutter and spread on a baking tray lined with baking paper. Bake for about 15 minutes. Cool on tray.

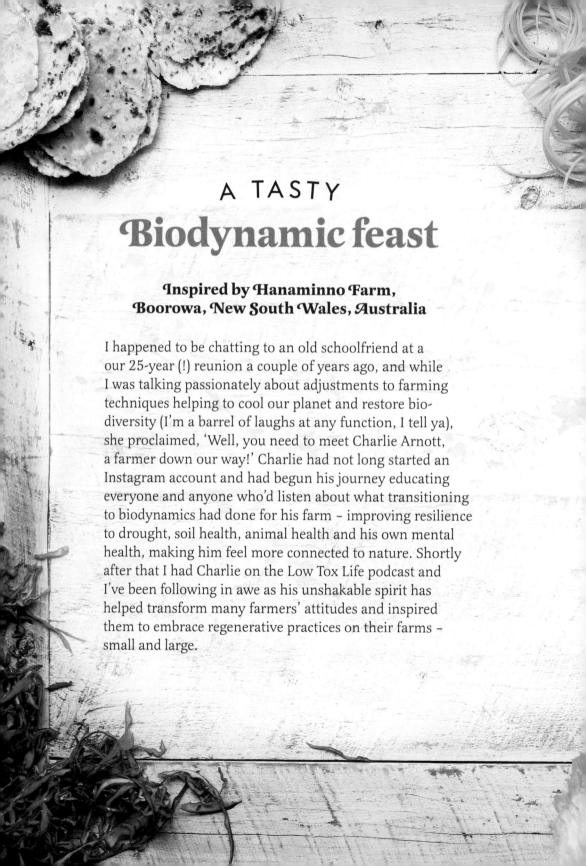

A TASTY
Biodynamic feast

Inspired by Hanaminno Farm,
Boorowa, New South Wales, Australia

I happened to be chatting to an old schoolfriend at a
our 25-year (!) reunion a couple of years ago, and while
I was talking passionately about adjustments to farming
techniques helping to cool our planet and restore biodiversity (I'm a barrel of laughs at any function, I tell ya),
she proclaimed, 'Well, you need to meet Charlie Arnott,
a farmer down our way!' Charlie had not long started an
Instagram account and had begun his journey educating
everyone and anyone who'd listen about what transitioning
to biodynamics had done for his farm – improving resilience
to drought, soil health, animal health and his own mental
health, making him feel more connected to nature. Shortly
after that I had Charlie on the Low Tox Life podcast and
I've been following in awe as his unshakable spirit has
helped transform many farmers' attitudes and inspired
them to embrace regenerative practices on their farms –
small and large.

Naturally, I wanted to include a little ode to Charlie's farm in this book. His property in Boorowa, New South Wales, wasn't always biodynamic, and a lot had to be done to make the transition, but now they wouldn't have it any other way. They produce beef, lamb and pork, all pastured/grass-fed, and they don't use any synthetic inputs on the animals, pasture or soil – nowhere.

To get a bit of feasting inspiration, I asked Charlie what was growing in the vegie patch at home. He said that he and his wife Angelica grow leeks, carrots, celery, parsley and garlic, mainly for inclusion in the bone broths Angelica makes every couple of days all year round. They also often have, dependent on the season, lettuce, rocket (arugula), tomatoes, pumpkins (squash), cucumbers, zucchini (courgettes), onions, kale, spinach, broad beans and peas. They have plenty of fruit trees in the garden, including medlars, from which they make a yummy paste.

'Biodynamic for me has helped connect the ponderable with the imponderable, the measurable with the immeasurable, the soil with the soul, and created a wonderful relationship with my most valuable business partner ... nature.'

So what shall we make with this bounty? I'm thinking pulled beef brisket and a few delicious little plates of vegie accompaniments. Some sweet potato flatbread might be nice if you're feeling like you want to be a little more technical and less rustic, but rest assured, you have lettuce cups for the easy, quick option. Sound like a plan?

A TASTY
Biodynamic feast

MENU FOR 8

Main
Pulled sweet-and-spicy brisket

Sides
Shredded purple 'minute pickle' cabbage

Carrot and beet slaw with smoky chipotle mayo

Two-ingredient sweet potato flatbread (optional)

Dessert
My upside-down fruit pudding cake with custard

Two-ingredient
sweet potato
flatbread
PAGE 274

Shredded purple
'minute pickle'
cabbage
PAGE 237

Pulled
sweet-and-spicy
brisket
PAGE 236

Carrot and beet
slaw with smoky
chipotle mayo
PAGE 237

Pulled sweet-and-spicy brisket

Main • Serves 8–12 • Prep time 10 minutes **• Cooking time** 6 hours

This is one of those dishes people think they couldn't possibly produce themselves. But once I got that smoky and sweet spice balance right, it wasn't hard at all.

Slow-cooked meats are a great way for kids to get all their B vitamins and amino acids. When I did the food plan for a daycare centre a few years ago, I put a lamb shoulder on the menu once a week and the kid absolutely loved it. Those little humans were satiated right down to their cells with slow-cooked meat, good mashed sweet potato and crunchy beans.

2 kg (4 lb 8 oz) shoulder
    beef brisket*
1½ teaspoons salt
¼ cup (60 ml) extra virgin olive oil
2 red onions, cut into quarters
1 cup (250 ml) dry alcoholic cider,
    or kombucha or kefir
1½ cups (375 ml) stock or
    filtered water
4 spring onions (scallions), finely
    chopped, to serve

Epic spice rub*
4 garlic cloves
2 tablespoons fennel seeds
2 tablespoons sweet paprika
1 tablespoon smoked paprika
1 teaspoon coriander seeds
1 teaspoon dried chilli flakes
    (optional)

Sauce
300 ml (10½ fl oz) tomato passata
    (puréed tomatoes)
¼ cup (60 ml) apple cider vinegar
3 tablespoons maple syrup
    or honey
1 tablespoon dijon mustard

Preheat the oven to 160°C (315°F).

Place all the spice rub ingredients in a mortar and grind coarsely with the pestle.

Sprinkle the beef generously with the salt. Heat the oil in a deep flameproof casserole dish over medium heat on the stovetop. Add the onion and beef, cooking the meat for about 3 minutes per side. Remove the meat from the casserole dish, leaving the onion. Cool the meat slightly, then cover with the dry rub, making sure you really get it 'in there'. Return the beef to the casserole. Pour in the cider and stock.

Put on the lid and transfer to the oven for 6 hours, spooning the cooking juices over the meat every 2 hours. (Alternatively, cook in a slow-cooker on low for 10 hours.)

Remove from the oven and transfer the beef to a plate or clean board. Return the casserole dish to high heat and add all the sauce ingredients. Bring to the boil, then reduce the heat to medium and simmer for 10 minutes.

Remove from the heat and return the beef to the casserole. Using two forks, pull the beef apart until it's nicely shredded.

Serve with the spring onion in a small bowl on the side.

***Notes:** Instead of brisket, you could use chuck or oyster blade (flat-iron/butler's) steak, or pork shoulder. Don't panic at the cost of stocking up the spices in your pantry. You'll have them for loads of future cooking projects.

Low Tox Life Food

Shredded purple 'minute pickle' cabbage

Side • **Serves** 8

This is the easiest, zestiest way to serve purple cabbage, in my humble opinion, and its sharpness makes a wonderful contrast to the creamy slaw and rich beef. It takes flavour contrasts to make a meal really sing.

700 g (1 lb 9 oz) purple cabbage, very finely chopped or thinly sliced using a mandoline
90 ml (3 fl oz) red wine vinegar or apple cider vinegar
1 teaspoon salt
¼ teaspoon black pepper
¼ teaspoon fennel and/or coriander seeds (optional),* crushed
juice of 1 lime
1 teaspoon maple syrup or honey (optional)
10 mint leaves, finely chopped
1 handful flat-leaf parsley, finely chopped

Place all the ingredients except the lime juice, maple syrup and herbs in a bowl. Using clean hands,* massage the cabbage well for a minute or so.

Refrigerate, uncovered, while you prep all the other bits and pieces, stirring in the lime juice, maple syrup and herbs just before serving. It's that easy! Store left-over pickles in a sealed jar in the fridge for up to 1 week.

*Notes: The fennel and coriander seeds are a great addition if you have them on hand. It's absolutely vital that you use clean hands to massage the cabbage, so that you can't accidentally transfer nasties that will grow and spoil the leftovers.

Carrot and beet slaw with smoky chipotle mayo

Side • **Serves** 8

3 small beetroot, peeled and grated
3 large carrots, peeled if not organic, grated
2 celery stalks, cut into 3 mm (⅛ inch) slices
1⅓ cups flat-leaf parsley or coriander (cilantro) or a mix of both, roughly chopped
¼ teaspoon black pepper
salt (optional), to taste*
½ quantity Smoked Chipotle Mayonnaise (page 183)

Combine all the ingredients in a medium bowl. Stir half the mayonnaise through. Transfer the rest of the mayo to a small bowl to serve on the side.

Lettuce cups

To serve • **Serves** 8

2 cos (romaine) lettuce heads

Carefully angle your knife downwards into the side of the lettuce above the stem, continue the whole way around, then pull the knife out. This will make it so much easier to remove each leaf without splitting them. Wash and dry the leaves carefully, then serve them in a bowl for people to fill with a little beef, cabbage and slaw.

Two-ingredient sweet potato flatbread

To serve • **Serves** 8

Add these if you fancy and have extra time (see page 274).

My upside-down fruit pudding cake with custard

Dessert • **Serves 8*** • **Prep time** 15 minutes • **Cooking time** 30–40 minutes

I made this one night with the ingredients I had in the house when I was taking dessert to a friend's for dinner. When her youngest son found out there wasn't enough for a third helping, he lay on the kitchen floor and banged his fists. Honest to god! Serve topped with a dollop of crème fraîche, coconut yoghurt, cashew cream, sour cream, ice cream or coconut cream.

Syrup
100 g (3½ oz) butter
¼ cup (60 ml) honey or maple syrup
¼ cup (60 ml) filtered water
1 heaped teaspoon ground cinnamon
½ teaspoon vanilla bean powder or 2 teaspoons vanilla extract
400 g (14 oz) apples or seasonal fruit,* cut into 3–4 mm (⅛–¼ inch) slices or pieces

Cake
3 organic pasture-raised eggs
80 g (2¾ oz) butter, melted
⅓ cup (80 ml) honey or maple syrup
1¼ cups (140 g) hazelnut meal
⅓ cup (45 g) coconut flour
¼ cup (35 g) tapioca flour
½ cup (125 ml) full-cream (whole) milk, almond milk or coconut milk
1 heaped teaspoon baking powder
2 teaspoons ground cinnamon

Preheat the oven to 180°C (350°F). Line a 23 cm (9 inch) cake tin with baking paper (or bake in the frying pan method).

Place all the syrup ingredients except the apple slices in a large frying pan (flameproof and nonstick if using for baking), over medium heat. Simmer for 1–2 minutes. Reduce the heat to low–medium, add the apple and cook for a further 3–4 minutes. Pour into the base of the lined cake tin, spreading the apple out evenly. Set aside. (Alternatively, remove the pan, with the apples and syrup, from the heat and set aside.)

Whisk the eggs in a medium bowl using hand-held electric beaters. Add the remaining cake ingredients and beat until combined. Spoon the cake batter over the syrup and apple base in the cake tin or frying pan.

Bake for 25–30 minutes, until a skewer inserted in the centre comes out clean. Cool in the tin for at least 10 minutes before turning out to serve (see tip below). Serve warm (how we prefer it) or cool, with cream, ice cream or custard (page 267).

***Notes:** If you're cooking for 10–12, I suggest making two of these. I used blood plums for the photo.

Pro tip: To turn out the cake, make sure it's almost cooled. Place a plate over the tin, then turn the tin upside down onto the plate, flipping in one swift go. Or just spoon it straight from the tin onto plates.

A DELICIOUS
Native American feast

Inspired by Spirit Farm,
Vanderwagen, New Mexico, USA

While researching indigenous wisdom (and mistakes) and
how indigenous farmers around the world are starting
to heal the land and their communities, often using food
education as a powerful tool, I came across the work of
Spirit Farm, New Mexico, a Native American educational
regenerative farm. Teach a man to fish and the rest takes
care of itself, as the saying (kind of) goes. I reached out
to ask a few questions, and the lovely James Skeet and I
had a great conversation about what they were working to
achieve, in the community and beyond, to reconnect Native
Americans to the land and to farming in such a way as to
build stronger communities and healthier landscapes.

**'Our vision for Healing the Soil is to improve the health of
Native peoples and Mother Earth (soil) by using cultural
traditions that change people's attitudes and actions with
regard to food and soil.'**

Low Tox Life Food

The Spirit Farm website describes how getting Native Americans involved in producing their own food, and connecting this activity to their cultural traditions and Mother Earth, 'elevates farming to a spiritual/cultural practice'.

'When we heal the land, we heal the people.'

This is particularly important given 20 per cent of Navajo adults have been diagnosed with type 2 diabetes, and it is estimated that half of all Navajo children will develop type 2 diabetes within their lifetime. 'There is an inextricable link between the impacts of colonisation across Navajo Nation and poor (physical, mental and spiritual) health outcomes. Eating more organic, nutrient-dense fruits and vegetables can help reduce the risk of many chronic diseases including Type 2 diabetes.'

Spirit Farm is proving that we can farm with little water, while regenerating soil and community wellbeing through composting, kind animal husbandry and companion planting, working to create a healthy 'whole' organism. As a result, it creates extraordinary hope and success.

They grow a lot of squash, corn, cucumbers, mint, tomatoes, beans, potatoes, chilli, capsicums (peppers), broccoli, beetroot and more, while also gathering local wild plants. Importantly, they intermingle a variety of crops to create resilience and ward off pests. Their chickens, turkeys, pigs and sheep provide healthy meat while also fertilising the vegetables.

So here's a delicious stew, corn tortillas, and a crunchy, fresh salsa for contrast. Take a break after this hearty, simple feast, then enjoy my indulgent but very simple almond 'blender' cake with a cup of tea.

Pork shoulder,
greens and
bean stew
PAGE 244

A DELICIOUS
Native American feast

MENU FOR 6

Main
Pork shoulder, greens and
bean stew

Sides
Spiced corn tortillas

Coriander and capsicum salsa

Dessert
Simple almond blender cake

Coriander and
capsicum salsa
PAGE 247

Spiced corn
tortillas
PAGE 246

Pork shoulder, greens and bean stew

Main • Serves 6*

You'll need to start this one the day before with a quick soak of the legumes. You can top the stew with finely chopped spring onions (scallions), and serve with sour cream on the side for anyone who fancies some. When friends are around I tend to beef up the 'little yummy extras' served with a main dish.

2 cups (350 g) cooked organic pinto or black beans (from 1 cup/195 g dried)*
squeeze of lemon or lime juice
¼ cup (60 ml) olive oil
250 g (9 oz) red onion, chopped
1 kg (2 lb 4 oz) pork shoulder, cut into 2.5 cm (1 inch) chunks
1 tablespoon tapioca flour or arrowroot (optional)
4 garlic cloves, roughly chopped
salt, to taste
1 rosemary sprig
3 thyme sprigs
1 chipotle chilli, finely chopped, or ½ teaspoon chipotle powder or 1 tablespoon chipotle hot sauce
3 cups (750 ml) chicken, beef or vegetable stock
400 g (14 oz) super-ripe tomatoes, chopped, or 1½ cups (375 ml) tomato passata (puréed tomatoes)
4 cups (180 g) baby spinach or collard greens (for perennial brownie points)
150 g (5½ oz) green beans, trimmed
2 cups fresh parsley or coriander (cilantro) leaves, to serve

The day before, place the beans in a large bowl and cover well with water, adding the lemon juice to enhance digestibility. On the day, drain the beans, transfer to a large saucepan or stockpot and cover well with fresh water. Bring to the boil over medium heat, then reduce the heat to low and simmer for 1 hour. (Get on with your life while they gently bubble away.) Drain and set aside.

Preheat the oven to 150°C (300°F).

Heat the oil in a flameproof casserole dish over medium heat and fry the onion until just browned. Add the pork and brown for 2–3 minutes. For a thick, glossy stew, add the tapioca flour, stirring to coat the meat. Add the garlic, salt, rosemary and thyme and fry for 1–2 minutes.

Add the chilli, stock and tomatoes. Bring to the boil, then remove from the stovetop, put on the lid, and transfer to the oven for about 3 hours, until the stew is thick and rich.

Just before serving, return the casserole to the stovetop and toss in the spinach and green beans, to finish with their delicious bright colour and crunch. Season with salt and pepper to taste, stir through the parsley and serve.

Done! Too easy, right?

*Notes: Double-batch this recipe for a big feast with friends or to freeze half for another day. For a fully vegetarian version, use 5 cups cooked legumes of your choice – I like a mix of black beluga lentils and black beans, or pinto beans and red kidney beans – soaking them in two large bowls before cooking.

Spiced corn tortillas

Side • **Makes** 12 tortillas about 15 cm (6 inches) wide, 2 mm (¹⁄₁₆ inch) thick

We've been making variations of these for our family taco night for a long time. They're great with the pork stew, too, with its southern American flavour profile.

2½ cups (625 ml) lukewarm filtered water
1 garlic clove, finely chopped
2 large red chillies, seeded and finely chopped
2 spring onions (scallions), very finely chopped
¾ teaspoon salt
2 cups (250 g) finely ground yellow or blue masa harina cornflour (cornstarch)
olive oil, for rolling and cooking

Pour the water into a large mixing bowl and add the garlic, chilli, spring onion and salt. Gradually add the flour, stirring it through with clean hands and continuing until the dough is soft and airy. If it seems too crumbly for rolling, work through another ¼ cup (60 ml) water. Too wet? Add another ¼ cup (30 g) cornflour.

Break the dough into about 12 portions and roll each into a ball. Cover with a clean damp tea towel (dish towel) for up to 1 hour before rolling out. Have a plate and clean dry tea towel ready.

Add a drop of oil to each of two small cast-iron or ceramic nonstick frying pans* then heat over medium–high heat.

Wipe a drop of oil onto two sheets of unbleached baking paper. Place a dough ball, between the sheets and roll out into a tortilla.

Peel off the baking paper and add the tortilla to the first pan. While it cooks, roll out your next tortilla ready for the second pan. Cook for 1–2 minutes each side, until light brown blisters appear.

Place the cooked tortillas on the prepared plate and wrap it in its 'blanky' (blanket – i.e. wrap the plate in the dry tea towel), adding them in a pile until all are cooked.

Serve with the stew and salsa. So good and delicious!

****Note:** You use two pans so that you can cook two tortillas at once. If you have a large hotplate and can do more than one at a time, I'm jealous. If you only have one pan that's fine – it will just take you a little longer to cook them all.

Low Tox Life Food

Coriander and capsicum salsa

Side ∗ **Serves** 6

Whenever I'm having something rich like a stew, I love topping it with some freshness for contrast or 'chasing' it with a salady salsa to cleanse the palate and stimulate stomach acid – notice the Frenchies always finish with a salad? Notice the Germans and eastern Europeans always include something like a sauerkraut or pickled cabbage? It may have been instinct back when these foods were paired together, but today we have the science. Just a stew can leave you heavy – enjoy this digestive stimulant and fresh flavour either with or after your stew.

⅔ cup (30 g) finely chopped
    coriander (cilantro)
2 large red capsicums (peppers),
    finely diced
2 small ripe tomatoes, finely
    chopped
2 cups (70 g) rocket (arugula),
    finely chopped
1 quantity Mum's Vinaigrette
    (page 193) or Cuban Kicker*
    (page 195)

Place all the ingredients in a bowl and toss together.

*****Note:** If using the Cuban Kicker dressing, you only need enough to just coat everything. Add little by little, to taste.

Simple almond blender cake

Dessert • **Serves 4–8**

This simple almond blender cake was born one year in Mauritius because although I wanted to keep my late grandmère's Sunday-afternoon cake tradition rolling on, I also wanted it to be a 'stick it all in a blender', no-fuss cake. The result is a very light and fluffy, almond-meal-based cake for gluten-free peeps. So easy.

4 organic pasture-raised eggs
½ cup (125 g) maple syrup
1½ cups (150 g) almond meal
2 tablespoons lemon zest
2 teaspoons apple cider vinegar
  or balsamic vinegar
1 teaspoon vanilla paste or
  powder
2 teaspoons baking powder
100 ml (3½ fl oz) extra virgin
  olive oil
⅓ cup (45 g) slivered almonds*

Preheat the oven to 180°C (350°F). Line a round 20 cm (8 inch) diameter cake tin with baking paper.

Place the eggs and sugar in a high-powered blender. Blitz for 1 minute. Add all the remaining ingredients except the olive oil and slivered almonds and blend a further 10 seconds. With the motor running, gradually add the olive oil over another 30 seconds.*

Pour the batter into the prepared tin and scatter the slivered almonds over the top. Bake for 30–35 minutes, checking at 20–25 minutes. The cake is cooked when a skewer inserted in the centre comes out clean. Cool in the tin for 10 minutes, then transfer to a wire rack to cool completely. Serve with a delicious tea.

*Note: If you can't get slivered almonds from a good source, just use finely chopped almonds as I did for the photo. The cake batter will seem quite runny, but don't worry, it will turn out great – airy, light and delicious! If you want to make a quick syrup to drizzle over the top, warm the zest of 1 lemon, ¼ cup (60 ml) lemon juice, ⅓ cup (80 ml) honey, and 30 g (1 oz) butter in a saucepan over medium heat for 3–4 minutes. Cool and drizzle over your cooled cake. To make decorative lemon slices, slice the lemon as thinly as possible, then bake in one layer on a baking tray in a 180°C (350°F) oven for 15–20 minutes.

Low Tox Life Food

A FARMER'S
Market feast

Inspired by Buena Vista Farm,
Gerringong, New South Wales, Australia

Oh, how I love what they're doing at Buena Vista Farm!
I have an Insta-crush on the place, and it was lovely to meet
Fiona Walmsley when I reached out for a little food story
about it for this book.

The farm has been in Fiona's family since her great-great-grandfather
rode in to the auction in Kiama on horseback in 1859, bid on it and
won, after having rented it for 18 years. Fiona and Adam moved back to
the farm with the intention of building a small, sustainable operation
that would support a young family. They started with laying hens and
meat chickens, and have gradually added bees, a small herd of grass-fed
beef cattle, a market garden, a kitchen garden, free-range pigs, geese
and ducks, and a commercial kitchen in which they make a range of
fermented foods for sale at their local weekly farmer's market. They also
run cooking workshops. Fiona's parents still live on the farm too, in a
house up the hill, 'which is terrific because Dad can usually fix things we
break, and shout over the back fence when the pigs are out'.

When I asked Fiona what it meant to be the current custodian of this
beautiful 7 hectares (18 acres) she had this to say: 'We feel incredibly

Low Tox Life Food

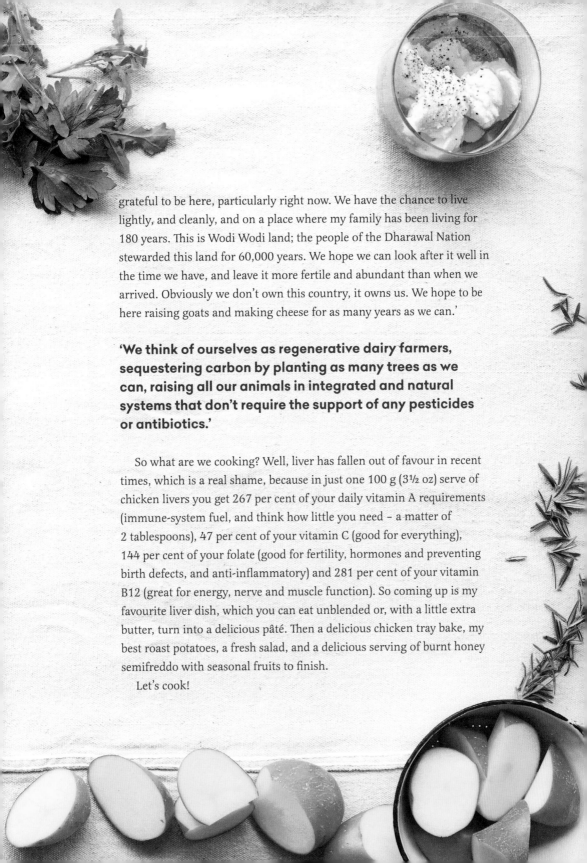

grateful to be here, particularly right now. We have the chance to live lightly, and cleanly, and on a place where my family has been living for 180 years. This is Wodi Wodi land; the people of the Dharawal Nation stewarded this land for 60,000 years. We hope we can look after it well in the time we have, and leave it more fertile and abundant than when we arrived. Obviously we don't own this country, it owns us. We hope to be here raising goats and making cheese for as many years as we can.'

'We think of ourselves as regenerative dairy farmers, sequestering carbon by planting as many trees as we can, raising all our animals in integrated and natural systems that don't require the support of any pesticides or antibiotics.'

So what are we cooking? Well, liver has fallen out of favour in recent times, which is a real shame, because in just one 100 g (3½ oz) serve of chicken livers you get 267 per cent of your daily vitamin A requirements (immune-system fuel, and think how little you need – a matter of 2 tablespoons), 47 per cent of your vitamin C (good for everything), 144 per cent of your folate (good for fertility, hormones and preventing birth defects, and anti-inflammatory) and 281 per cent of your vitamin B12 (great for energy, nerve and muscle function). So coming up is my favourite liver dish, which you can eat unblended or, with a little extra butter, turn into a delicious pâté. Then a delicious chicken tray bake, my best roast potatoes, a fresh salad, and a delicious serving of burnt honey semifreddo with seasonal fruits to finish.

Let's cook!

A FARMER'S
Market feast

MENU FOR 6

Starter
Chicken livers on sourdough

Main
Roasted garlic, herb and apricot chicken tray bake

Sides
My bestest roast potatoes

Fresh goat's cheese, leafy local greens, seasonal fruit and classic dressing

Dessert
Burnt honey semifreddo with seasonal fruits

Roasted garlic, herb and apricot chicken tray bake
PAGE 255

Chicken livers on sourdough
PAGE 254

My bestest
roast potatoes
PAGE 256

Fresh goat's
cheese, leafy local
greens, seasonal fruit
and classic dressing
PAGE 257

Chicken livers on sourdough

Starter * **Serves** 6-8 * **Prep and cooking time** 15 minutes

These livers are so delicious and nourishing and, frankly, my family would happily forget the rest of the feast and just eat these with a salad and some toast or crackers for dinner.

80 g (2¾ oz) butter

300 g (10½ oz) red onion, roughly chopped

1 kg (2 lb 4 oz) organic chicken livers

1 rosemary sprig

2 garlic cloves, crushed

150 ml (5 fl oz) tomato passata (puréed tomatoes)

⅓ cup (80 ml) chicken stock

1 tablespoon finely chopped dried cranberries*

½ teaspoon salt

½ cup roughly chopped flat-leaf parsley, to serve

6–8 slices sourdough bread*

Heat half the butter in a large frying pan over medium heat and sauté the onion until soft and translucent. Add the livers, rosemary and garlic and pan-fry for about 5 minutes, until the livers are browned each side.

Add the tomato passata, stock, remaining butter and cranberries, then pan-fry for a further 5–7 minutes, until the liver is cooked through (I always just cut through the thickest one and check. Chef friends will no doubt laugh at me when they read this, but it works for me).

Voilà! Season to taste, pop in a serving bowl, top with the parsley and serve with the sourdough bread.

*Notes: Instead of the cranberries you could use cranberry, plum or crabapple jelly. Honey would work too. I of course serve this with gluten-free sourdough, but if you can eat gluten, choose your sourdough and enjoy.

To make chicken liver pâté Double the butter, then whiz in a blender or food processor. Store in the fridge and eat within 3–4 days.

Roasted garlic, herb and apricot chicken tray bake

Main * **Serves** 8 * **Prep time** 10 minutes active, 40 minutes passive * **Cooking time** 1 hour

2 garlic bulbs

extra virgin olive oil, for roasting, plus 2 tablespoons extra, for rub

1⅔ cups (50 g) coriander (cilantro)

½ cup (10 g) flat-leaf parsley

½ teaspoon fennel seeds

150 g (5½ oz) tomatoes

1½ teaspoons salt

1.6 kg (3 lb 8 oz) chicken pieces*

1 large red onion, cut in half and then 3 wedges each half

½ cup (125 ml) stock of your choice

60 g (2¼ oz) butter or 1 tablespoon extra virgin olive oil

12 dried apricots or pitted prunes, or 6 pitted dates, cut in half

Preheat the oven to 200°C (400°F).

Place the garlic bulbs on a roasting tray and douse them in olive oil. Roast for 45 minutes, then remove from the oven and set aside to cool. Turn the oven off.*

Once the garlic is cooled, squeeze the roasted cloves from their skins and into a food processor.* Add the coriander, parsley, fennel seeds, tomato, extra olive oil and salt, then pulse until a paste forms. Rub this all over the chicken pieces, then place them in a roasting tin. Pop them to bed in the fridge overnight if you can. Otherwise continue with the recipe.

Reduce the oven temperature to 180°C (350°F).

Arrange the onion around the chicken pieces. Pour the stock into the corners of the tray, to ensure it sinks to the bottom. Cut the butter into slices and dot on top of the meat. Add the apricots, arranging them around the chicken. That's it.

Roast for 1 hour and it's ready to serve, straight from the roasting tin.

*Notes: I like to roast the garlic a couple of days before when I'm cooking something else so that it's ready for me to make the paste super quick. Use a mixture of chicken thighs and legs – whatever you fancy. You could also use a hand-held blender to blend the garlic paste in a jug.

Still strapped for time?
* Cook in the oven on a less busy night while you're making a stovetop evening meal. Pop in the fridge and reheat the next evening in no time.
* Serve with steamed greens and butter, a salad and roast potatoes (see page 256), or my Caramelised Onion Quinoa or Cauliflower Purée (recipes on the lowtoxlife.com).

My bestest roast potatoes

These will definitely help to make you famous with your friends. This isn't a promise I make lightly, but I have a secret weapon. To achieve the super-crunchy potato with light clouds of fluff on the inside, olive oil and butter aren't going to cut it. Animal fats are the key, as is the two-step process described below. I cannot wait to hear about your success with these – #lowtoxfoodbook.

8 desiree sebago, maris piper
    or russet potatoes (about
    2 kg/4 lb 8 oz)
1½ teaspoons salt
½ cup (125 ml) extra virgin olive
    oil, lard or tallow

Preheat the oven to 220°C (425°F).

Wash the potatoes and cut them in half. Place them in a large stockpot, cover with cold water and add the salt. Place over medium heat and bring to the boil, then reduce the heat to medium–low and simmer for 5 minutes to parboil them. Strain in a colander and leave for a couple of minutes to let all the steam off – this is key. They must be dry before the next step. While they're drying off, place the lard or tallow in a roasting tin and place in the oven for about 5 minutes.

Cut the potatoes in half again and scrape all over the exposed flesh with a fork, to rough them up and create some crumbly edges. These bits will catch the fat and crisp up to epic heights during cooking.

Add the potato pieces to the super-hot fat in the roasting tin, placing them on a flesh side and spooning a little fat over them to coat the other sides. They should sizzle as they hit the tin. Roast for 45–60 minutes, turning them halfway through cooking, until roasted to your liking. You're done. Enjoy!

Fresh goat's cheese, leafy local greens, seasonal fruit and classic dressing

Side ● Serves 6

200 g (7 oz) fresh goat's cheese, crumbled
1 lettuce head, leaves separated, washed and torn into smaller pieces
60 g (2¼ oz) rocket (arugula) and/or foraged local greens (see page 228)
100 g (3½ oz) seasonal fruit*
2 tablespoons finely chopped mint
⅔ cup (105 g) hazelnuts, roasted*
¼ quantity Mum's Vinaigrette (page 193)

Combine all the non-dressing ingredients in a large flat salad bowl. Toss the vinaigrette and serve.

*Notes: In summer, pitted cherries are delicious, as are nectarine wedges. To roast hazelnuts, see the note on page 228.

Burnt honey semifreddo with seasonal fruits

Dessert • **Serves** 10–12

¾ cup (185 ml) local honey

600 ml (21 fl oz) organic thin (pouring) cream or coconut cream

8 organic pasture-raised egg yolks

2 organic pasture-raised eggs

½ teaspoon vanilla bean powder

¼ teaspoon grated or ground nutmeg

Topping

2 cups (300 g) pitted cherries or your favourite seasonal fruits, chopped*

fresh berries and local edible flowers in season,* to serve

grated or ground nutmeg, to serve

Line a 24 cm (9½ inch) cake tin or 11 x 27 x 9 cm (4¼ x 10¾ x 3½ inch) loaf (bar) tin with baking paper (it will mould to the tin better if you scrunch it up well first, then spread it out to line the tin. I use two strips of paper at right angles, to get good coverage and to have plenty to fold over the top).

Combine half of the honey and 2½ tablespoons of the cream in a small saucepan and cook on high until the mixture smells super caramelly (almost burnt), about 4 minutes. Pour immediately into a room-temperature bowl to cool.

Half-fill a medium saucepan with water and bring to a gentle simmer over low heat. Place the egg yolks and remaining honey in a medium metal bowl that will sit securely on top of the saucepan without touching the water. Place the bowl over the simmering water and beat with hand-held electric beaters until the mixture is pale, creamy and frothy (taking care not to burn the electrical cord). Remove the bowl from the saucepan and set aside.

Pour the remaining cream into a deep medium bowl and beat until thickened but not too stiff. Gently fold the cream and the cooled burnt honey mixture into the beaten egg mixture. Everything should now be in one bowl.

Pour into the prepared tin, then cover and freeze for 3 hours or overnight.

When ready to serve, remove the semifreddo from the freezer,* take out of the tin by pulling on the paper, then remove the paper and place the semifreddo on a plate or cake stand. DO NOT PANIC if the paper sticks. Just wait a couple of minutes for the semifreddo to soften, and it will peel off super easily.

Scatter the fruit and edible flowers over the top and sprinkle with nutmeg.

*Notes: To roast hazelnuts, see the note on page 228. When cherries are out of season, try finely diced pear, sautéed in a pan with a little butter and vanilla bean powder, then cooled to room temperature. For the photo, I used figs, about four. In spring/summer, you could use berries and small locally growing edible flowers such as elderflower. You can keep the semifreddo in the freezer for 3–4 days before serving.

A SIMPLE
Sustainable feast

Inspired by Roebuck Farm,
Taranaki, New Zealand

One of my favourite types of people to interview on the Low Tox Life podcast is a regenerative farmer who also teaches others how to farm. No one is better placed to explain the incredible effect of converting to regenerative methods, and that's why some of my most popular shows have been with Joel Salatin, Charlie Arnott, Paul Grieves, Nick Ritar and a farmer Nick introduced me to, Jodi Roebuck of Roebuck Farm, Taranaki, New Zealand.

Jodi grew up a surfer and designer with a mum who had a passion for gardening, so when he became interested in how people were producing food around the world, he took it upon himself to travel and learn from as many of them as possible. Today, Roebuck Farm has become an international beacon for modelling the alliance between sustainable, traditional growing principles and modern innovations. The thriving market garden and restoration grazing farm sells its produce locally and regenerates pasture diversity through stock management. The workshops teach these principles through highly interactive on-farm activities.

Through degenerative agriculture, Jodi explains, 'we have lost a lot of our nutrition and our topsoil whether it's crops or grazing'. What really excites him about regenerative agriculture is the chance to run a thriving farm while also improving the landscape.

'It might be a new concept, but it's really been around for millennia. It's a bit more work, for sure, but it's worth it if you think about the big picture.'

So what are we cooking? A simple family feast here, with 'moussaka', wilted lemony greens and a delicious custard with seasonal fruit to finish.

Wilted lemony
greens
PAGE 266

A SIMPLE
Sustainable feast

MENU FOR 6

Main
Almost moussaka

Side
Wilted lemony greens

Dessert
Lemon custard with seasonal
fruits and toasted honey nuts

Almost
moussaka
PAGE 264

Almost moussaka

Main • Serves 6

This makes a delicious family meal, and is perfect for doubling up so you have one to freeze (especially if, unlike me, you have a decent-sized freezer) or if you want to serve 10–12 people at a bigger gathering. I hope you enjoy it.

600 g (1 lb 5 oz) eggplant
  (aubergine), cut into 1 cm
  (½ inch) slices
salt, for salting eggplant, plus
  1 teaspoon extra for cooking
3 heaped tablespoons butter
1 onion, roughly chopped
1 kg (2 lb 4 oz) minced (ground)
  lamb, or 5½ cups (500 g)
  chopped mushrooms or
  4 cups (800 g) cooked brown
  lentils
1 carrot, diced
¾ cup (105 g) chopped celery
1⅓ cups (120 g) chopped Tuscan
  cabbage (cavolo nero)
1 large zucchini (courgette),
  grated
1 cup (250 ml) tomato passata
  (puréed tomatoes)
2 garlic cloves, finely chopped
½ cup (30 g) chopped parsley
1 rosemary sprig
1 heaped tablespoon dried
  mixed herbs
1 cup (250 ml) stock

White sauce
60 g (2¼ oz) butter
2 tablespoons coconut flour
60 g (2¼ oz) tapioca flour
700 ml (24 fl oz) milk of your
  choice
1⅓ cup (120 g) grated
  Parmigiano Reggiano

Preheat the oven to 200°C (400°F). Lightly oil a roasting tin.

Lay the eggplant slices on the prepared roasting tin. Salt them generously on both sides to extract water and bitterness. Set aside for 10 minutes and pat dry with a clean tea towel (dish towel) to remove the water that comes out of the slices.

Heat the butter in a large saucepan over medium heat. Fry the onion for 10 minutes until softened and golden brown, then add the lamb, mushrooms or lentils, along with carrot, celery and extra 1 teaspoon salt, and cook for 3–4 minutes.

Add the Tuscan cabbage, zucchini, tomato passata, garlic, herbs and stock. Increase the heat to high and cook for 10 minutes. Reduce the heat to low and simmer, covered, for about 30 minutes, then remove the lid and cook for 15 minutes to thicken the juices a little (or cheat by adding 2 tablespoons tapioca flour or arrowroot to thicken in a minute or two).

Meanwhile, bake the salted and dried eggplant slices for 20 minutes and set aside. Keep the oven on.

To make the dairy white sauce, melt the butter in a medium saucepan over medium heat. Pour in the flours and stir until doughy. Cook for 30 seconds, until you can smell 'pastry vibes'. Remove from the heat. Gradually add half the milk a tiny bit at a time, whisking well with each addition. Return to the heat and gradually whisk in the remainder of the milk. Keep whisking until the sauce is thick and creamy.* Stir through 1 cup (70 g) of the cheese and set aside.

Or, to make the dairy-free white sauce, place all the ingredients in a high-powered blender and blend until smooth.

To assemble the moussaka, spread the lamb mixture in a 25 x 30 cm (10 x 12 inch) glass, enamel, cast-iron or ceramic baking dish. Top with the eggplant slices, then pour the white sauce over the top. Scatter the remaining cheese or extra nutritional yeast over the sauce and bake for about 30 minutes, until golden brown.

*Note: If your dairy-based white sauce gets lumpy, you can smooth it out using a hand-held blender.

Variation

Dairy-free white sauce

1 small head cauliflower, chopped into 2 cm (¾ inch) florets, steamed until soft
⅓ cup (80 ml) coconut milk or nut milk
¼ teaspoon salt
black pepper, to taste
¼ cup (15 g) nutritional yeast, plus extra to top

Wilted lemony greens

Side ∗ **Serves** 6

This is my favourite greens dish – so simple, nourishing and tangy. I could eat bucketloads of it every day. My standard simple go-to is to fry a handful of mince with onion and have it with a huge helping of these delicious wilted leaves.

½ cup (125 ml) filtered water
350 g (12 oz) Tuscan cabbage
(cavolo nero), fibrous bottom
5 cm (2 inches) composted,
the rest roughly chopped
160 g (6½ oz) wild dandelion or
amaranth, chopped*
50 g (1¾ oz) butter or
3 tablespoons extra virgin
olive oil
juice of 2 lemons
½ teaspoon salt
150 g (5½ oz) goat's cheese or
crème fraîche

Heat the water in a large saucepan over medium heat. Add the chopped greens (don't worry, they will shrink in volume considerably). Sauté the greens for 2–3 minutes, until they wilt and the water has evaporated.

Reduce the heat to low, then add the butter, lemon juice, salt and goat's cheese and sauté a further 3–4 minutes.

*Note: If you can't get wild dandelion or amaranth, use collard greens or silverbeet (Swiss chard).

Lemon custard with seasonal fruits and toasted honey nuts

Dessert • **Serves** 6

seasonal fruits (e.g. berries in spring/summer, peaches in summer, pears in autumn)

Lemon custard

600 ml (21 fl oz) coconut cream or 400 ml (14 fl oz) full-cream (whole) milk plus 200 ml (7 fl oz) organic thin (pouring) cream

zest of 1 lemon or lime

1–2 vanilla pods, split lengthways and seeds scraped, or 1 heaped teaspoon vanilla bean powder

4 organic pasture-raised egg yolks

2 organic pasture-raised eggs

2 tablespoons tapioca flour, arrowroot or cornflour (cornstarch)

2½ tablespoons honey or maple syrup

Toasted honey nuts

1½ cups nuts, mixed or your favourite kind, chopped*

1 tablespoon softened butter

1 tablespoon honey

½ teaspoon assorted sweet spices (e.g. cinnamon, vanilla)

To make the custard, heat the coconut cream, lemon zest and vanilla in a medium saucepan over medium heat until just boiled.

Meanwhile, whisk the egg yolks and whole eggs, tapioca and honey in a medium bowl until well combined. Then, very gradually, while whisking constantly, pour the hot coconut cream mixture into the egg mixture. (The whisking is imperative, to prevent the eggs cooking.)

Pour the whole mixture back into the saucepan and return to medium heat, stirring constantly until it thickens enough to coat the back of a spoon. Pour back into the bowl and cool in the fridge until ready to use, or serve warm with a pudding. Or for an indulgent treat your family will kiss your feet over, serve it as a coconut vanilla 'soup' with strawberries.

Preheat the oven to 180°C (350°F). Line a baking tray with baking paper.

Place the nuts in a small bowl. Add the butter, honey and spices and mix well with your hands to combine. Spread the coated nuts on the prepared tray and bake for about 15 minutes, until light golden brown. Cool on the tray.

When ready to serve, chop the fruit, if needed. Fill serving bowls with custard and scatter the fruit and toasted nuts over the top. Voilà – simple, delicious dessert is served.

*Note: I love hazelnuts for this dish. See page 293 for a photo of this dish.

AN ORGANIC
Olive and grain feast

Mount Zero Olives, Laharum, Victoria, Australia

A couple of years ago it dawned on me that whenever I bought organic grains or legumes, they tended to come from overseas. Research shows that around 85 per cent of a food's environmental impact happens before it leaves the farm gate, so finding a good regenerative organic producer is important, but local really is the holy grail. This made finding Mount Zero especially exciting.

Jane and Neil Seymour, and their son Richard who joined them in the business in 2005, are inspiring land custodians who produce beautiful biodynamic olives, pulses and grains. Their olive grove, which comprises 6000 Spanish manzanilla and gordal olive trees and lies at the base of Mount Zero, the northernmost summit of the Grampians, was planted in the 1940s, making it one of oldest in Australia. Their website describes their operation in this way:

'Here we practice biodynamic farming techniques and have the international Demeter certification. The grove is self-sustaining in its farming practices – feeding the trees directly from the soil humus rather than chemical inputs, and our energy supply is sourced from off-grid wind and solar generators.'

What are we cooking, you ask? It's gotta be something using delicious legumes, hasn't it? I've always wanted to perfect my own falafel, and I think I've finally done it – you be the judge. You can either serve them with an array of fresh vegies on a platter or jazz things up for a bigger feast with the recipes I've put together here. We're finishing the feast off with a new creation: my Chocolate Mousse Cake made with olive oil. My husband says it's the most delicious dessert I've ever come up with. Proceed with glee – it will be worth the effort.

Sweet potato, beetroot and lemon purée
PAGE 273

AN ORGANIC
Olive and grain feast

MENU FOR 6

Main
Falafel

Sides
Sweet potato, beetroot and lemon purée

Oven-roasted eggplant

Chopped herb, tomato and cucumber salad

Two-ingredient sweet potato flatbread

Dessert
Chocolate mousse cake

Oven-roasted eggplant
PAGE 273

Falafel
PAGE 272

Two-ingredient
sweet potato
flatbread
PAGE 274

Chopped herb,
tomato and
cucumber salad
PAGE 273

Falafel

Main ∗ **Serves** 6 ∗ **Makes** 30–35 ∗ **Prep time** 25 minutes active,
24–36 hours passive (soaking chickpeas) ∗ **Cooking time** 5 minutes

You'll need to start the day before by soaking the chickpeas overnight. The key with this feast is to get everything else ready to serve before you cook the falafel, given they're so quick to fry.

2 cups (400 g) dried chickpeas, soaked in water with a squeeze of lemon juice overnight*

200 g (7 oz) red onion, cut into chunks

2 handfuls parsley stalks and leaves

1 handful coriander (cilantro) stalks, leaves and roots, roots washed

2 teaspoons ground cumin

¾ teaspoon ground cardamom

1 teaspoon salt

½ teaspoon black pepper

2 tablespoons chickpea flour (besan) or teff flour*

4 garlic cloves

1 teaspoon baking powder

1½ cups (375 ml) extra virgin olive oil, for deep-frying

1 quantity Garlicky Tahini Parsley Sauce (page 184)

Preheat the oven to 100°C (200°F).

Drain the soaked, uncooked chickpeas, place in a food processor and pulse for a few seconds to break them down a little. Add all the remaining ingredients except the baking powder, pulse for 5 seconds then stop, scrape down the sides of the processor and pulse again. Repeat until you have a green chickpea dough that will just hold together. It will be a bit fragile, but if it's crumbly or completely falling apart, add a splash of water. If it's too wet, add another tablespoon of flour. Add the baking powder and pulse for a few seconds to combine, then set aside to rest.

Roll heaped tablespoonfuls of the mixture into falafel about 3 cm (1¼ inch) wide and 1.5 cm (⅝ inch) thick, and lay them gently on a clean board. Continue until all the mixture is used up. (It's much less stressful to form all the falafel before frying than to cook them as you go.)

Heat the olive oil in a deep, wide, flat-based saucepan (a crumb of the mixture dropped in should sizzle immediately).

Using a wide flat spatula, pick up a few falafel and carefully place them in the hot oil, cooking ten at a time for 2 minutes each side, or until deep golden brown. Remove to a baking tray and keep warm in the oven. Repeat until all the falafel are cooked. Once the oil is cool, strain it and store in a jar in the fridge to use a second time.

Serve with the garlicky tahini parsley sauce.

*Notes: I soak chickpeas for 2 days at room temperature, in water with a squeeze of lemon juice in it, as I find it's better for digestion. Use a deep bowl with lots of water, as they will expand a lot. Teff is a very fast-growing, planet-friendly grain.

Sweet potato, beetroot and lemon purée

Side * **Serves** 6

---

250 g (9 oz) sweet potato, roughly chopped
    into chunks
250 g (9 oz) beetroot, peeled and cut into quarters
¼ cup (60 ml) fresh lemon juice
2 pinches of salt
½ teaspoon ground cumin
½ teaspoon ground sumac
2–3 tablespoons goat kefir or sour cream (optional)

Place the sweet potato and beetroot in a medium–large saucepan, cover well with cold water and bring to the boil over medium heat. Boil for 20 minutes, or until the sweet potato is tender.

Drain the vegies (retaining and cooling the water for plants) and pop them in a food processor. Add the remaining ingredients and pulse until they form a smooth purée. Add a glug of goat kefir or sour cream if you have some and want to make it creamy. Transfer to a serving dish and you're done.

Oven-roasted eggplant

Side * **Serves** 6

---

2 large eggplants (aubergines), cut into 6 mm
    (¼ inch) slices
⅓ cup (80 ml) extra virgin olive oil

Preheat the oven to 200°C (400°F).

Lay the eggplant slices in a shallow roasting tin (or two tins if necessary). Salt them generously on both sides to extract water and bitterness, right there on the tray. Set aside for 5–10 minutes.

Using a clean tea towel (dish towel), wipe the salt and moisture off the eggplant slices, then pour the olive oil over them, coating them all well. Roast for 30 minutes or until golden brown.

Chopped herb, tomato and cucumber salad

Side * **Serves** 6

---

300 g (10½ oz) vine-ripened tomatoes, roughly
    chopped into small cubes
200 g (7 oz) cucumber, roughly chopped into
    small cubes
1⅔ cups (50 g) chopped flat-leaf parsley
1 cup local leafy greens (I used rocket and baby
    red sorrel)
Garlicky Tahini Parsley Sauce (page 184) or
    Mum's Vinaigrette (page 193), to taste

Toss all the ingredients together and dress lightly with some garlicky tahini parsley sauce or Mum's vinaigrette.

Two-ingredient sweet potato flatbread

Side • **Makes** 12 • **Prep time** 30 minutes • **Cooking time** 90 seconds each flatbread

Apart from the oil used for frying, and salt if you want to add it, this versatile flatbread is made from sweet potato and flour, and gluten-free flour works a treat. It makes a great gluten-free roti or naan to BYO (Australian for bring your own) to your local Indian restaurant or to enjoy with curries at home (see, for example, the simple fish curry, chicken spinach curry or 'set and forget' lamb saag on the Low Tox Life website). It develops those little 'blisters' and a nice flakiness when served fresh and hot, to give you an 'I can't believe it's not gluten-containing roti' vibe.

It also works fine stored in the fridge and used as a wrap for school lunches, as a simple vehicle for an egg and avocado roll for brekkie, or for a corn-free soft taco option if you have to avoid corn. The options are endless, and I hope you love them as much as we do.

Remember, the first time you make anything fiddly like this, it won't be easy. The problem is, we often don't try again, which means we don't allow ourselves to become proficient to the point we find it easy. Instead, we usually abandon it with 'Well, that was hard, I'm never doing that again.' I found it hard the first time too, but the second time it felt super easy. The third time I was like 'How awesome is this?' Let yourself be the same. And the photos over the page will help with a couple of the steps.

For the best possible results, you will need:
* a well-seasoned nonstick cast-iron or ceramic frying pan
* a rolling pin (or once in an Airbnb I used a tall round bottle of olive oil instead)
* a large marble or granite chopping board or benchtop for rolling.

*Notes: Either orange or purple sweet potato will work well. For gluten-free flour, use either a ready-mixed 1:1 baker's flour (e.g. Bob's Red Mill or Wholefood Collective), or mix ½ cup (65 g) buckwheat flour, ¼ cup (35 g) tapioca flour and ¼ cup (25 g) almond meal.

Fridge: Refrigerate cooked flatbread and use over the next 2 days. Quickly reheat on a pan for a few seconds each side or in a toaster on medium, or use cold as a wrap. There are multiple roads to success.

Freezer: Freeze the dough balls for up to 3 months so they're on hand to defrost, roll out and cook at a later date – hooray! After defrosting, I find each needs an extra ½ teaspoon of flour worked into it before dusting it to roll out. To freeze, dust dough balls with flour, then arrange in a glass container and freeze. Defrost overnight in the fridge or at room temperature for 1 hour.

Pro tip: For some reason, using cold mash makes the flatbread dry, whereas warm mash seems to ensure a yummy result. I can't wait to see yours – #lowtoxfoodbook

1 sweet potato (about 300 g/
10½ oz), unpeeled*
1 cup (150 g) gluten-free 1:1
baker's flour,* plus extra for
dusting
¼ teaspoon salt (optional)
olive oil, coconut oil or ghee, for
greasing and frying

Place the whole sweet potato in a saucepan large enough
to hold it. Cover with cold water then bring to the boil. Boil
for 25–30 minutes, until you can easily insert a fork in the
centre (like sticking a fork in a peeled ripe banana). Drain
and cool for about 5 minutes, until still hot but cool enough
to handle safely. Carefully peel off all the skin and cut off
any rough bits or bumps (compost them). Mash with a fork
until almost smooth (or use a hand-held blender with the
sweet potato in a jug).

Measure out 1 cup (250 g) mashed sweet potato.
Transfer to a large bowl and add the flour and salt. Mash
the sweet potato into the flour (see page 276) and mix until
just combined – overworking it can make it a little dry. If
it's super sticky though, and feels too 'wet' and mashy, add
extra tablespoons of flour, one at a time, until it feels like
a super-light dough.

Heat 1 teaspoon of the oil in a medium low-tox nonstick
frying pan (or in each of two frying pans if you have them)
over high heat until it just reaches smoke point, then reduce
heat to medium.

Break the dough into 3 cm (1¼ inch) balls and dust
them with flour. Oil a rolling pin and roll out a dough ball
to about 2–3 mm (1⁄16–1⁄8 inch) thick and 15 cm (6 inches) in
diameter, rolling it once away from you, then turning the
disc 90 degrees and rolling it away from you again, until it's
the right size (see page 277). Pick up the disc with a wide
flat spatula and place it in the prepared frying pan.

Cook for 1 minute each side, then flip again and cook
for another 1 minute each side, meanwhile rolling out your
next dough ball. Repeat until the dough is used up. As each
flatbread is cooked, place it in a bowl wrapped in a tea
towel (dish towel) to keep it from drying out or getting cold,
adding to the pile each time one is cooked.

Serve immediately with curries, soups, or a Middle
Eastern spread of falafel and vegies like this, or cool and
keep in the fridge to use as a wrap over the next couple
of days. Or do as I did this morning, and reheat one in the
toaster to serve with a couple of fried eggs and wilted
spinach for brekkie.

Mash the sweet potato
into the flour and mix
until just combined

Oil a rolling pin
and roll out each
dough ball

Chocolate mousse cake

Dessert * **Serves** 6–8 * **Prep time** 25–30 minutes * **Cooking time** 25–30 minutes

1 cup (200 g) rapadura, panela, coconut or maple sugar
5 eggs, separated
165 g (5¾) dark chocolate (70% cacao), roughly chopped
1½ tablespoons Dutch-processed unsweetened cocoa powder
½ cup (125 ml) olive oil, plus extra for greasing
¼ cup (60 ml) full-cream (whole) milk or coconut milk (optional)*
2 tablespoons hazelnut or pecan meal

*Notes: You'll only need the milk on emergency stand-by in case your chocolate splits during melting. You will totally know if this is happening to you! This milk save has been bulletproof for me over years of carelessly taking my eye off ganache chocolate, and if I can help you live a less stressful dessert-making life then I will. To fold it in, you just fold it in, David. Some of you will get this joke. Some won't and I'm afraid our friendship will be strained ...

Preheat the oven to 170°C (325°F). Line a 23 cm (9 inch) spring-form cake tin with unbleached baking paper and grease the paper with olive oil.

Separate the sugar into small bowls, one with 75 g (2½ oz) and the other with 125 g (4½ oz). Place the egg whites in the bowl of an electric mixer and the yolks in a medium bowl.

Half-fill a small saucepan with water and bring to the boil over medium heat. Rest a large bowl on the saucepan, without it touching the water, and add the chocolate. Reduce the heat to low and warm the chocolate until it's almost melted, stirring carefully with a wooden spoon now and then. Remove from the heat and stir in the 75 g (2½ oz) sugar.

Between stirs while the chocolate is melting, whisk the cocoa powder into the egg yolks until thick and well combined.

Gradually drizzle the olive oil into the melted chocolate mixture, whisking constantly. Does it look like curdled chocolate sick-up or silky smooth? For the first scenario, heat the milk until just warm, then add tablespoons, one at a time, to the curdled mess, stirring gently and watching for it to come together. You might need it all or only a couple of tablespoons.

Whisking constantly, slowly add the melted chocolate mixture to the egg yolk mixture until well combined.

Using the electric mixer, beat the egg whites on medium–high speed until soft peaks form. Add half the remaining sugar and beat for 10 seconds, then add the remaining sugar and beat for a final 10 seconds, or until the sugar is just combined and the mixture looks glossy and rich.

Gently fold* the chocolate mixture, then the hazelnut meal, into the egg white mixture until just combined – don't stir.

Pour into the prepared tin and bake for 30–35 minutes, until there's just a hint of wobble in the centre. Serve hot as a dessert with custard, cream or ice cream, or chilled as a mousse cake.

Low Tox Life Food

Tips for saving time, waste and stress

A bountiful vegetarian feast

How to prepare everything as a feast:
Ever wondered what order to make everything so that all the dishes come together at the right time? Here's my process for attacking multiple-dish cooking. This will help you to plan and map out your own timings, and will remove a large part of the stress from the delicious experience of providing food for your favourite people.

Planning about what you can prepare in advance, and what you're happy to do while guests are there, makes it much less stressful. Bringing a friend into the kitchen and being super clear on what you need them to do can be a lovely way to break down that barrier between cook and guests.

To further reduce any pressure, you could decide to prepare the brussels sprouts dish in advance and serve it cold. That way, it's just the fritters that are hot, and if you've already prepped the mix in the morning, it's simple to get them cooked.

A day or two before
* Make the Spiced Pumpkin Pie. Pressure averted.
* Make the Tahini, Macadamia and Lemon Cream and pop in a jar in the fridge, ready to use.
* Make the Pesto Dressing – it always tastes better that way anyway. Put it in a jar with a thin layer of olive oil on top to keep it bright green. Ready.
* Measure out the hazelnuts and roast them. Set aside in a jar.

That morning
* Chop the kohlrabi and apple and pop in a bowl of water with a squeeze of lemon.
* Measure out the rocket (and wild greens, if using).
* Have the salad bowl out and ready.
* Prepare the fritter mixture so it's ready to fry. Keep in the fridge. If frying to order later stresses you out, you can fry in advance and then simply pop under the grill (broiler) for 2 minutes each side to reheat and serve.
* Prepare the brussels sprouts, fennel and onions.

When cooking
* Get the brussels sprouts in the oven.
* Start frying the fritters halfway through the brussels sprouts cooking time.
* Spoon the tahini macadamia cream onto the platter so it's ready for the brussels sprouts when they come out.
* Strain the kohlrabi and apple, pop them in the waiting salad bowl with the rocket and mix through the Pesto Dressing.
* Finish off the dishes and serve.

Produce brainstorm: Did you know you can roast kohlrabi? Chop a couple of bulbs into 2.5 cm (1 inch) cubes, coat well with olive oil, add a sprinkle of dried herbs if you fancy, and roast in a 220°C (425°F) oven for about 50 minutes or until golden brown, stirring halfway through the cooking time. Season with salt. It makes a perfect side dish or base for a substantial salad.

Kitchen effort maximisation tip: If you have a big family, never do a single batch of fritters. Double it up and you've got quick-grab snacks and school lunchbox goodness. They freeze really well too, for those busy weeks.

Leftovers tip: Use left-over roast vegies to bulk up a leafy salad the next day, or blend them into any left-over soup with a bit of extra water, milk or stock. You can also toss them into a casserole to bulk it up. If you can't think of anything right now, freeze them so they don't get wasted, but label them and use them within the week – otherwise you'll probably end up consigning them to compost heaven.

A tasty biodynamic feast

Produce brainstorm: With cabbage, don't just think slaw and pickles. Cut thick wedges of it, douse them in olive oil, roast in a 180°C (350°F) oven for 30 minutes, then drizzle over my delicious mayonnaise (page 183) or tahini sauce (page 184). Or chop finely and add to soups. For a detoxifying boost, add cruciferous vegies to your soup or stir-fries whenever you can. It's time to get excited about all the things you can do with versatile cabbage.

Kitchen efforts maximisation tip: It can be a most excellent thing to have a couple of freezer meals in reserve. Why not do a double batch of the brisket and freeze half? Defrost and reheat down the track, and serve with a grated carrot salad and chopped cucumbers with lettuce cups for a 'fast feast'.

When you shred the cabbage or grate the carrot and beetroot, do double to use in salads and so on over the next few days.

Leftovers tips

* This feast makes delicious leftovers for wraps or lettuce cups the next day.
* Toss left-over cabbage in with some sautéed greens the next day.
* Freshen up left-over slaw by mixing in spring onion (scallion) and fresh parsley.

A delicious Native American feast

Produce brainstorm: Corn isn't just for on the cob, even though that's delicious. Pop fresh kernels into Adaptable Fritters (page 204). Or barbecue (grill) corncobs on all sides, then cut off the kernels and mix them with sautéed zucchini (courgette), mint and fresh parsley for a delicious side. Or add a cup to left-over roast chicken, with vegies, stock, garlic and fresh herbs for a simple bowl of winter comfort food.

Kitchen maximisation tips: Make a double quantity of tortilla dough, then freeze half in a ball, tightly wrapped in wax paper or foil to protect it. Once it's thawed, I work in 1 tablespoon water before dividing into 12 to make the new batch. Double the stew and freeze half for a busy week.

Leftovers tip: Reheat the left-over corn tortillas in the toaster or under the grill (broiler) for a couple of minutes to enjoy with a couple of eggs and wilted greens for breakfast. Or freeze cooked tortillas and thaw them to enjoy on your next taco night.

Turn left-over stew into soup for lunch the next day. Reheat, add some stock, lentils and the juice of a couple of lemons, then simmer until the lentils are cooked.

A farmer's market feast

Kitchen effort maximisation tip: Double the livers and blend half with extra butter while still hot. That way, you have enough pâté to serve warm with bread now and to have ready for the week's meals, all with very little extra effort.

Leftovers tip: Left-over chicken definitely lends itself to reincarnation as chicken soup, or take out any remaining dried fruits and add 1 cup (250 ml) tomato passata (puréed tomatoes) and ½ cup (125 ml) stock to make a pasta sauce (or serve it with rice or quinoa). Reheat left-over livers the next day to enjoy with your favourite toast or crackers and a salad.

Produce brainstorm: Goat's cheese has got to be one of my favourite foods. I add a dollop to a tomato-based stew for tang before serving, or to sautéed greens for some creaminess, or I crumble it over salads or into wraps, or serve it as a treat on crackers with figs or quince or cherry jam. It's one of those ingredients that can make something simple taste fancy.

A simple sustainable feast

Produce brainstorm: Don't forget all the great things you can do with leafy greens – see Chapter 3 for loads of ideas.

Kitchen effort maximisation tip: If you have the space and ingredients, make two moussakas and freeze one uncooked, ready for a busy time. Pop it in the fridge two days before serving, then transfer to the benchtop for 1 hour before heating in a 180°C (350°F) oven for at least 30 minutes.

If you're not a fan of washing and chopping leafy greens, do double the prep and keep half in a glass container in the fridge to use for a pie or quiche, soup or stew over the week. Or wilt them and either pop them in the fridge then toss in with some other sautéed greens the next day, or freeze for a later soup or stew. I love that extra motivation and ease of knowing you can say 'Here's something I prepared earlier' and get underway a little faster.

Leftovers tip: Moussaka is super easy to enjoy the next day if there's any left. In our small family of three, when I make this, it's off to school for my son's lunch and I enjoy it for a day or two after for my work lunch. Delicious – and it always tastes better the next day, too.

An organic olive and grain feast

Pro tip: If you make all the dishes for a big feast, take the pressure off by preparing the Falafel (or the falafel mixture), Sweet Potato, Beetroot and Lemon Purée, Oven-roasted Eggplant and Two-ingredient Sweet Potato Flatbread dough balls all the day before.

Produce brainstorm: Chickpeas are great for gut bugs. A lot of people with digestive weakness need to rebuild tolerance, so over a month, try a teaspoon of something like hummus one day, build up to two, then three, then a couple of carrots dipped in a couple of tablespoons. This gets most people swinging again. If your gut is healthy, you can use chickpeas to add fibre and prebiotics to soups, curries, stews, salads or dips, or roast them in the oven as crispy salty snacks.

Kitchen effort maximisation tip: Try making a double batch of falafel. They keep well in the fridge for 3–4 days and are perfect for salads, lunchboxes and snacks.

Leftovers tips: Pop left-over sweet potato purée or roasted eggplant in your next soup. The purée also makes a yummy dip for the next 2–3 days. Toast left-over flatbread for brekkie, lunch or tacos.

Conclusion

Well, it's been quite a journey, but here we are now, at the end of it.

If you're looking to take your food sourcing to the best possible level for your good health and the planet's, I hope you've found some ideas and inspiration here. If you're brand new to looking into your food choices, how things are made, where they come from and how we can fix it, I hope you've arrived at this point optimistic, and fuelled for whatever your first steps ahead look like. You'll probably still pop into a supermarket sometimes as I do; we'll probably eat food from time to time, that we don't know the exact origin of or way it is grown. Remember: it is never about perfection, it's about progress.

One thing I know for sure, and that I hope I've been able to show you as we've travelled through this book together, is that farmers are one of our biggest tickets out of this disaster we've inflicted on our natural world. And the best bit about it is that we pay them our respects with every meal we make from scratch in our own kitchens – for ourselves and the people we love.

It's going to take some big mental and cultural shifts to return produce once again to its rightful high status, tossing aside the hot new launch from the food industry giants. And it will be hard to ensure serious investment dollars at every level in food production, from human wellbeing to animal welfare, biodiversity protection and overall planet health. Here we are, though – you and me – taking steps to do better, to do more, and to chink our glasses at the start of each meal, say 'We've got this' and enjoy the bounty of our efforts.

Remember kindness to yourself when, for whatever reason sometimes, you're making the best choice you can when you'd rather be making a different choice. Remember kindness towards those who don't yet understand or hold different beliefs. Simply lead with delicious-ness, let them ask for the recipe or farm you source from, or share info about a wonderful regenerative farming workshop coming up near you or online. Be the ripple of positive change through the generous example of sharing your food and stories about great work being done rather than your opinions. From our overlapping love of good food and a great story about a farmer we know, we will create epic, collective change and give more and more farms permission to rewrite their stories.

See you at the virtual table that unites us all,

Alex

Notes

Introduction

8   I'd find one piece of research that said almonds …: 'Wild Soil® farming – distinct and superior to organic® almonds', Wild Soil Almonds, wildsoilalmonds.com/pages/wild-soil-farming; Isla Binnie, 'Climate-friendly almond farmers coax life from drying Spanish soil', Reuters, 27 May 2020, reuters.com/article/us-climate-change-farming-spain-idUSKBN2331JR; avocados were not only creating horrible human rights abuses …: Joanna Blythman, 'Can hipsters stomach the unpalatable truth about avocado toast?', *The Guardian*, 12 August 2016, theguardian.com/commentisfree/2016/aug/12/hipsters-handle-unpalatable-truth-avocado-toast; avocados were a hardy tree that required little pest control …: 'White Buffalo Land Trust: regenerative organic agriculture in Santa Barbara County', OPN Connect Newsletter 163, 23 April 2020, OPN: Organic Produce Network, organicproducenetwork.com/article/1046/white-buffalo-land-trust-regenerative-organic-agriculture-in-santa-barbara-county

Chapter 1: How did we get here?

20   colourant with known links to hyperactivity …: Jun Yan, 'Hyperactivity in children linked to food coloring', Psychiatric News, 2 November 2007, psychnews.psychiatryonline.org/doi/full/10.1176/pn.42.21.0019; to treat meat with carbon monoxide …: 'H.R. 3115 (110th): Carbon Monoxide Treated Meat, Poultry, and Seafood Safe Handling, Labeling, and Consumer Protection Act', GovTrack (US), govtrack.us/congress/bills/110/hr3115

25   the role lobbyists from various food associations played …: Denise Minger, *Death by Food Pyramid: How Shoddy Science, Sketchy Politics and Shady Special Interests Have Ruined Our Health*, Primal Blueprint, Malibu, 2014; In her book *Death by Food Pyramid*, Denise Minger …: Denise Minger, 'The new USDA dietary guidelines: total hogwash, and here's why', Denise Minger (blog), 4 February 2011, deniseminger.com/tag/food-pyramid; how Luise Light, head nutritionist …: Luise Light, 'A fatally flawed food guide', 2004, cited at 'USDA nutritionists ignored + food pyramid corrupted = an epidemic of obesity and diabetes', Schultz Family Farm (blog), 14 September 2015, farmerglenblog.wordpress.com/2015/09/14/usda-nutritionists-ignored-food-pyramid-corrupted-an-epidemic-of-obesity-and-diabetes

28   we have about 60 years of healthy topsoil left …: Chris Arsenault, 'Only 60 years of farming left if soil degradation continues', Reuters, 6 December 2014, reuters.com/article/us-food-soil-farming-idUSKCN0JJ1R920141205

32   post-farm processing contributes to 18 per cent …: 'Processed food consumption statistics', Statistic Brain Research Institute, 28 February 2018, statisticbrain.com/processed-food-consumption-statistics, Jennifer M. Poti et al., 'Is the degree of food processing and convenience linked with the nutritional quality of foods purchased by US households?' *American Journal of Clinical Nutrition*, vol. 101, no. 6, 2015, pp. 1251–62, academic.oup.com/ajcn/article/101/6/1251/4626878

34   Some of the biggest industrial food producers …: 'General Mills to advance regenerative agriculture practices on one million acres of farmland by 2030', news release, General Mills, 4 March 2019, generalmills.com/en/News/NewsReleases/Library/2019/March/Regen-Ag; 'Cargill to advance regenerative agriculture practices across 10 million acres by 2030', Successful Farming, 16 September 2020, agriculture.com/cargill-to-advance-regenerative-agriculture-practices-across-10-million-acres-by-2030

36   A sizeable percentage of all food emissions globally …: Hannah Ritchie, 'Food production is responsible for one-quarter of the world's greenhouse gas emissions', Our World in Data, 6 November 2019, ourworldindata.org/food-ghg-emissions

Chapter 2: What's best for our planet?

45   the Geneva Gas Protocol, which prohibited …: 'Geneva Gas Protocol, 1925', *Britannica*, britannica.com/event/Geneva-Gas-Protocol

47   Walter James, Lord Northbourne …: John Paull, 'Lord Northbourne, the man who invented organic farming, a biography', *Journal of Organic Systems*, vol. 9, no. 1, 2014, orgprints.org/26547/12/26547.pdf

48   J.I. Rodale (1898–1971) championed …: 'Our story', Rodale Institute, rodaleinstitute.org/about/our-story; Nathanael

Johnson 'Regenerative agriculture': world-saving idea or food marketing ploy?', Resilience, 15 April 2019 resilience.org/stories/2019-04-15/regenerative-agriculture-world-saving-idea-or-food-marketing-ploy

52 If we can see farms as an important site for reversing …: Austin Wang, 'Research shows we're running out of topsoil', The Rising, therising.co/2019/04/05/research-shows-we-are-running-out-of-topsoil; 'Global study reveals time running out for many soils, but conservation measures can help', Science Daily, 14 September 2020, sciencedaily.com/releases/2020/09/200914115905.htm; In their book Sacred Cow …: 'The book', Sacred Cow, sacredcow.info; The net total emissions on the farm …: Paige L. Stanley et al., 'Impacts of soil carbon sequestration on life cycle greenhouse gas emissions in Midwestern USA beef finishing systems', Agricultural Systems, vol. 162, 2018, pp. 249–58, sciencedirect.com/science/article/pii/S0308521X17310338?via=ihub

55 compacted soil that allows water to run off, taking topsoil with it into rivers …: '20-year study shows levels of pesticides still a concern for aquatic life in U.S. rivers and streams', 11 September 2014, usgs.gov/news/20-year-study-shows-levels-pesticides-still-concern-aquatic-life-us-rivers-and-streams; A 2019 UK report …: 'State of nature 2019', State of Nature Partnership, nbn.org.uk/wp-content/uploads/2019/09/State-of-Nature-2019-UK-full-report.pdf; Victoria Balfour, 'Bringing biodiversity back into farming', Sustainable Food Trust, 6 December 2019, sustainablefoodtrust.org/articles/bringing-biodiversity-back-into-farming

56 believed by Dutch and German scientists to be responsible for a massive loss of insect population …: Caspar A. Hallmann et al., 'More than 75 percent decline over 27 years in total flying insect biomass in protected areas', PLoS ONE, vol. 12, no. 10, 2017, article no. e0185809, journals.plos.org/plosone/article?id=10.1371/journal.pone.0185809

57 Project Drawdown describes 'drawdown' as the future point …: 'Drawdown framework', Project Drawdown, drawdown.org/drawdown-framework

61 In one study, holistic planned grazing …: Megan B. Machmuller et al., 'Emerging land use practices rapidly increase soil organic matter', Nature Communications vol. 6, 2015, article no., 6995

62 Seaweed can grow up to 60 times faster …'How seaweed can help us tackle climate change', Climate Council, 31 March 2016, climatecouncil.org.au/seaweed-climate-change; Sylvia Hurlimann 'How kelp naturally combats global climate change', 4 July 2019, Science in the News blog, Harvard University Graduate School of Arts and Sciences, sitn.hms.harvard.edu/flash/2019/how-kelp-naturally-combats-global-climate-change

65 Corn, beans and squash, known as the 'Three Sisters' …: Tracy Heim, 'The Indigenous origins of regenerative agriculture', Climate Blog, National Farmers Union (US), 12 October 2020, nfu.org/2020/10/12/the-indigenous-origins-of-regenerative-agriculture; coined the term 'regenerative organic' to describe …: 'Regenerative agriculture', Terra Genesis International, regenerativeagriculturedefinition.com

68 Biodynamic farming …: 'Biodynamic principles and practices', Biodynamic Association, biodynamics.com/biodynamic-principles-and-practices

70 These preparations and the composting treatments …: J. Fritz, 'Results of scientific trials', In: Ueli Hurter (ed.), Agriculture for the Future: Biodynamic Agriculture Today, 90 Years Since Koberwitz, Verlag Am Goetheanum, Dornach, Switzerland, 2014, pp. 201–14

72 Agroforestry …: 'Agroforestry, growing food and trees together', Tree Plantation, treeplantation.com/agroforestry.html; Chris Hill, 'Farmer reaps green rewards by growing wheat in an apple orchard', Eastern Daily Express, 28 August 2020 edp24.co.uk/business/farming/agroforesty-pioneer-stephen-briggs-at-agriteche-event-1-6812620

73 Permaculture …: David Holmgren, Essence of Permaculture, revised edn, Melliodora Publishing, Hepburn Springs, Victoria, 2002, files.holmgren.com.au/downloads/Essence_of_Pc_EN.pdf

75 This quote from permaculturist Robyn Francis …: Robyn Francis, 'Do nothing, or as little as possible', Permaculture College Australia, Djanbung Gardens, permaculture.com.au/do-nothing-or-as-little-as-possible-permaculture-perspectives-robyn-francis; Holistic management …: 'About us: our mission', Savory, savory.global/our-mission

78 What about methane? …: 'Fast facts', Savory, savory.global/fast-facts

79 Silvo-farming …: Steve Gabriel, Silvopasture: A Guide to Managing Grazing Animals, Forage Crops, and Trees in a Temperate Farm Ecosystem, Chelsea Green, White River Junction, Vermont, 2018

82 Natural sequence farming …: 'About Peter Andrews', Farming Secrets, farmingsecrets.com/experts/peter-andrews; Peter Andrews, Natural Sequence Farming, nsfarming.com/andrews.htm; Paul Newell & Garry Reynolds, 'NSF – principles and applications', Natural Sequence Farming, nsfarming.com/Principles/principles2.html

83 Conservation agriculture or no/minimal till …: 'Conservation agriculture: the 3 principles', Food and Agriculture Organization of the United Nations, 13 March 2014, fao.org/resources/infographics/infographics-details/en/c/216754

84 Thanks to overfishing and climate change …: Fiona Harvey, 'Oceans losing oxygen at unprecedented rate, experts warn',

The Guardian, 7 December 2019, theguardian.com/environment/2019/dec/07/oceans-losing-oxygen-at-unprecedented-rate-experts-warn; we can work to restore balance and regenerate oceans …: Sarah Bedolfe, 'Seaweed could be scrubbing way more carbon from the atmosphere than we expected', Oceana, 6 October 2017, oceana.org/blog/seaweed-could-be-scrubbing-way-more-carbon-atmosphere-we-expected; Seaweed grows between …: See note for page 62 ; Scientist and author Professor Tim Flannery …: Richard Schiffman, 'How "third way" technologies can help turn tide on climate', 26 October 2015, Yale Environment 360, 'e360.yale.edu/features/how_third_way_technologies_can_help_win_the_climate_fight

85   In Paris, in the 15th arrondissement …: Caroline Harrap, 'World's largest urban farm to open – on a Paris rooftop', *The Guardian*, 13 August 2019, theguardian.com/cities/2019/aug/13/worlds-largest-urban-farm-to-open-on-a-paris-rooftop

86   Ron Finley, a celebrated urban gardening pioneer …: 'The Gangsta Gardener, Ron Finely', Ron Finley Project, ronfinley.com; Far to the north-east, in Detroit …: Dave Leblanc, 'Urban farming returning Detroit to its roots, but not without challenges', *Globe and Mail*, 7 July 2016, theglobeandmail.com/real-estate/bring-detroit-back-to-its-roots/article30767484; In Sydney, Australia, one of my favourite …: Pocket City Farms, pocketcityfarms.com.au

89   Excitingly, though, research published by the Rodale Institute …: 'Farming systems trial', Rodale Institute, rodaleinstitute.org/science/farming-systems-trial

Chapter 3: Change starts with us

107   In the US, for example, around 60 per cent …: Filippa Juul et al., 'Ultra-processed food consumption and excess weight among US adults', *British Journal of Nutrition*, vol. 120, no. 1, 2018, pp. 90–100, cambridge.org/core/journals/british-journal-of-nutrition/article/ultraprocessed-food-consumption-and-excess-weight-among-us-adults/5D2D713B3A85F5C94B0C98A1F224D04A; 50 per cent of Australia's diet …: Tegan Taylor, 'What is ultra-processed food and how do I avoid it?', ABC News, 19 June 2019, abc.net.au/news/health/2019-06-19/ultraprocessed-food-what-is-it-and-how-do-i-avoid-it/11216306

109   If global food waste was a country …: 'Tackling Australia's food waste', Department of Agriculture, Water and the Environment, Australian Government, environment.gov.au/protection/waste-resource-recovery/food-waste; landfill, which is responsible for about 16 per cent …: 'Carbon emissions from waste measured in EPA greenhouse gas inventory', Waste Management World, 26 April 2012, waste-management-world.com/a/carbon-emissions-from-waste-measured-in-epa-greenhouse-gas-inventory

110   The dirty dozen and clean 15 fruit and veg: 'EWG's 2020 Shopper's Guide to Pesticides in Produce™: Methodology', EWG, 25 March 2020, ewg.org/foodnews/summary.php

114   We saw a few years ago, when quinoa took off …: Joanna Blythman, 'Can vegans stomach the unpalatable truth about quinoa?', *The Guardian*, 16 January 2013, theguardian.com/commentisfree/2013/jan/16/vegans-stomach-unpalatable-truth-quinoa

130   A little fat from wholefood sources …: Julia Layton, 'How does dietary fat help us absorb vitamins?', How Stuff Works, health.howstuffworks.com/wellness/food-nutrition/vitamin-supplements/fat-absorb-vitamins.htm

148   whose carbon emissions have three times the impact …: Hannah Ritchie, 'Food waste is responsible for 6% of global greenhouse gas emissions', Our World in Data, 18 March 2020, ourworldindata.org/food-waste-emissions

160   David from the Grow Network …: 'David the Good', 'Composting the SCARY stuff – meat, dairy, bones, and human waste!', Grow Network, 15 July 2019, thegrownetwork.com/composting-meat-dairy-bones-sewage

Chapter 4: Let's cook!

221   Their Vegetable Systems Trial, for example …: Gladis Zinati, 'Webinar: Vegetable production and soil health', Rodale Institute, YouTube, 14 November 2019, youtube.com/watch?v=VximNfpTOoA; St Luke's farm-to-hospital partnership …: Debbie Burke, 'Organic farming flips healthcare paradigm', Local Flair, 24 July 2017, flairmag.com/organic-farming-flips-healthcare-paradigm

Further information

Books

Stephanie Anderson *One Size Fits None: A Farm Girl's Search for the Promise of Regenerative Agriculture* (University of Nebraska Press, Lincoln, 2019)

Peter Andrews *Back from the Brink: How Australia's Landscape Can Be Saved* (ABC Books, Sydney, 2006), *Beyond the Brink: Peter Andrews' Radical Vision for a Sustainable Australian Landscape* (ABC Books, Sydney, 2008)

Gabe Brown *Dirt to Soil: One Family's Journey Into Regenerative Agriculture* (Chelsea Green, White River Junction, Vermont, 2018)

Rachel Carson *Silent Spring* (Houghton Mifflin, New York, 1962)

Charles Einsenstein *Climate: A New Story* (North Atlantic Books, Berkeley, 2018)

Damon Gameau *2040: A Handbook for the Regeneration* (Macmillan Australia, Sydney, 2019)

David Holmgren *Permaculture: Principles and Pathways Beyond Sustainability* (Holmgren Design Services, Hepburn Springs, Victoria, 2002)

Charles Massy *Call of the Reed Warbler: A New Agriculture, a New Earth* (Chelsea Green, White River Junction, Vermont, 2017)

Nicole Masters *For the Love of Soil: Strategies to Regenerate Our Food Production Systems* (Integrity Soils, Huntly, New Zealand)

Denise Minger *Death by Food Pyramid: How Shoddy Science, Sketchy Politics and Shady Special Interests Have Ruined Our Health* (Primal Blueprint, Malibu, 2014)

David R. Montgomery *Dirt: The Erosion of Civilizations*, 2nd edn (University of California Press, Berkeley, 2012)

Bruce Pascoe *Dark Emu* (Magabala Books, Broome, 2014)

Michael Pollan *The Omnivore's Dilemma: A Natural History of Four Meals* (Penguin Press, New York, 2006), *Cooked: A Natural History of Transformation* (Penguin Press, New York, 2013)

Weston A. Price *Nutrition and Physical Degeneration: A Comparison of Primitive and Modern Diets and Their Effects* (Paul B. Hoeber, New York, 1939)

Diane Rodgers & Robb Wolf *Sacred Cow: The Case for (Better) Meat* (BenBella Books, Dallas, 2020)

Joel Salatin *Folks, This Ain't Normal: A Farmer's Advice for Happier Hens, Healthier People, and a Better World* (Center Street, New York, 2011)

Allan Savory *Holistic Management: A Commonsense Revolution to Restore Our Environment*, 3rd edn (with Jody Butterfield, Island Press, Washington DC, 2017, first published 1988)

Vandana Shiva *Soil Not Oil: Environmental Justice in an Age of Climate Crisis* (North Atlantic Books, Berkeley, 2015), *Biopiracy: The Plunder of Nature and Knowledge* (North Atlantic Books, Berkeley, 2016) and *Staying Alive: Women, Ecology, and Development* (North Atlantic Books, Berkeley, 2016)

Rudolf Steiner *Agriculture Course: The Birth of the Biodynamic Method, Eight Lectures by Rudolf Steiner*, trans. George Adams (Rudolf Steiner Press, Forest Row, East Sussex, 2004, first published 1958)

Other resources

Gather – a documentary that shines the light on indigenous farming practices, people and the injustices many have faced

Kiss the Ground – a wonderful documentary on the importance of shifting to a regenerative way of farming and how farmers, soil and climate scientists are putting the wheels in motion, kisstheground.com

The Regenerative Journey – the podcast of biodynamic farmer and educator Charlie Arnott, charliearnott.com.au/podcast

Dr Walter Jehne – this former CSIRO scientist, climate scientist and soil microbiologist doesn't have a book or movie, but do yourself a favour and look online for one of his lectures on climate change, soil as a carbon sponge and restoring water cycles. They're often long, but he's a gifted explainer of the most complex of things and you will be mesmerised.

Fussy Eating Bundle – see lowtoxlife.com/shop-low-tox-products

Lemony custard
with seasonal fruits
and toasted
honey nuts
PAGE 267

The thankyous

Thank you to my husband Ollie, and son Sebastien for supporting me in this project and always knowing when I just needed to buckle down and get some deep thinking and solo time for writing – as well as knowing when I needed cuddles and dinner cooked for me. Thanks to my mum, dad and sister Nat for your ongoing cheerleading.

Thank you to Jane Morrow, my publisher at Murdoch Books, for helping me search my soul until this book became as clear as day to me. You are a legend. Thank you to Justin Wolfers and Megan Pigott, also at Murdoch, for helping me bring this book into being with your incredible smarts and vision. Nicola Young – is there a better editor out there? Doubt it. Your attention to detail and counsel are so appreciated. Jacqui Porter from Northwood Green – your design talents have brought this book to life in such a beautiful way. Thank you to my book-shoot crew dream team – photographer Cath Muscat, stylist Lucy Tweed and chef Vikki Leigh. Best fun and beautiful work.

Thank you to Costa Georgiadis. As I started to pen the composting section of the book I stopped immediately and reached out to you, to do justice to such an important action in our day. Thank you for inspiring us all to ditch the word 'waste' and instead say 'resource', and use our scraps to create life on earth.

Thank you to the farms and farmers who inspired the feasts – Maria Rodale and the Rodale Institute, Spirit Farm, Charlie Arnott's Hanaminno Farm, Mount Zero Olives, Roebuck Farm and Buena Vista Farm. Thank you to these pioneers of methods helping to regenerate our planet, restore healthy water systems, sequester greater and greater percentages of carbon over time, and bring biodiversity back to paddocks, plains and forests. You are legends, as are the many farmers around the world undertaking regenerative farming methods. A new day is dawning, and that day includes rapid healing of the planet beyond our current wildest dreams. And to the First Nations people, Native Americans and people of colour whose stories have not yet been told, I promise that I will find and tell as many of those stories as I can.

And thank you to Christine Schwedhelm, my first naturopath 17 years ago – if you hadn't insisted I try going gluten-free, who knows where I'd be now! Funny how life works out, hey?

Low Tox Life Food

Index

Low Tox Life Food

Published in 2021 by Murdoch Books, an imprint of Allen & Unwin

Murdoch Books Australia
83 Alexander Street
Crows Nest NSW 2065
Phone: +61 (0)2 8425 0100
murdochbooks.com.au
info@murdochbooks.com.au

Murdoch Books UK
Ormond House
26–27 Boswell Street
London WC1N 3JZ
Phone: +44 (0) 20 8785 5995
murdochbooks.co.uk
info@murdochbooks.co.uk

For corporate orders and custom publishing, contact our business development team at
salesenquiries@murdochbooks.com.au

Publisher: Jane Morrow
Editorial Manager: Justin Wolfers
Design Manager: Megan Pigott
Designer: Northwood Green
Editor: Nicola Young
Photographer: Cath Muscat
Stylist: Lucy Tweed
Home Economist: Vikki Leigh Moursellas
Illustration: Northwood Green, Creative Market
Production Director: Lou Playfair

Text © Alexx Stuart 2021
The moral right of the author has been
asserted.
Design © Murdoch Books 2021
Photography © Cath Muscat 2021

ISBN 9 781 76052 579 8 Australia
ISBN 9 781 91163 289 4 UK

A catalogue record for this
book is available from the
National Library of Australia

A catalogue record for this book is available from the British Library

Colour reproduction by Splitting Image Colour Studio Pty Ltd, Clayton, Victoria
Printed by C&C Offset Printing Co. Ltd., China

OVEN GUIDE: You may find cooking times vary depending on the oven you are using. For fan-forced ovens,
as a general rule, set the oven temperature to 20°C (40°F) lower than indicated in the recipe.

TABLESPOON MEASURES: We have used 20 ml (4 teaspoon) tablespoon measures. If you are using a 15 ml
(3 teaspoon) tablespoon add an extra teaspoon of the ingredient for each tablespoon specified.

MIX
Paper from
responsible sources
FSC® C008047